AF660848

A PRACTICAL HANDBOOK
ON
TRAINING

A PRACTICAL HANDBOOK ON TRAINING

E.D. SETTY

ANMOL PUBLICATIONS PVT. LTD.
NEW DELHI - 110 002 (INDIA)

ANMOL PUBLICATIONS PVT. LTD.
H.O.: 4374/4B, Ansari Road, Daryaganj,
New Delhi-110 002 (India)
Ph.: 23278000, 23261597
B.O.: No. 1015, Ist Main Road, BSK IIIrd Stage
IIIrd Phase, IIIrd Block,
Bangalore - 560 085 (India)
Visit us at: www.anmolpublications.com

A Practical Handbook On Training

© Reserved

First Edition, 2003

Reprint, 2009

ISBN 81-261-1440-1

PRINTED IN INDIA

Printed at Mehra Offset Press, Delhi.

Dedicated

to

The Hon'ble Chief Minister of Andhra Pradesh

Nara Chandrababu Naidu

A Staunch Proponent of Training

CONTENTS

FOREWORD

Training of personnel in all fields of development activities has, in the recent past, gained considerable importance. It is a necessary human input for development. The diverse categories of adults who are trained constitute a different audience from that of a school or university. The success of any training programme depends importantly on five factors: the participant (learner), the trainer (teacher), the sponsoring organisations of the participants and the training institute and, the training technology employed. Training essentially is an interaction between the participant and the trainer. Learning very much depends on the climate that is created by the five factors mentioned above.

Training is an essential human resource development activity. It is an investment on people since people are primary in all endeavours in life in making things better. Training is for action, accomplishment, improved performance, managing men and material. It is behaviour to be taught and learnt. The very existence and progress in life in all spheres of life is based on informal and formal training. Training is to meet one's needs and contribute to development. It is well nigh impossible to imagine how life would be minus training. Man is born with genetically transmitted potential. We may call this as nature and nurturing this biological endowment that takes place right from the infancy upto adulthood and beyond the adult stage is the process of training the individual to fit him to meet his needs and work towards the progress of the community. In development administration, training has become an indispensable necessity with increasing innovations and new ways of accomplishing needs and expectations of people. It is to bring about an extended self in the individual with a concern for the amelioration of all segments of people in the society. Training attempts to bring about an attitudinal change to work towards 'Unto This Last'. We may speak at length about various dimensions of training but it is enough to say that minus training it would be groping in the dark. Training is light that leads you towards continuous betterment of life. Even in the epic period, for instance, in the Mahabharatha, the Pandava and Kaurava princes were trained in archery. We cannot imagine a soldier or a general in the army without having undergone training in knowledge and skills related to warfare. They are trained especially in discipline, commitment and determination to serve their country. Training, principally, focuses on three areas: knowledge, skills and attitude. For any effective management, the above three components are essential. One can imagine what happens and the consequences of any performance short of or want of one of the three elements. One may have knowledge in a particular area, but lacks skills to use that knowledge and also inclination to use it (attitude). In another case, one has skill but lacks the needed knowledge and proper attitude. Still in another case, one is positively inclined ready to perform but lacks knowledge and skills. They are to be in the proper functional composition and balance meeting the needs of administration and development. The whole operation in life is learnt behaviour. Training may be called as neo-socialization creating an environment to acquire needed new knowledge, develop requisite skills and also to learn conducive interpersonal behaviour in managing people in getting things done.

Training makes you realize where you are and where you should go and what you should do. It gives you an idea that still miles to go by. Sometimes, training throws some glimmering light on future. Training opens new vistas of knowledge. It makes you feel humble and modest in the area of intellectual exposure. Training is an opportunity for the participant to compare his ideas, views, convictions and knowledge. Training provides means for reflections. Training of personnel assumes greater significance and importance when it comes to development administration. We may think of several analogies likened to the import of training. Training is a kind of intellectual refreshment. Training is just like irrigating a crop periodically. It is reminding and helping people what they are expected to do and how to do. Training invigorates the spirit of commitment. It is drawing strength from each other. Training is sometimes a fine soothing breeze. Sometimes, it opens your eyes, kindles and injects your imagination. It is something like dawn from darkness. Training provides intellectual, social and cultural contacts among the participants and faculty. Training generates flow of new ideas. It is a testing ground for the experience of the participants. Training is going into the open and receiving the sunlight. Learning in groups provides a comparative perspective. It is an opportunity for the personnel to tune with changing times and demands. It tells you that there is something better to learn and apply that learning and make things better.

"A PRACTICAL HANDBOOK ON TRAINING" is a comprehensive text critically examining all aspects and suggesting the way to go about the entire training activity. It would serve as a road map guiding the principal organisations and the personnel involved in training in achieving maximal development of human resources which would in turn contribute to the establishment and sustaining of good governance. I congratulate Dr. E.D. Setty, Consultant, Dr. MCR HRD Institute of AP, Hyderabad for the efforts he has made in writing this valuable guide on training.

—P.V.R.K. PRASAD, IAS
Director General
Dr. MCR HRD Institute of AP &
Ex-Officio Special Chief Secretary
to Govt. of Andhra Pradesh

PREFACE

"No Man Can Teach A Person Unless He Wants To Learn"

There are number of books on training but the one in your hand is rather distinct. It is a practical guide covering the whole course of training activity right from the assessing of training needs, designing and offering of training and evaluation of training. The critical side of the book spells out some pitfalls and lacunae one finds at various phases of training programmes offered today at some of the training institutes.

Training, in a broad sense, is a continuous process in life, equipping oneself with knowledge, skills and a desired pattern of behaviour to be effective as an individual and a member in the society. Training in a job or activity is a process of imparting new knowledge, and developing skills and attitudes and values among employees in order to make them effective and efficient in their job through instruction, practice, demonstration and other techniques either on the job or in a formal training situation.

The book begins with Functions of Training highlighting a Three-Pronged Approach to training briefly indicating courses for personal growth and efficacy, courses for interpersonal relations and managerial skills and courses covering substantive technical areas focusing on knowledge and skills for professional growth. These training programmes will meet the development expectations on the part of the organisations. In respect to the functions of training, illustrative training titles and outlines are provided in Appendix-I (A) & Appendix-I (B).

The chapter on Assessment of Training Needs provides

guidelines as to how one has to go about assessing the training needs in an organisation spelling out the learning objectives related to the performance objectives on the part of the individual employees. The assessment of training needs includes job analysis, organisation analysis and manpower analysis, complemented with a questionnaire in Appendix-II.

The most important phase in training activity is designing the right and appropriate type of training programmes. Guidelines in Chapter-3 under Designing of Training Programmes are provided as to how to go about designing a training programme in respect to the learning objectives, and training objectives and the kind of training that is to be offered to the employees. The chapter also includes an interesting and educative and stimulating list of multi-ways to ruin a training programme.

Chapter-4 looks into Psychology of Adult Learning contrasted with learning on the part of children. It discusses in detail all dimensions of adult learning with limitations thereof.

Chapter-5 highlights the significance of communication in training. Here the emphasis is on the effective way things are to be communicated whichever may be the training method used in a programme. Each method that the faculty uses should bring in clarity in concepts and facilitate right type of understanding and reflection as intended in terms of learning and training objectives. This chapter spells out in detail the key elements in communication.

We may consider Chapter-6 dealing with training methods as a major one in the book. In this chapter, we discuss almost all the methods and their relevance and the way in which they are to be used in a training programme. It briefly looks into the issues of training methodology, how one has to decide which method is applicable to meet a particular objective in training or the learning that is expected on the part of the participants. Methods relevant to the three types of training: (i). On the Job, (ii). In the Classroom and (iii). Off the Classroom are discussed elaborately. While speaking of training methods, in Appendix-III, one will have a comprehensive idea of various aspects of training methods at a glance. Interestingly the Training Methods at a Glance covers all the aspects and dimensions of each method.

Chapter-7 looks into the way in which audio-visual aids are to be used complementary to lecture or discussion in the classroom.

In the entire training programme, the course director plays a significant role. Chapter-8 speaks of the role of the course director and the way in which he has to direct the course under his charge.

Similar to the course director who is himself a trainer there are other faculty who play the role of a trainer and chapter-9 looks into what should be the profile of a trainer and the way in which he has to build rapport with the participants and the way in which he has to create learning environment in the classroom.

Some of the training institutes often go in for Guest Faculty. Chapter-10 briefly looks into the way in which the guest faculty is to be utilized as an expert in a particular field of training and how guest faculty would be made a PRO of the training institute. It also looks into the limitations in respect to the contribution of a guest faculty in a training programme.

It is rather a normal practice to provide the participants with reading material. In terms of quality and the form in which the reading material is provided to the participants varies a great deal. Chapter-11 reflects on the ways in which the reading material is provided to the participants and how it should be.

Since training is not one man's or one institute's business, several institutes and individuals at various stages are involved in a training programme. Chapter-12 focuses on Issues in Adult Training reflecting on the participants the trainer, sponsoring organisation, training institute and the training technology employed in the course of a training programme.

In the entire gamut of training activity, the training institute plays a vital role. In Chapter-13, we look into the training institute as a professional agency and how it should be and the kinds of role and expertise that is expected on the part of the functionaries in a training institute right from the top executive down to the research associate and how constantly they have to expand their knowledge and skills in several dimensions which are the necessary requirements in order to make training professional a significant contributor to the growth and development in all organisations.

Similarly Chapter-14 looks into the role of a sponsoring organisation and how it has to go in for assessing the job analysis and training needs on the part of the employees, it sponsors for training and the way in which the organisation is to make use of the trained personnel.

As a new way of advancing one's knowledge Chapter-15 looks into the revolutionary means of computer based learning, its significant advantages and its economy in respect to cost of training.

Finally, Chapter-16 discusses the importance of evaluation of training programmes and the different types of evaluation which are part of the cycle of training. As supplement to Chapter-16 in Appendix-IV some evaluation instruments are included.

Training Methods—At A Glance in Appendix-III presents all the facets of each training method. It is quite comprehensive and handy for a trainer to understand the nature, function, advantages, limitations and the requisite skill to use each method.

Every effort has been made to provide guidelines as to how one could effectively run the entire course of training activity. It is believed that this book would serve as a very handy instructive guide to the academics, trainers, training institutes, sponsoring organisations and to the student community who specialize in training and development.

—AUTHOR

ACKNOWLEDGEMENTS

The author would like to express his profoundest thanks and gratitude to Sri P.V.R.K. Prasad, IAS, Director General, Dr. MCR HRD Institute of AP & Ex-Officio Special Chief Secretary to Govt. of Andhra Pradesh for his valuable Foreword and inspiring guidelines in writing this book. The author feels deeply thankful to Sri M. Yanadaiah, Senior Stenographer, Dr. MCR HRD Institute of AP for his continued and meticulous work in preparing this Manuscript. He takes this opportunity to express his sincere thanks to Dr. MCR HRD Institute of AP for the facilities the Institute provided him in preparing the manuscript for the book and expresses his indebtedness to the sources named and unnamed from which he has borrowed some ideas and concepts.

October 9, 2002 —E. D. SETTY
Dr. MCR HRD Institute of AP Ph.D.
Hyderabad

1

FUNCTIONS OF TRAINING

Though there is a great deal of writing in respect to function of training, it may not be superfluous and out of place here to briefly touch upon it, since the whole question here revolves around aiding the staff towards better performance wherein training is an investment on people.

Training in a broad sense is a continuous process in life to equip oneself with knowledge, skills and desired patterns of behaviour to be effective as an individual and as a member in the group. Training in a job or activity is again a process of imparting new knowledge and developing skills, attitudes and values in people in order to make them effective and efficient in their job through instruction, practice, demonstration or other techniques either on the job or in a formal training situation.

In view of increase in the on-going activities, introduction of new activities of technical and non-technical nature, growth in the size of organization, induction of new incumbents to a variety of jobs, knowledge and skill demands of new jobs, problems of inefficiency, low productivity and low production, and problems of human relations in the organizational setting, training of the personnel has become a necessity and of late it has assumed greater significance and importance. Training as a remedial measure is also directed towards individual development, competence and efficiency.

Further, the following are the emerging factors necessitating training.

i. Computers

ii. Information Technology

iii. Multinational interaction

iv. Globalization

v. Cultural contact

vi. New Rules and Regulations being brought in

vii. Increased awareness and expectations on the part of the public

viii. Emerging of new ideas, systems, new ways of doing things, and attempts to make things better.

ix. Training as a function in administration

x. Training as a function in development

xi. Training as a necessary input in making things better

xii. Training towards individual growth and development

xiii. Training towards streamlining of organisations

Looked at from any angle irrespective of individual qualifications and capabilities, training has become a necessary component. It has become as a continual process, improving and revamping the human resources, building capabilities in order to ensure satisfactory performance in all endeavours related to administration and rendering services and supplies to the public.

Training in the Context of Professional Staff in Government

None at any level denies the need for a relevant kind of training. Training does not straightaway imply that there is something deficient and wanting in the individual to be trained. Being professional staff is one thing and competent, effective and efficient is another. Change being a natural and continuous phenomenon in all spheres of life, training has to be a life-long activity. The Government, public and private sector organisations have recognized and emphasized the need for providing training opportunities to the staff for their personal growth and professional competence and better performance.

The need for a particular kind of training may be felt and articulated by a professional staff in respect to the job he/she has to do and the standard of excellence he/she sets for himself/herself. It is not possible always for the individual to come up clearly as to what exactly and precisely he/she needs in terms of training. If it were to be a specific skill as computer use, one could specify, but in areas dealing with socio-economic development and efficient administrative knowledge and skill needs are diverse. Some of these fields in the case of professionals and subject-matter specialists are gray areas seemingly known and unknown. And so, one of the ways to stipulate and recommend the kinds of training that may be provided to the professional staff is to move from the expected, anticipated performance and the end-product of certain comparable excellence on the part of the staff. This is a supervisory and management assessment and decision, based of course on the role of a particular department /organisation or the whole government as a unified system.

Reward Anticipated and Follow-up of Training

Training is not to be taken as an isolated, single-time activity, but as a process of organizational development. It has pre-training and post-training phases. People some times look forward to some rewards, recognition in whatever form it could be after the training and some may consider training itself as a reward.

In order to make the training serve its purpose and to make the participant really benefit from the training for his own development and contribute to departmental objectives, the concerned department may have to do its part.

A Three-Pronged Approach to Training

In consonance with every department / organisation's approach to Human Resource Development in all fields of administrative and socio-economic development, a three-pronged and an integrated approach to training is recommended. This three-pronged approach focuses simultaneously on individual staff's personal growth, inter-personal relations and professional growth in substantive functional areas. Sensitizing the individual, promoting the inter-personal relations and enriching the professional competence would, it is believed, meet the mandates of any organisation. The essential learning situations which go under different nomenclature as seminars, workshops, labs and training course are clustered under three areas referred to above. As shown in the diagram (Please see Training Schema), the course in each cluster has distinct and at the same time unifying characteristics motivating, strengthening and reinforcing the other clusters, thus facilitating knowledge of the self, understanding of and working with others with excellence in one's own respective functional areas.

TRAINING SCHEMA

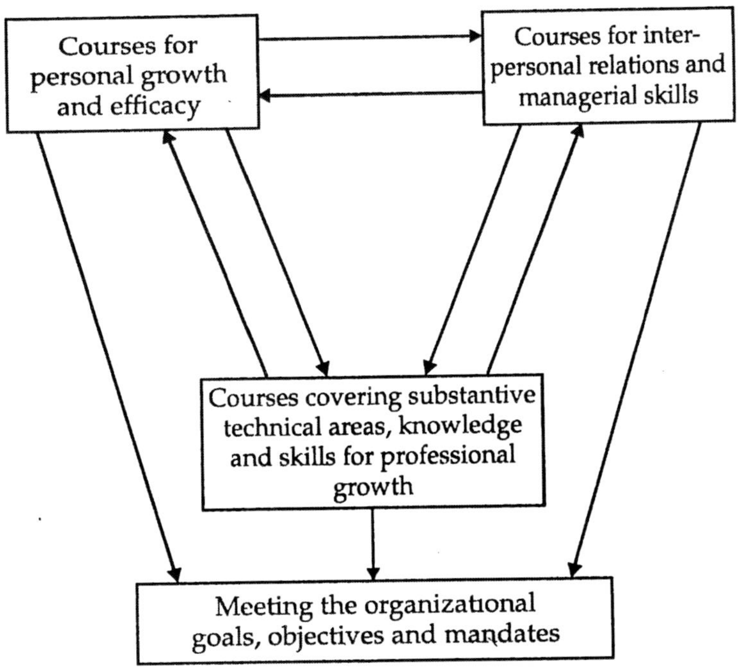

Duration of Courses

While considering the duration of course, we may have to reckon with three constraints; time, cost and resources. Most of the courses are elastic in their nature. They could be condensed into a few hours and a couple of days or they could be full-length courses. It is the content of the course and also the level of the participants that matter. Duration of the course also depends on the question, whether it is a basic course or a refresher one. In view of the time, and resource constraints, one may have to compromise, sacrifice certain content, details, field visits and strike a balance. As Francis Bacon speaks of books: Some books are to be tasted, some are to be swallowed and a few are to be chewed and digested. Similarly, one may think of assigning relative importance to courses and the duration of courses. Training courses are not to be organized for the namesake as a cosmetic touch. Duration or time is one of the significant factors in the impact of a training programme on the participant.

Courses for Personal Growth and Efficacy[1A]

Most of the training programmes as mentioned above funnel down to three areas, one dealing with personal growth and development, second focusing on interpersonal relations, and the third covering subject area specializations. As a kind of illustration, we will briefly look into the three types of courses which put together make a wholesome kind of training. One may call this kind of approach an integrated system of training wherein the individual's growth and development and helping him to advance in his area of expertise / specialization and focusing on interpersonal relations which is a significant contributing factor in any kind of activity where the group is involved.

Under three headings, we just include illustrative training programmes that fall within these three areas.

Laboratory for Personal Growth

It is experiential learning and the experience that the participant gains in the small group setting, much of it cannot be explained in words. However, if we were to describe the process, it helps the participants in (a) articulating the un-articulated, (b) making the invisible visible, and (c) owning up the disowned and (d) acting the withheld. It is said that growth of a man into being lies by directing his effort to extend these four boundaries in his own life space. The Lab is geared to answer the specific needs for the mobilization of the self and the system in which the individual functions.

Further, the experience-based learning would help individuals and systems to develop socio-psychological infrastructure for anchoring major programmes of change and development. It also enables individuals and systems acquire a realistic appraisal of internal resources and constraints to action and mobilize themselves for alternative action choices which can break the pattern of stagnation and usher in new ways of maximal utilization of human resources in the organization.

Management of Motivation

Motivation is a drive, an urge fuelling and propelling an individual into action. It is interesting to reflect upon what motivates us and others and how to motivate others. Irrespective of the levels at which individuals operate, super-ordinate or subordinate, knowledge of factors that motivate people is highly essential. This knowledge facilitates individual satisfaction, promotes understanding of others, fosters healthy inter-personal relations and leads to higher productivity and production. Knowledge of how to motivate your colleagues and subordinates towards coordination and better performance is a psychic tool in management. It is ignorance of this knowledge that leads to misunderstanding, prejudices and miss and under utilization of human resources in an organization.

Communication

Communication assumes various forms and the entire business of human society depends on multiple modes of communication. It plays a basic, essential role in all walks of life. Communication is the ongoing process by which people attempt to share meaning via the transmission of messages. Management constantly is interested in the work performance and the way jobs are done with and through other people in order to achieve the mission, vision, values and goals. Communication provides a common silken thread for all management processes of planning, organizing, leading, controlling and proper coordinating. The management of people through small groups and teams demands continuous communication.

Leadership

Leadership is an important social tool for initiating action, motivating people, mobilizing resources, directing and accomplishing a task. Leadership is task related. It plays the role of guiding and building confidence among people towards better performance. Leadership in different degrees and modes operates in every social system. It is a process of influencing and directing task-related activities of group members. Motivational skills are critical components of leading. It plays a role in organisation and human resources development. One can think of self-inspired leadership and motivated leadership.

Personality Development

Personality is the sum total of ways in which an individual reacts and interacts with others. Heredity and environment may be said as two interacting factors that mould the personality of an individual. Physical stature, facial attraction, sex, temperament, muscle composition, reflexes and energy level and biological rhythms are the result of the heredity factor. Environment is related to culture and upbringing. Situational factors influence the effects of heredity and environment on personality. The core trait in a personality of an individual is his character. We have extensive studies on personality formation and behavioral patterns related to each type of personality. Though the foundation is laid in shaping of one's personality in the formative period, it is possible to bring about changes in the attitude or behaviour of an individual especially in his interpersonal relations, mode of working with other people and communication. The study of personality is not only in the interest of one individual but it is essential for any official to understand the personality of others which is a kind of clue for the individual working with another individual or a group.

Courses in Inter-Personal Relations and Managerial Skills[1B]

Right from the family, small group to a large and complex organization, most of the functions are collective. The quality of work, productivity and the harmony that is generated in the work environment depend on mutual understanding and inter-personal relations among the members in the group. The need for cultivating and fostering healthy, productive relationship in a multi-regional, multi-cultural, multi-lingual and multi-religious personnel composition as obtaining in the governmental organizations is greater. Effective functioning is a learned behaviour and this learning environment is created through training.

Knowledge, skills, methods, techniques, understanding and leadership are the ingredients that are the requisites to work with people and to make people work effectively and efficiently. The courses that are suggested under this cluster focus on building functional inter-personal relations, enhancing supervisory capacity, developing communicative skills and abilities, to introduce and sustain desirable change, managing conflicts incidental to changes in the organization.

Inter-Personal Relations

Public development functions are collective activities that are carried on by a mixed group of people, occupying varied positions of authority and with diverse personal and cultural orientations. To bring about unison in thinking and action amongst such a diverse group is a task wherein you cannot apply force and accomplish things. The only means is to educate and motivate people towards enlightened, cooperative participatory action with personal commitment in accomplishing a public task. The course addresses this issue.

Management of Change and Conflict

Economic and social development implies change and some kinds of change are welcomed and some resisted. It is not only facing change and conflict in the clientele system, but more often we have to face it in the organization itself, when desirable changes are attempted. For instance, one change that is presently attempted in the State of Andhra Pradesh is 'Janmabhoomi' and socio-economic development necessitating streamlining the entire administrative strategies and bringing about changes in the work behaviour of officials in the departments. There is need to prepare people to accept and sustain desirable changes in the organization. The course on Management of Change and Conflict provides an insight into the psychology of human behaviour either favouring or resisting a change phenomenon and the ways to effectively induce a change and handle conflicts that often arise as a result of values, traditions, practices, vested interests and wrong perceptions.

Human Resources Management (HRM)

The personnel in the various organisations and departments of government with their intellectual and psychic endowment constitute the human resources. They are a precious resource. The personnel on their own can and may perform their roles efficiently, but more often they need direction, guidance, appreciation and motivation to do their jobs better. Efficient utilization and management of people in the organization is the responsibility of the management. But people cannot be used as building blocks mechanically. It is an art to work with people and make them more efficient and productive and the HRM course addresses itself to such a task.

Training Methods and Skills (TMS)

It may be said that knowing a thing is knowledge and communicating it is skill. What is attempted in this course is development of communicative skills among professional experts and subject-matter specialists. Some of them who have an aptitude to be trainers could be trained in training methods and skills who could function as resource persons for in-house training programmes and also serve as trainers in respect of training programmes.

This training of trainers (TOT) programme would enhance the training capabilities of the staff to be trained and also sharpen their verbal and non-verbal skills of communication. The TMS course may be organized at least once in a year and senior and middle level staff, around 10 to 15 may be trained who would really be a rich resource and an asset to any Institute.

Performance Appraisal

Performance appraisal is the systematic description of the job relevant to strengths and weaknesses of an individual or a group. It serves two major purposes in organizations. (1) Improving the job performance of employees and (2) Providing information to employees and managers for use in making decisions such as administration, placement, selection-promotion, financial rewards, incentives or compensation etc. The essential purpose in this systematic and periodic appraisal is the accurate measurement of human performance. It attempts to reduce if not to eliminate human bias and prejudice by means of a system that is subject to impartial review and check.

Team Building

Most of the activities in organizations are collective in nature carried on by teams ranging from 8-10, each individual playing a specified role and coordinating with others in carrying out a particular activity. Team members synchronize their efforts towards translating a designed objective. Team building can be within groups or at the inter-group level where activities are inter-dependant. The teams may go by different names such as committees, project teams, self-management teams and task groups. The most vital role of an organization is to build teams and foster them towards accomplishing of organizational tasks.

Supervisory Training

A supervisor may be called a manager in action who often is in close physical contact with the employee. He has a dual task: Get things done by the employees and at the same time guide, train the employees and also keep up their morale. His is to answer the management and also be friendly with his subordinates. His is no easy task. He is to be competent professionally and at the same time effective in human relations. The supervisory training course focuses on making a good supervisor a better supervisor.

Courses for Professional Growth

As the very title of this cluster of courses stands, the selective courses that are included here chiefly focus, the following courses under subject specialization are only illustrative since there are number of subject areas wherein courses could be offered for further advancement in a particular field.

1). *Modern Techniques and Computer Applications in Social Research*

As the title describes, the participant in this course will be exposed to the latest techniques including computer aided statistical package in carrying out social research.

2). *Project Planning and Implementation*

The course focuses on the information, knowledge, skills and techniques required to plan sound development projects.

3). *Poverty Focused Development Planning*

What is called poverty in the economic sense is a complex phenomenon in any society. It has social, cultural and psychic dimensions though economic attribute is visible and usually the one that is looked into. There is what is called culture of poverty. Mere money alone cannot reduce or eliminate poverty. To alleviate one has to work through several intricate and deep-rooted barriers. The approach is through education, skill development, motivation and facilitating the poor to wriggle out from the clutches of poverty. The course tries to open up means towards this end.

4). *Programme Planning*

It deals with the principles, philosophy and guidelines that one has to bear in mind while planning a development programme. In the set of priorities in programme planning the place of primacy is given to the beneficiary group, who and how many and to what extent they will be benefited.

5). *System Analysis for Integrated Systems Management*

The course focuses on the inter-connected, inter-dependent and mutually influencing sub-systems in a system of activity. Knowledge of system analysis would help towards effective management and bring about an integrated development economizing the cost of any project.

6). *Sustainable Development*

The need that we have to address today is not only development, but more importantly sustainable development. This concept of sustainability relates to physical resources, economic structure, technology, environment, social institutions, and the consumption pattern of the people. The course draws attention to all these factors that impinge on sustainable development.

7). *Sustainable and Environmentally Sound Development*

This course draws the attention of participants to plan sustainable development especially in the fields of agriculture, industry, land and forest use and tourism safeguarding the environment.

8). *Management of Agricultural Extension*

Agricultural extension as an applied non-formal education spans from research lab to farm encompassing several layers of administration and line agencies. Managerial aspects are pivotal in delivering of services and goods to the farmers on time in the right way. The course addresses the managerial aspects of agricultural extension.

9). *Planning and Promotion of Integrated Area Development*

Area, a district, a sub-district, a region, a tribal or coastal region is the unit of development in this approach. It is a multi-project development in a selected geographic area.

10). *Promotion of Self-Employment*

The course looks into several means and ways of promoting self-employment as the basis for income generation leading to minimum quality of life, supported by country case studies.

11). *Small Industry Sickness Prevention and Rehabilitation*

Some small enterprises started under pressure of targets, ill-planned, ill-equipped and wrongly located and due to mismanagement or want of finance, raw material, infrastructural facilities and finding no market for the goods and services, fall sick. The course addresses the ways to prevent sickness and rehabilitate the sick enterprises.

12). *Small Industry Management Consultancy*

As the title of the course says, it is a specialized field and of a multi-disciplinary nature. It is optional to the industry development staff.

13). Information Storage and Retrieval Systems

It may be called informatic science highly useful to the librarians and people working in the information centres. It deals with providing accessibility to the users employing the latest techniques.

Relative Importance of Courses

The importance of any training course is dependent on the need felt for it and so, one may accord importance to different courses. The three clusters of courses recommended for the staff, as mentioned earlier, focus on person, group and subject – two courses on personal growth and efficacy, five on inter-personal relations and others on substantive subject technical areas.

*Note:- **Please see Appendix-I(A) & Appendix-I(B) for model courses under each head Personal Interpersonal relations and Managerial skills.***

2

ASSESSMENT OF TRAINING NEEDS

In assessing the training needs of an employee we are not only to look at his role and functions related to his tasks but we should also get an idea from the superordinate and subordinates in respect to interpersonal relations and communication on the part of the employee. In assessing training needs we not only look into the needs of the present but into the future too.

In most of the cases the training institutes or the organisations do not go in for a real methodological assessment of training needs. Depending on the operations in the organisation and the level of the employees and their functions, training needs are assumed just like the kind of menu for the breakfast, lunch or dinner. May be it is true, that some of the training needs are common and can be assumed. But it would be ideal at least to go in for regular assessing of training needs at certain intervals depending on the feedback received from the trained employees and the organisations. If training were to be serious input and investment towards human resources development it is to be accorded a significant place in the entire gamut of organisation development.

It is common knowledge that you have to take into account both organization needs and the employee role oriented, job oriented needs at present and also of the near future. It is interesting to note that there are only three areas which constitute the contents of any training programme. The contents of all courses relate to and funnel down to three areas:- Knowledge, Skills and Attitudes or behaviour. To know is Knowledge, to do is Skill where as the way you do speaks of your Attitude i.e., how the individual looks at things, interacts with people. In respect to the three areas which constitute all training programmes, the methodology of imparting differs. In case of knowledge it is just giving information related to learning and relearning about any aspect. When it comes to skills, it is doing skills to be broadly divided into two areas:- Technical and Social. The learning here, is practice-oriented of course, based on knowledge in the field in question. The difficult area in training is bringing about attitudinal change i.e., change in the behaviour of the individual. Attitude is the subtle and manifest aspect of knowledge and skills used and the way the individual does work on his own and the way he works with others. In simple terms the manner in which the individual does his work as a solo or in the group reflects his attitude, attitude towards his work and individual with whom he does his job. The individual may be quite knowledgeable and equally skilled too in the particular knowledge area but the way he performs the job, attitudinally makes a difference.

Speaking of imparting of knowledge and enhancing knowledge on the part of a participant we may just take the example of rural or urban development. Knowledge is to be enhanced on the part of the participant or speaking of knowledge, let's take for example the kind of knowledge and skills and attitude expected of rural development professional in respect to the following areas:

Rural Development Professional (RDP): Profile

Awareness

1. He should be aware of the issues and problems centering around rural development.
2. He should be aware of the strengths and limitations of the client community.
3. He should be aware of proper timing of various activities i.e., when to do what.

Understanding & Ability

1. He should be a strategic planner.

2. He should be able to understand the community with which he is to work.
3. He should be able to understand people, interact with them, educate and motivate them towards desired change.
4. He should have respect and concern for the culture, values, attitudes and the knowledge of the people.
5. He should be able to recognize consistency and usefulness of indigenous knowledge system in its own way and as adapted with newly attempted technology or innovation.
6. He should have an understanding as to the need, structure and functions of the support system, and be skilled enough to coordinate and secure assistance from such a system.
7. He should have an appreciation for the complimentary, integral role of NGOs.
8. He should be able to map out problems and their causes.
9. He should be able to coordinate a number of activities.
10. He should be able to understand the technical aspects of programmes as to how to do them.
11. He should be able to understand/appreciate people's reaction/feedback and be able to use them for improving programmes.
12. He should be able to supervise, monitor and evaluate the programme activities.
13. He should have the ability to draw the people's attention to factors which they may otherwise overlook, but which they need to take into account when deciding what to do.
14. He should be able to avoid arousing resentment by attempting to decide for people something they feel they have the right to decide for themselves.

Knowledge to be enhanced about

1. The community – people, their way of life, their value system, culture and tradition, their resources, their knowledge, their needs/problems, social stratification.
2. Alternatives towards problem solving.
3. Planning process, planning techniques, programme planning, setting objectives, targeting of achievements, means of implementation, data needs, allocating resources.
4. Utilizing material and human resources.
5. Socio-economic, religious, political organisations and their functioning.
6. Suitable technologies.
7. Support system for Rural Development.
8. Integrating voluntary efforts with government programmes.
9. Local leadership and its utilization.
10. Monitoring, supervision/coordination, evaluation of programmes.

Specific Knowledge and Skills

1. He should have the knowledge, understanding and appreciation of sectoral, internal, external and national economies working toward right blend of economic policy for rural development.
2. He should be skilled enough in organizing and building new communities.
3. He should have an insight into environmental problems accruing as a result of ill-conceived and hastily implemented rural development programmes.
4. He should have qualities that of an effective leader.
5. When conflict arises, he should be able to perform the role of a patient listener, a negotiator and a counselor.

6. Even when people have already chosen a project, and need only a little encouragement and help to go ahead, he should be able to check that the project will meet a real and permanent need.
7. When forming a group he should be able to anticipate any major difficulties the group is likely to face and to help the group to think out how they can be avoided.
8. He must be able to carefully choose the most favourable situations in which to work.
9. In times of need, he should be able to consult others (colleagues, superiors, community people etc.) and give due credit to their opinion/contribution.
10. He should have knowledge about scientific fact-finding – collection of facts and figures, analyzing and interpreting and reporting the same.

Attitudes to be enhanced about

1. Community
2. People's knowledge
3. People's way of doing things and the 'why' behind things
4. Local leaders
5. Local factions
6. Local institutions
7. Own superiors
8. Own colleagues
9. National policies and programmes

Knowledge may relate to any domain of information technical or non-technical. In one sense, knowledge is all the time growing and expanding, knowledge is not static and as mentioned it is ever growing and changing. The concept of skills sometimes appears nebulous and vague. We may just mention here some requisite kind of skills expected on the part of an employee whether he is at the lower or at the apex level. The following skills are to be enhanced among the individuals for better understanding and performance.

Skills to be enhanced

1. Interaction
2. Appreciation
3. Fact-finding/Data Collection
4. Identification
5. Prioritization
6. Integration
7. Coordination
8. Delegation
9. Consultation
10. Negotiation
11. Counseling
12. Organisation
13. Analysis
14. Interpretation
15. Reporting
16. Extension
17. Demonstration
18. Supervision
19. Evaluation

The entire training is related to what the participant is to learn in order to perform his role or carry his tasks effectively i.e., the performance objective is related to the learning objective. If the employee is to perform the way in which he is expected to perform he is to learn that part of requisite knowledge, skills and the attitude or behaviour conducive and facilitating his role. There is an organic link between the performance objectives and learning objectives. The following are a few examples.

PERFORMANCE OBJECTIVES Vs. LEARNING OBJECTIVES*

Sl. No.	*Performance Objective*	*Learning Objective*
1.	Cause-problem identification	• To identify problems & their cause • To rank problems according to their nature.
2.	Assessment of needs	• To understand short and long term needs • To prioritize needs
3.	Programme Planning and project formulation	• To gain practical knowledge/skill in planning • To understand interdisciplinary nature of planned activities • To integrate various approaches
4.	Education and motivation	• To understand clients' ethos, needs, • strengths • To mobilize groups towards attitudinal change • To learn skills in organizing and building new communities
5.	Institutional network analysis	• To understand structure and functions of various institutions • To learn the way these institutions influence development and change
6.	Participatory development promotion	• To understand the indigenous knowledge system and its relation to the change proposed • To recognize the consistency and usefulness of such knowledge system • To learn to plan close to people's expectations
7.	Environmental planning	• To gain insight into environmental problems accruing as a result of ill-conceived and hastily implemented programmes
8.	Planning for effective support system	• To understand the need, structure & functions of support system for RD • To gain knowledge and skills to coordinate and secure assistance from such system

(Contd .)

9.	Monitoring and evaluation	• To understand technical aspects of programme activities • To understand "WHAT, WHEN AND HOW" in project implementation
10.	Planning in collaboration	• To understand the integral and complimentary role of NGOs • To learn the way to encourage and strengthen working with NGOs
11.	Development administration	• To understand ideal administrative organisational set up facilitating development

* *Source*: Thanks are expressed to the unknown author of the above table.

Organisation Analysis*

Organisation analysis involves a study of the entire organisation, its objectives, its resources, the allocation of these resources in meeting its objectives, and the total socioeconomic-technological environment within which the organisation exists. This kind of analysis helps answer the question of broad content areas. In so doing, it largely determines the training philosophy for the entire organisation.

The first step in an organisation analysis for training purposes is to obtain a clear understanding of both short and long term goals. Long-term objectives need to be established in broad areas for the entire department/company; next specific goals and strategies should be stated for the various components of the organisation (divisions, departments, section-down to the lowest subgroup) as a means of achieving these broad objectives. It is because of the constantly changing nature of development and the business environment. Short-term goals and strategies may change radically from one review to the next; but if the long-term goals are the result of careful thought, they will help stabilize organisation-training

* *Source:* Adopted from Bernard B.M. Bass, Janes A. Vaughan, *Training in Industry: The Management of Learning*, Wadsworth Publishing Company, Inc. Belmont, California, Tavistock Publications, Ltd., London, great thanks are expressed to the authors and the publishers.

plans, since they will change much less rapidly than will short-term goals. One of the major limiting factors of this approach to date has been the seeming inability to translate many general objectives into more detailed and specific operational targets.

A second step in an organisation analysis is an inventory of the organisation's attempts to meet goals through its human and physical production resources. Various efficiency indexes can be derived to determine the adequacy of specific workflows, so that a detailed examination of inputs and outputs of the total system is possible. The focus, of course, will be on the human contribution to these indexes. Although in the past the human inputs were measured or rather estimated in terms of physical exertion, it is now clear that the psychological costs of the job as reflected in individual feelings, beliefs, emotions and attitudes must be included as more precise measuring factors. Automation and information technology have already brought about significant changes in the nature of these costs in many organisations as employees now find themselves having significant interaction with machines as well as other men. Managers relating to a computer may present a completely different kind of problem from that faced by the worker relating to an automated (controlled) production line.

The final step is an examination of the business enterprise an organisation is operating in a distinct social, economic and political environment, which it can usually influence to some extent, but not control. A business enterprise is more than a collection of buildings, physical equipment, materials, and people. It is a social organisation and, as such, involves the employees' awareness of belonging to an identifiable group, their interaction among members of the group, and the non-members' perception of the group as a group. Thus, an organisation is said to have a certain 'climate' which influences and in turn is influenced by the total environment of the organisation.

The climate of an organisation is, in essence, a reflection of its members' attitudes toward various aspects of work, supervision, department procedures, goals and objectives, and membership in the organisation. These attitudes are learned; they are a product of the members' experiences both within and outside the work environment. Thus, a training programme may be designed to effect certain changes in the organisational climate; however, the change process is a two-way street, since the prevailing organisational climate-especially the attitudes towards employee development will largely determine the training programme's success.

For instance, in management development, training is primarily considered a line responsibility. A man's boss is his main teacher. The staff expert can only help and advise. Yet, operational demands too often leave line management little time to do a good job of developing subordinates. Moreover, the subordinate may be superior in every respect to the man who is supposed to be developing him. Actually, few managers are in a position to observe their subordinates as they perform their jobs, with the result that they are seldom able to coach them effectively.

Numerous studies show that lack of management support for the objectives of a particular training programme reduces or eliminates its potential for serving the organisation. Formal training is likely to be ineffective if the course work runs counter to management ideology. In one study, foremen from two divisions of a large company were given supervisory training. In the first division, employees, after their training showed increased satisfaction with their supervisors. Three foremen from this division said, in turn that they had received considerable encouragement from their bosses. In the second division, employees expressed a greater dissatisfaction with their foremen following training; these supervisors reported that they had not been encouraged by their bosses.

An International Harvestor foremen who received two weeks of training designed to increase consideration for their subordinates all showed improvement in attitudes toward consideration immediately following the training programme. However, six months later, only those foremen who believed their bosses wanted them to be considered maintained their new attitudes towards their staffs. A deterioration in human relations also resulted when a supervisory training programme came into conflict with union norms, when recruitment for the programme was poor, and when the programme itself became a matter of indoctrinating a captive audience rather than educating individuals.

Ideally, the attitudes and actions of higher-level management need to be consistent with the course content of the supervisory training programme. Top management needs exposure to the programme and its objectives, so that it will actively support them as well as reinforce what is learned in the training programme. One of the most common suggestions arising at the end of the typical supervisory training programme is, "I sure wish my boss could take this programme; he needs it more than I did".

Often, training must be supported by other organisation actions to bring about desired changes. For instance, a supervisory-training programme directed at reducing employee absenteeism achieved this goal when supervisors at the end of their training received uniform data about the absence of their own personnel.

Another important consideration, particularly in management development, is an organisation's need to project the major trends in what it will require during the careers of its current management force. Current training programmes and plans for subsequent management development programmes must consider the changes taking place in business and development management. They must also pay increased attention to how to apply the physical and social sciences to business administration, to the non-market responsibilities of management, to long-range planning for the successful administration of technically advanced industries, and to the different types of careers for management trainees in the same firm.

Job Analysis*

Job analysis for training purposes involves a careful study of jobs within an organisation in a further effort to define the specific content of training. It requires an orderly, systematic collection of data about the job or position; and its purpose is to spell out, in as much detail as possible, what tasks constitute the job, how they are to be performed, and what behaviour (skills, knowledge and attitudes) the job holder must have to perform certain specified tasks.

Job analyses are fairly straightforward for production and other lower-level jobs in an organisation, though they become

* Please see Appendix-II for a model evaluation instrument to assess the training needs of employees in an organisation.

increasingly complex as an individual moves to higher levels with less clearly defined duties and responsibilities. An expert can analyze the job following a standardized procedure; observing the operator at work, actually performing the job, and asking the operator questions about the job.

In the collection of job information for the purpose of formulating training programmes, particular attention must be focused on performance standards required of employees, the tasks in which they will be engaged, the methods they will use on the job, and, most important, the way they have learned these methods.

Especially, in developing programmes that train workers to place complex equipment in operation and then maintain it analysis must consider the component tasks the operators must learn to complete the final performance.

For the purposes of analyzing the need for training, many different ways of collecting job information are available. These include the following:

1. Observations in the context of manufacturing and production activities. (Were these obvious evidences of production inefficiency, such as excessive tools breakage, failure to meet schedules, too much scrap, poor methods, wasted time, large numbers of grievances, high absenteeism, and excessive turnover? Were dramatic incidences on the part of individuals or a group that reveal poor personnel relationships, emotionally changed attitudes, frustrations, lack of understanding, or personal limitations? Do these situations imply training needs?).
2. Management requests for training of employees.
3. Interviews with supervisors and top management personnel to accumulate information about production problems, as well as interviews with employees concerning problems encountered in production or areas in which they feel they need training.
4. Group conferences with interdepartmental groups and training advisory committees to discuss organisational objectives, major operational problems, plans for meeting objectives, and areas in which training could be of value.

5. Comparative studies of good versus poor employees to underline the bases for differentiating successful from unsuccessful performance.
6. Questionnaire surveys.
7. Tests or examinations of job knowledge of current employees; analyses of samples of their work.
8. Supervisors' reports on the performance of employees.
9. Personnel records.
10. Business and production reports.
11. Review of literature concerning the job.
12. Actually performing the job.

For most of the jobs in an organisation, one can follow relatively standardized procedures and obtain very satisfactory job analyses. On the other hand, an analysis of a top executive or a secretary's job in a government department is not so simple. Much of his time may be spent in interpersonal interaction and thinking, so that it is extremely difficult-often impossible to determine by observation when he is working on a specific task. The complex and ambiguous nature of the managerial function makes it difficult for the manager to describe just what he does, how he does it, and when he does it. Furthermore, it is impractical to have someone perform the manager's job for analytical purposes.

The knowledge that job analysis of managerial positions is extremely difficult should not deter us from seeking better ways to perform these analysis. From those performed to date, we have a fairly clear picture of the general characteristics of the manager's job. For example, the typical manager is a solver of unprogrammed problems; in other words, the problems he must solve constantly change, and he deals largely with unknowns rather than knowns. He must perform a wide variety of functions, including planning, coordinating, evaluating, negotiating, supervising, and investigating. He must be skilled, then, in gathering information, defining problems, searching for alternative solutions and translating his understanding into decisions for action and ultimately into action itself. The organisational setting in which he works makes his position unique. Typically, he operates from a power position in a pyramidal structure. He is blessed (or cursed) with varying amounts of authority over others, though he is peculiarly dependent on those beneath him even while seeming to be independent. From a somewhat delicate position, then, he must perform his functions through his influence on other people.

His job is further complicated in that the typical manger is not the top manager; he is dependent not only on his subordinates but also on his peers and superiors. In a sense, he is always an apprentice to someone and must deal with difficulties from above and below, as well as all around him. Finally, he is a teacher and therefore needs a clear understanding of the significant principles of learning involved in developing subordinates.

Manpower Analysis

Manpower analysis focuses on the individual in a given job, rather than on the job itself. Three basic issues are involved in a manpower analysis for training purposes.

First, through appropriate observation, supervisory evaluation, and diagnostic testing, we need to determine whether performance is substandard and training is needed. Second, we need to know whether current employees are capable of training, and we need to know the specific areas in which they may require training, in order to minimize training time. Finally, we need to ask whether current employees with substandard performances can improve their work through appropriate training or should be transferred to make room for those who can already do the job. At the same time, we must consider whether engineering modifications in the job may bring employee performance upto standard, whether, instead, new equipment or processes may be the solution, or whether training seems the wisest course.

Job-knowledge tests, work samples, diagnostic psychological tests, and performance reports provide the kind of information we need to help us choose from the above possibilities.

When the executives of a marketing firm became disturbed by reports on their salesmen's ability to calculate percentage discounts and markups for their customers, they arranged for the "hundred-problem arithmetic test" to be given to approximately 300 of the men. While no correlation was found between their rated merit as salesmen and their ability to add, subtract, multiply, divide, or calculate decimals, some of the areas diagnosed confirmed management's concern. Half of the examinees needed help in addition, subtraction, multiplication and division, while nearly three-fourths were below any minimal standard of proficiency in calculating fractions, percentages, and decimals.

Review and Revision of the Training Programme

If the training programme is to remain current and viable, then the three kinds of analyses described above must be carried on continuously. The very essence of organisational life is change, thus a training programme must be reviewed constantly and revised in the light of changes in the organisation's resources, its objectives, its internal organisational climate, and the total environment within which it operates. Furthermore, these analyses, to be effective, cannot be done in an "armchair" manner; they must be integrated in a carefully designed and carefully executed research programme.

Although this kind of programme is expensive to pursue in the higher levels of an organisation and often produces far from ideal results, there is still reason to be optimistic. Despite the erratic growth of knowledge concerning management, a substantial amount of it has been developed. Each of the fundamental and classic disciplines such as psychology, sociology, mathematics, statistics, and economics has contributed modern analytical tools that are directly applicable to the study of management and its organisation. In addition, many newer disciplines – such as operations research and systems analysis-have added to this body of knowledge. Although a widely accepted scientific doctrine of management cannot be described in more than general terms, there is, at least, this core of analytical methods and tools, which were founded in basic disciplines and tested in actual management settings. The intelligent use of these methods, however, demands a well-grounded, basic education that will help the manager recognize their operational limits and adapt them to the particular conditions of many different business decisions.

3

DESIGNING TRAINING PROGRAMMES

Designing training programmes is one of the most pervasive, yet the most misunderstood activity to be found in the field of human resource development. As human resource development is concerned with learning particularly in work settings, the task of designing is crucial.

There are a few significant parameters which are to be taken into account while designing any training programme. We will briefly look into these parameters which enrich and facilitate a training design in terms of its efficacy in operation.

Introduction

Before we go into the details, in the introductory part, it is to be mentioned the relevance of the particular training programme and the context in which it is to be used in order to bring about changes in the functioning of the personnel who are expected to contribute to development or betterment. The specific contribution of the training programme is to be highlighted and it takes us to the Identification of Needs.

The following aspects are to be taken care of:

- Analyze task, Job or function
- Determine the target participants

- Discover gap in actual and required performance
- State training needs and their priorities
- Specify required knowledge, skills and attitude

The above analyses may be done through

- Discussions with the concerned
- Examination of records

Learning Objectives

One is to be very clear as to what is expected in terms of learning on the part of the participants. This learning is equipping the participants may be with additional information, new skills, are trying to bring about desirable attitudinal change among them. Once we are very clear as to what is to be delivered in terms of the content to the participants the rest of the things will be clear. We should have a clear idea as to the learning objectives in the particular programme which has bearing on the training objectives and relevant training methods; otherwise, the programme will not be ideal or systematic. In many cases, the learning objectives or the training objectives are simply assumed. When you have a group of participants, the knowledge requirement, skill requirement or the desirable attitude on the part of the participants may not be uniform. Though, they are from a particular level, their potential in the three areas (Knowledge, Skill, Attitude) may vary from person to person. While designing a training programme, we have to keep in view the job or the function or the activity to be carried out by the individual or group and what kind of knowledge, or skill or the kind of attitude that is required which will facilitate a satisfactory discharge of functions or completion of a particular task. It cannot be an ad-hoc approach. It is a question of spending resources in terms of finance, personnel and time. More often, the designers of training programmes assume as to what is required on the part of the participants and with that kind of assumption, they include modules in the training programmes. As we have mentioned earlier, this kind of learning objectives to be quite objective, one has to go in for interviewing a sample of prospective participants in respect to the requirements for the present job operations and the future requirements. This kind of a process starting from understanding of the requirement on the part of the participants in three areas (Knowledge, Skill, Attitude) in a realistic way would facilitate designing the training programme with appropriate modules and using related training methods.

Determination of Training Objectives

The training objectives obviously are related to the task to be performed and the learning that is expected on the part of the participants. In respect to training objectives there may be a principal or a central objective or the main objective of the training programme and further the training objective also may be detailed. While determining the training objective the following aspects may be taken care of:

- Decide learning to be achieved
- State aims in learner-behaviour terms
- Specify objectives in terms of
    - Performance with action expected
    - Conditions provided under which the performance is to be carried out
    - Standards of performance expected

Unless we have clarity in respect to the above aspects we will not arrive at clear objectives of the training programme.

Further in the course construction, the following factors may be taken into consideration:

- Determine syllabus and scope
- Decide subject sequence
- Determine training activities
- Decide aids in presentation
- Write or collect lesson plans

This is to be convenient for learner to concentrate, providing adequate duration for fuller understanding.

While designing the training programmes, the following types of training may also be kept in mind:-

- Institutional / In company
- On-the-job / Off-the-job
- Individual / Group
- Formal / Informal
- Immediate / Future
- Short / Long-range

Further, the nature of the training programme also is to be determined for example, whether the programme is:

- Informational
- Skill development
- Attitude modifications
- Approach moderation
- Habit changer
- Whether the emphasis of the programme is general
- Functional
- Job-oriented or
- Problem specific

Curriculum

While designing training programmes it is relevant here to have some idea of Concept of Curriculum.

Curriculum is a total concept while syllabus is specific. Syllabi of several aspects constitute the curriculum. Curriculum is from the teaching point and not from learning angle. The following may be considered as the objectives of a curriculum:

(i) Imparting of new knowledge or providing information.

(ii) Removing wrong knowledge or information that the participant had learnt already.

(iii) Imparting of new skills and removing wrong habits or skills.

(iv) Curriculum aims at increasing competence. It aims at

creating and maintaining motivation and interest on the part of the participant / trainee.

(v) It attempts changing attitudes and undesirable values on the part of the participants.

(vi) It aims at working towards a sense of healthy curiosity.

(vii) It attempts to develop motives of competence and need for achieving excellence.

(viii) It encourages participants from passive learning to active learning and from close-minded to open-minded.

In a very broad sense what you call curriculum embraces the following: ***cognitive, emotive, conative*** aspects in respect to the task.

Usually a curriculum is developed based on the job analysis covering knowledge component and motivation aspects. As mentioned earlier one of the aims of curriculum is reinforcement of right response and extinction of wrong response. Curriculum also aims at minimal level of inputs to reach maximal number of objectives. A curriculum is expected to be pragmatic and it should make people innovative and further it should develop adoptability on the part of the participants. Curriculum is not just syllabus of a course. It is a comprehensive tool which looks into physical requirement, staff, analysis of the training requirement, the people who are to be trained, the duration of the programme and the evaluation of thereof.

A curriculum is a kind of a total guide. And it is not to be taken as something static. Depending on the need and objectives of training and learning, curriculum may change but you need to have for any kind of a programme a curriculum which gives direction and specifies the parameters within which training is to be carried out.

Designing of courses is not one time affair like constructing a house. Based on the feedback from the participants and the feedback from their superiors in terms of their performance in the organisation and the course directors and the faculty discover lapses or shortcomings in the programme they have designed and operated. One may have to think of improving the selection of modules, the structure of the course or the sequence of topics and the exercises and methods that may be employed in order to improve the delivery of that programme. Therefore, there is to be a constant concerted effort in designing a training programme. It is not to be casual, the attempt is to bettering as you move on from making the training programme as an effective tool to increase knowledge, skills and desirable attitudes on the part of the employee towards making things better.

Critical Events Model

Any training programme is a process which goes through in a circular form, as the accompanying diagram shows, any training design is subject to continuous change towards consistency and betterment in terms of methodology, imparting of new knowledge, developing new skills and also attempts made towards desirable attitudinal change on the part of the employees in an organisation. In a sense, it is a nonstop journey all the time, improving all the components of training activity.

In general, almost all the training institutes follow this critical path, but in some cases for example, identification of organisational needs, and evaluation and obtaining feedback from the participants are not strictly followed and done. In some cases you have more assumptions made and taking things for granted.

Some of the job related/role related requirements will be known in the area of knowledge, social and technical skills and desired attitude. Therefore, depending on the demands of the job, the emphasis will be more on one of these three areas. For example, a Public Relations Officer (PRO) should have knowledge of people as to who is who and how one is to be received, treated and informed and he should also have interpersonal interactive skills, wherein his language, communication matter a great deal and also warmth and the way in which he interacts with the people. Here the emphasis is on his friendly or welcoming attitude. In simple terms, a greeting smile on his face facilitates a healthy and friendly interaction. Knowledge not only about the people with whom he interacts but also of the organisation that he represents matters a great deal. The PRO is to be the main source of information about the organisation and the way he builds up the image of the organisation. He should have that kind of talent. Here, talent is not simple knowledge, but it is skill spiced with a positive disposition.

In respect to organizing any training programme normally and usually we follow certain process right from the beginning to the end of conducting and evaluating the effectiveness of the training programme. The following Critical Events Model speaks of an ideal way of planning and organizing training programmes.

THE CRITICAL EVENTS MODEL

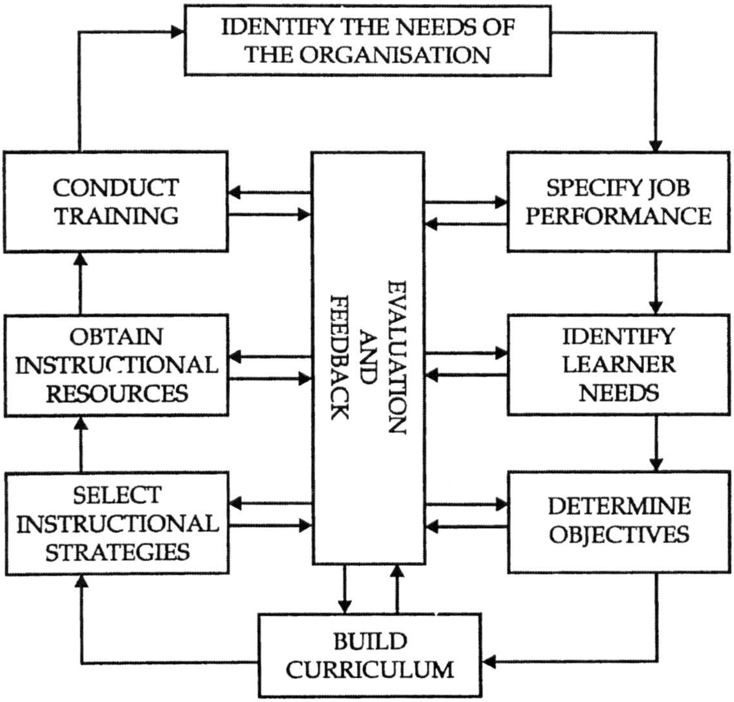

Source:- Leonard Nadler, Designing Training Programmes, Addison-Wesley Publishing Company Inc., U.S.A.

Though, one may have to follow the procedure or the process mentioned above, in actuality it is seldom adhered to in several cases. Though, one has to go through the whole process, sometimes in some cases, certain stages in terms of preparation may be skipped. For instance, selection of instructional strategies, obtaining of instructional resources, even identification of learner needs may be assumed or taken for granted. Often, the programme may mainly focus on the duration of the training programme with already identified selective modules. In respect to a particular category of personnel to be trained once or twice, we go through the process of organisational needs, job requirements and the role that is to be performed by individual employees. In such cases, there may not be a need to rigorously go through some of the stages in organizing a training programme.

Here is an illustrative list of the ways in which a training is ruined.*

MULTIPLE WAYS TO RUIN A TRAINING PROGRAMME

1. Teach them what you think you teach best, and not what they need to learn.
2. Argue with the participants.
3. Eat and drink too much.
4. Argue with co-faculty.
5. Do imitations.
6. Apologize in advance for the poor quality of your material.
7. Handout your lecture notes at the start.
8. Repeat what the previous speakers did.
9. Make them discover slowly what you can tell them fast.
10. Clutter yourself with equipment you can't use.
11. Start and finish at the wrong times.
12. Don't vary the pace.
13. Let a speaker go on for more than half an hour.
14. Borrow good material that does not quite fit.
15. Tell them what a skilled performance looks like, then stop.
16. Fail to brief your guest speakers.
17. Expect the course members to read the literature sent them in advance.

---

* Grateful thanks to the author of the above.

18. Believe that reaction-sheets tell you how much they have learned.
19. Expect to get it right first time.
20. Give assessments to their managers when they were not called for.

The following material presents in brief the important elements in designing and conducting training programmes.

TRAINING DESIGN PLANNING

OBJECTIVES
- Based on needs
- Stated in terms of expected outcome of learner behaviour & instructor achievement
- In terms of performance, condition, standard

SUBJECT CONTENT
- Based on objectives
- Under-standable to learner
- Of benefit to organization

SCHEDULE
- Convenient for learner
- Proper length-frequency
- Convenient to production schedule
- Organisational task requirements

LOCATION
- Within / outside
- Adequate facilities
- Minimum interruptions
- Minimum cost

CONDUCTING

TRAINERS
- Knowledgeable in subject
- Interested in teaching
- Respected by learners
- Skilled in teaching
- Ability to guide, coach

METHODS
- Varied
- Maintain learner interest
- Get group involvement
- Help learners learn

AIDS
- Audio visuals
- Simple and should be made out of practical situations.

EVALUATING IN RELATIONSHIP TO OBJECTIVES

Reaction	Learning	Behaviour	Results
How well did learners like the course?	To what extent did participants appreciate the relevant knowledge provided, skills discussed and demonstrated and the desirable attitudes emphasized.	To what extent the change expected is perceivable.	What final results were achieved? The significance in the quality of work.

STEPS IN DESIGNING AND CONDUCTING TRAINING PROGRAMMES

I. Identify Needs

- Analyze Task, Job Or Function
- Determine The Target Trainees
- Discover Gap In Actual And Required Performance
- State Training Needs And Their Priorities
- Specify Required Knowledge, Skills And Attitude.

Through

- Discussion With Concerned
- Examination Of Records

II. Determine Aims and Objectives:

- Decide Learning To Be Achieved
- State Aims In Learner-Behaviour Terms
- Specify Objectives In Terms Of:
    - Performance With Action Expected
    - Conditions Provided Under Which The Performance Is To Be Carried-Out
    - Standards Of Performance Expected

III. Formulate Plans

Course Construction

- Determine Syllabus And Scope
- Decide Subject Sequence
- Determine Training Activities
- Decide Aids In Presentation
- Write Or Collect Lesson Plans

Schedule

- Convenient For Learner To Concentrate
- Adequate Duration For Fuller Understanding

Location

- Institutional / In Company
- On-The-Job / Off-The-Job
- Individual / Group
- Formal / Informal
- Immediate / Future
- Short / Long-Range

Types

- Orientation
- Introduction
- On-The-Job
- Progressive
- Refresher
- Retraining
- Appreciation
- Advanced / Specialized

Nature

- Informational
- Skill Development
- Attitude Modification
- Approach Moderation
- Habit Changer

Emphasis

- General
- Functional
- Job-Oriented
- Problem Specific

IV. Organize and Administer Trainees

- Ascertain Level, Age, Experience, Qualification
- Mix Of Age, Sex, Status For Effectiveness

Trainers

Select Ones

- Knowledgeable In Subject
- Interested In Training
- Respected By Learners
- Skilled In Training
- Having Ability Later To Guide, Coach
- Having Authority And Approachability

Methods

- Varied To Suit Input Of Knowledge Skill And Attitude
- Maintain Learner's Interest And Involvement
- Sequencing And Structuring To Help Learning
- Inbuilt Feedback To Trainer/Trainee
- Suiting Time, Cost And Training Facilities

- Meets Job Environment, Participant Make-Up, Trainer Make-Up, Training Setup.

Aids

- Strengthen Learner's Learning
- Proper For Training Facilities, Environment
- Simple And Economical

V. Assess Effectiveness

- How Well Did Learners Like The Course?
- To What Extent Participants Learnt Fact, Principles And Development Of Skills And Attitudes.
- Is Design Right In Terms Of Content, Method, and Sequence?
- Is Training Effective In Terms Of Time Allocated, Reading Material And Facilities?
- Does It Meet Requirements Of Job In Terms Of Applicability?
- What Final Results Are Achievable In Terms Of Application Or Change In Behaviour?
- Whether Specific Learning Objective Was Met?
- Is Training Balanced On Cost-Benefit Analysis?

VI. Follow-Up

- Explore Further Personal Development
- Organize-On-The-Job Further Help, Guidance, Coaching
- Extend Help In Practical Applications
- Provide External Assignment And Attachments
- Conduct Informational Conferences
- Arrange Diagnostic Meetings
- Get Encouragement For Adjustment And Achievement
- Extend Help Of Superiors And Colleagues

4

PSYCHOLOGY OF ADULT LEARNING

LEARNING is : **"what we do to ourselves".**

TRAINING is : ***"what we do to others".***

Concept

Learning is the process by which the individual acquires various habits, knowledge and attitudes that are necessary to meet the demands of life in general. It means, (i) modifying and changing one's behaviour with reference to achieving a particular goal, (ii) establishing new relationships between a stimulus and response, (iii) development of a method for dealing with our problems; it is the development of a technique.

In short, learning involves changing capacities into abilities. Modifications which occur when we learn are dependent upon what happens to us as individuals. They are produced by the effects upon us of changes in stimulation, by activity, by practice, by special training, by observation or by a combination of these.

Aim of Learning

The **aim of learning** involves either **acquisition of knowledge,** understanding thereby intellectual and emotional modification and control, and the **acquisition of skill** involving sensory-motor modification and control. Under knowledge are comprehended the following sub-divisions:- (i) **Perception**: Refers to the acquisition of specific knowledge about objects or events directly stimulating the senses at any particular time. Perceptions involve cognition (knowledge). (ii) **Conception:** It means the acquisition of organized knowledge in the form of concepts or general ideas which transcend any particular percept. (iii) **Associative Learning:** Involves deliberate recall and recognition of past experience. One has habit or automatic memory due to associations. (iv) **Appreciation:** Refers to the acquisition of ideals, attitudes or dispositions characterized by an emotional tone.

Factors Influencing Learning

In any learning situation, the following three factors must be taken into account:

1. The **Physiological Factor** involving the organism and its receptor-effector system, the relative perfection of the sense organs and the general tone of the organism. The organic defects if any, like visual, auditory etc., and the fatigue state of the individual etc., can influence learning.
2. The **Psychological Factor** involving the motivational condition of the organism, both extrinsic and intrinsic.
3. The **Environmental Factor** in terms of the atmospheric and physical conditions, time of the day etc.,

It is, therefore, necessary that in any adult learning situation, the following factors must be known:

(i) The need of the learner in terms of his desire to learn;

(ii) His learning readiness in terms of physical and mental maturation;

(iii) Individual variations in terms of capacities, age, intelligence and motivational level.

Above all, the situation of the learner must be taken into account as individual learners belong to different home environments having different levels of intellectual stimulation. It is also necessary to assess the individual's attitude to learning situations.

The sufficiently mature adult may learn almost anything for which he has had adequate earlier preparation, i.e., provided he puts his mind to it or provided he has not developed emotional impediments.

The Adult and his capacities

Certain facts about the potentialities of the adult must be known before inducing him to any learning situation.

An adult is an individual who has completed his growth and is ready for his status in society with other adults. There are different views about the stage of early adulthood. According to some, the early adulthood stage would be between 21 and 40 years and middle age, between 40 and 60 years. But, some feel that the early adulthood stage is between 18 and 35 years and middle age from 35 to 60 years. Whenever an individual passes through one stage of development to another, changes can be seen in three areas: in his **perceptions**, in his **feelings** and in his **actions**. Every stage of development is associated with certain expectations and individuals have to develop the potentiality to adjust to these changing expectations.

The peak of physical efficiency is generally reached in mid twenties after which there is a slow and gradual decline in general fitness upto the age of 40 or 45 years when the rate of decline begins to accelerate. In physical **strength**, the individual is at his peak between the ages of 20 and 30 years. In **learning new motor** skills, the adult in his early twenties is superior to the one who is approaching middle age. With regard to **mental** abilities, genetic studies of intelligence have revealed that there is a slow but continuous rise in intelligence test scores upto the mid twenties after which the curve begins to flatten out and remains thus until the fifties. The peak is retained upto the middle age. It may take the young adult longer to learn than it did when he was younger but the quality of learning does not suffer.

The mental resistance to change appears with advancing age but is generally not apparent before middle age. In all levels of education, the younger the individual, the more ready he is, to accept new ideas and new practices.

The successful development of any individual from one stage

of development to another depends upon his capacity to master the developmental tasks that go with the particular stage of development. Some of the developmental tasks for early adulthood are: completing formal education, getting started in an occupation, selecting and learning to live with a mate, starting a family and providing for the material and psychological needs of one's children, finding a congenial social group, taking civic responsibilities and developing a satisfying philosophy of life.

Learning Process

There are many theories which have been propounded to explain the learning process. These theories are an attempt to find out how learning takes place. The important theories centre around trial and error learning, learning by conditioning and learning, learning by conditioning and learning by association and learning as conceived by Gestalt psychologists. Some of these theories have also put up some laws to explain the learning process. The contemporary theories by and large centre around the principles of conditioning. This is particularly so because learning by conditioning lends itself to both precise and highly quantified formulations.

I. Trial and Error Learning:- This learning process, as the name implies, involves attempting at a task blindly and as a result of continuous number of trials, the organism reaches the goal. Trial and error learning involves random activity, gradual reduction of useless movements and finally reaching goal. One of the pre-conditions in this kind of experimentation is a reward in terms of food that the organism gets at the end of the trial. This theory also brought in certain laws to explain the trial and error process.

(i). **Law of Effect:-** If the activity gives satisfaction of success, then that activity is fixed in and established. On the other hand, when a particular movement does not yield result, a feeling of disappointment and dissatisfaction helps towards discarding that particular movement.

(ii). **Law of Frequency:-** When any activity is repeated a certain number of times, there is a tendency for the same to be permanently established.

(iii). **Law of Recency:-** Any activity which has just recently been undertaken has an advantage of being repeated once again for the simple reason that it is fresh in the experience of the organism.

(iv). **Law of Readiness:-** This is interpreted to mean that a preparatory state is an important condition influencing learning. If the organism is set for a given kind of behaviour, then engaging in that behaviour pattern is rewarding.

II. Learning by Association:- Verbal learning is understood from the point of view of association theory. This involves that ideas get associated because of certain factors and therefore, the learning gets facilitated. Three laws have been proposed to explain the association of ideas.

(i). **Law of Continuity:-** When two events occur independently, though in a particular sequence of time, it has the capacity of being associated. This involves the dependence/between the observed variable and the antecedent condition, e.g., Lightening and Thunder.

(ii). **Law of Similarity:-** This also involves association on the basis of certain similar characteristics between one object and another or one word and another.

(iii). **Law of Contrast:-** This involves association between opposite events. When the relationship between two objects are opposite in character, learning gets facilitated, e.g., Black and White.

III. Gestalt Theory:- In this, perception is considered as basic to the learning process. It involves the perception of the learning situation accurately in order to get an insight into the problem. Most of their learning experiments demonstrate that learning involves insight. The learning phenomenon can be understood only in terms of organisation of the learning situation. According to them, learning takes place when the relationship between the different parts get reorganized into new patterns or better Gestalts. Learning situations are problematical. They, therefore, give rise to tensions in the organism making it to put in attempts to reduce the tension. They also proposed certain laws to explain learning.

(i). **Law of Similarity**:- This is similar to the law under association learning.

(ii). **Law of Proximity**:- It is similar to the law of recency where recent events, because of the temporal proximity, are recalled better.

(iii). **Law of Closure**:- Closed areas are more stable than unclosed areas; therefore, more readily form figures in perception. This law is similar to the law of effect, as it conceives of the end-result in learning.

The insight which is emphasized in Gestalt learning depends upon past experience. Insight is possible only if the learning situation is so arranged that all necessary aspects are open to observation. In any teaching operations, the end-result must be known before the commencement of any learning. Trial and error, though not of a motor type, is present in the course of achieving insightful solution.

Conditioning:- Conditioning experiments were initiated by Pavlov. The conditioned response theory explains learning among children and also animals. This conditioning process can be applied generally to the various day-to-day occurrences in individual's life. Conditioning simply means the establishment of a connection between a response and a stimulus which has no natural connection with it. The main emphasis in this process is that it is possible to condition a primary response with a conditioned stimulus by associating the primary stimulus with the conditioned stimulus. For example, by associating food (primary stimulus) with bell (conditioned stimulus), it is possible in course of time to elicit the primary response (saliva) for the conditioned stimulus (Bell) alone. In short, a situation can be substituted by another situation in eliciting a response. This theory utilizes the principle of substitution in explaining the process of learning.

There are other theories of learning which go by individual investigators like Guthrie, Skinner, Hull, Tolman, Lewin. Apart from Lewin and Tolman, the other theories take conditioning as a basis of learning.

All these theories have many things in common and quite a few things are unique. All the theories seem to imply the importance of goals, motivation, selection of alternate responses, reinforcement of the selected responses and gradual improvement in responses.

Learning Principles

As a result of various experiments on human or animal subjects based on the different theories of learning, some basic principles of learning have emerged which have practical bearing in any learning or training situation. Before going through the principles, it may be worthwhile to recapitulate the aim of learning as applicable to training situations.

1. The aim of any **training** programme must be specified and the behaviour of individuals must be **shaped** and **modified** so that they can perform the tasks required as members of an organisation.
2. **Shaping** and **modifying** are the key words of **Training** and indeed of all education.

The main question is: how can a Training programme provide an opportunity in which individuals can learn **new behaviour, new perceptions, new orientations** – which may require some isolation from every day pressures from the organisation.

The training process involves the actual procedures and techniques used in **shaping** and **modifying** behaviour, including teaching of certain **skills, knowledge and attitudes.**

1. *Repetition and Practice*

Repetition can facilitate the learning of a task. A training situation should be designed so that repeated practice of skills is possible. The amount of practice required depends upon the kind of task involved, training techniques and individual trainee differences.

The trainer must determine the optimal schedule of practice for the particular activity with which he is concerned and he must also consider the size of practice units (spaced for massed repetition).

2. *Task Guidance*

Learning is facilitating when the behaviour of the learner is controlled through 'Guidance'. 'Guidance' here refers to any procedure employed to ensure that the trainee performs a task or works through a problem in a way which the trainer considers correct. The trainer needs to determine the kind of information which, in particular training situations, can be best used by the learner and he must decide upon the best method of presenting this information to him.

3. *Learning to Discriminate*

The trainee must learn to discriminate certain classes of behaviour and to respond similarly within these classes.

Learning to discriminate between classes and to generalize within classes is considered a basic learning process involved in the formation of concepts.

4. *Extinction*

The modification of behaviour through learning sometimes involves removing certain behaviour from a trainee's repertoire.

The process whereby a task response loses strength as a result of lack of reinforcement is called response extinction. This is slower than the process of acquiring a response. Extinction is more rapid with continuous than with intermittent reinforcements.

In the development of attitudes, it is often advised that procedures be designed to permit trainees to let off steam. It is desirable in these procedures to permit no reinforcement to occur, so that these attitudes can undergo extinction. Otherwise, it may be that the release of hostile expression is reinforcement enough to guarantee its continuance.

Forgetting is not equivalent to extinction. Forgetting involves decrease in response proficiency as a result of the non-occurrence or disuse of the response over a course of time.

5. *Training Sequence*

In the learning of a task, certain sequence of task performance is more effective for the learner than others.

One of the major problems of effective training is arranging the successive task in such a way that the behaviour is efficiently learned. A good trainer will then have to organize a task into the most effective sequence of learning. Decision regarding use of whole or part method of learning depends on the nature of the tasks.

6. *Learning and Effort*

As a task response if learned and the learner becomes increasingly skillful, there is a reduction in the amount of effort required to perform it. A trainer should be aware of this stage of performance if it occurs in the tasks with which he is concerned, so that he can permit the learner to drop out unnecessary responses and cues which were required in the earlier phase of training.

7. *Meaningfulness of material*

Learning is facilitated when the tasks to be learned are meaningfully related.

Training sequences therefore should be organized around **connecting principles** whenever possible. The trainer should be aware of principles which do relate material meaningfully and those which do not.

In attitude and morale training, it appears that free exchange of opinion should be encouraged if such discussion helps to develop meaningful relationships which facilitate further learning.

8. *Aversive consequences*

For learning, stimulation by unsuccessful or aversive consequences of the learner's behaviour appears to be less effective than positive reinforcement. In learning situations, reproof, penalty or withdrawing privileges have not been favoured because of their undesirable consequences on the individual. Training under the control of rewarding consequences is preferable to training under the control of punishment.

9. *Plateaus*

In many training situations involving complex behaviour, the learner reaches a stage in which he exhibits no apparent learning progress or increase in task efficiency. An important function of the trainer is to analyze the characteristics of this stage of learning in his training programme to guide the learning behaviour.

10. *Learning to Learn*

Much can be gained in certain training programmes if the learner is taught how to learn. The training of a **set to learn** can be of important practical significance for job situations in which the individual must adjust rapidly to changing problems.

A significant influence appears to be systematic variations in the learning situations presented to the trainees.

11. *Active Learning*

Learning that takes place by active responding permits more effective control by the trainer than does that which takes place through passive observation.

Training procedures which require a trainee to respond actively by summarizing a problem (or a lecture) in his own words may be effective learning procedures of this kind. Despite the apparent advantage of trainer control, that active responding permits, many training programmes rely almost exclusively on a lecture method which does not make available to the trainer the behaviour he is interested in 'shaping'.

12. *Transfer of Training*

The aim of training programme is a dual one – to train for a specific task and also for transfer of training to subsequent tasks.

13. *Motivation and Motivating Conditions*

The influence of the considerations for learning so far listed are enhanced or depressed by motivating conditions.

For the practical purpose of modifying behaviour a trainer may distinguish between the motivational possibilities that a trainee brings to the learning situation as a result of his past experience and the motivational conditions that can be built into the training programme. It is a good practice for the trainer to assess the motivational states with which trainees enter a training programme. It is even more important for the trainer to determine what motivating conditions he can introduce into his training programme in order to enhance the effect of such variables as reinforcement. Trainers often suggest that this can be accomplished by **setting up conditions** of **competition** and **cooperation** in a training programme.

How behaviour gets started, is energized, is sustained, is directed, is stopped and what kind of subjective reaction is present in the organisms while all this is going on will amount to a study of motivation. Motivation in brief determines the **direction** of action, its **vigour** and persistence. A motive as defined by habitual usage as something (a need or a desire) that causes a person to act. Motives can function in three levels as it can be conscious or unconscious – (i). where the individual is aware and is willing to tell, (ii). Where he is aware but, not willing to tell and (iii). Where he is not aware and hence not able to tell. To motivate is to cause the release of energy to a desired goal. In order to motivate an individual, the following three factors must be known:- (i). the **goal** that is to be realized, (ii). the **energy** or **effort** that is to be released, (iii). the tool or method that is to be used to direct and control the energy. It is possible for us to manipulate the motives through incentives. Motives are subjective whereas incentives are objective. The incentives can be financial or non-financial (socio-psychological) in nature. Incentives bolster an activity in a particular direction.

Hull distinguishes between primary (PR) and secondary reinforcement (SR).

PR is a process of need reduction.

e.g., jumping reaction from a charged grid is closely followed by need reduction – need being avoiding injurious effect of shock.

SR results when stimuli closely associated with PR became effective in reducing needs.

e.g., Infant ceases crying when fed.

Cuddling replaces food and becomes SR.

Variables associated with Reinforcement

In classical conditioning, Conditioned Stimulus (CS) is followed by Unconditioned Stimulus (US) and during the period of acquisition, the US is always present and hence the **reinforcement is continuous.** In operant behaviour which is more characteristic of every day life, **reinforcement is anything but continuous.** Consider the gambler for example, who for years responds to the lure of the horse races despite the fact that reinforcement in the form of picking a winner is all too infrequent. Life is replete with intermittent rewards.

Applied to Learning

The least complicated situation is that in which the animal is reinforced according to a certain predetermined schedule, say every 2 or 5 minutes. B.F. Skinner classifies such schedules under the category of **interval reinforcement,** since the fundamental variable is the time interval involved. The shorter the interval, the more rapid the rate of response, with speed of acquisition falling off rapidly with very long intervals. In interval reinforcement, extinction is slower. (Finding eatables in a jar – mother hiding it always results in extinction. But occasional finding involving not hiding in between, extinction is slower).

A second type of intermittent reinforcement makes use of **fixed ratio** schedules. Here the animal determines its own schedule of reinforcement in the sense after so many trials say 20 – the animal is reinforced.

Secondary Reinforcement

Skinner prefers to emphasize the concept of **generalized reinforcers** by which he means a variety of conditions that may become associated with primary reinforcers. Money is generalized reinforcer par excellence. Money becomes associated with a variety of primary reinforcers.

If the primary reinforcement is negative (punishment), then any secondary reinforcer associated with it, will be negative.

If the original primary reinforcers are positive, the generalized reinforcers are also positive. For example, in the case of phobias, the original or primary condition of reinforcement may no longer be present or remembered, but the presence of stimuli associated with the original reinforcement will reactivate the original emotional response.

Some of the methods of motivating are by praise and blame induced by prestigeful persons, competition with one's own standard, rewards and punishments in concrete for, knowledge of results or progress, social motivations in terms of approval, recognition, status etc.

14. General

Trainer must be aware of the differences that exist between individual trainees with regard to speed of learning, capacity to discriminate, motivational state and age etc.

A pleasant instructor can elicit pleasant experiences. The personality of the trainer may have enhancing or hampering influence on the learning process. Thus to contribute to good morale and to individual satisfaction it is important for a trainer to be aware of this sort of conditioning.

Methods of Measuring Memory

The phenomenon of memory seems to contain learning, retention, recall and recognition. Retention takes the form of memory. The memory process is measured by recall, reproduction, recognition and relearning. In **recall** the subject must demonstrate that he can remember what has been learned without the aid of additional stimulus cues. In **reproduction** he must show, by a drawing or by rearranging objects in their original order, that he can remember what was originally learned or perceived. In **recognition** the subject must demonstrate that he can remember which of several alternatives were originally learned when all are presented together. In **relearning** the amount of time or number of trials saved is measured for the relearning of a passage which had been learned in the past.

(i). **Whole and Part Method:-** Learning can also be facilitated either by whole method or by part method. The whole method involves attempting at the task as a whole. The part method involves learning the tasks in convenient meaningful parts. In view of the difficulty in the former and disadvantages of the latter, a mediating method has been proposed wherein a person learns part by part at the same time tries to link the parts at each phase of learning. Whether a person should use whole or part method of learning depends to a great extent on the nature of the task.

(ii). **Recitation Method**:- It means checking up one's self by being one's own inquisition from time to time. The outstanding advantages are that it will create a feeling of accomplishment, errors get detected and eliminated and reproduction becomes facilitated.

Forgetting:- The first curve of retention to get an idea of the nature of forgetting process was presented by Ebbinghaus. Ebbinghaus's curve of retention is interesting not only because it shows the general nature of forgetting but the initial period of rapid 'drop off' followed by negatively accelerated loss in time.

There are various causes of forgetting. They could be classified as follows:

(i). **The time Factor**:- The retention curve mentioned above has suggested that the retention goes on diminishing with the passing of time.

(ii). **Atrophy through disuse**:- Where a particular skill acquired, if not put to use, may lose its memory by sheer disuse.

(iii). **Interference**:- There are two types of interference: (a). Retroactive Inhibition, (b). Proactive Inhibition

a). **Retroactive Inhibition**:- In this process what is learnt presently will disturb what was learnt earlier. The effect of the present activity is thrown back upon an earlier activity. This results in the present learning inhibiting what was learnt earlier.

b). **Proactive Inhibition**:- In this process, just the reverse of what happens in the retro-active inhibition takes place. Here, the past learning interferes with the learning of the present.

The other causes of forgetting which are pathological in nature can be classified into **exogenic** and **endogenic** causes. Exogenic causes could be severe injure to the brain such as shock resulting from a fall etc., which can affect the memory process badly.

Endogenic are due to causes from within, which may be mainly unconscious in nature or some emotional blocking in the individual resulting in recall amnesia.

In training the faculty may bear in mind the factors, the situations, the conditions that facilitate learning on the part of the trainees. It is knowing the learner, the subject and making a systematic effort and using appropriate methods and creating a learning environment to facilitate the learner to learn.

[*Source:-* Adopted with grateful thanks from 'Psychology of Adult Learning' by Dr. B.C. Muthayya, Formerly Director of Psychology, National Institute of Rural Development, Hyderabad-30.]

5

COMMUNICATION IN TRAINING

The entire activity in training is through communication in diverse forms: verbal, non-verbal, using of audio-visual aids. It is not only the means and modes of communication that are used in training, the physical environment, the setup of the classroom, and other materials related to audio-visual aids can be taken as part of communication. It is what the participants, hear, see and experience i.e., the total environment in a training institute could be taken as a medium of communication. In a training programme depending on the learning needs and training objectives, we use different methods and each method whether it is lecture, case study, panel or any other kind of method or technique that is used in training will have a different mode of communication. It is not only the language and the content but the way in which the learning environment is created constitutes an effective communication.

The training methods may be likened to the musical instruments. By themselves they will not operate and it depends on the operator. In order to play each musical instrument one should have the skill to tune it to the RAGA of the song. When a faculty uses several methods they should synchronize and should result in symphony as in the case of orchestra that is the symphony that results in concord on the part of the participant. Each method that the faculty uses should bring in clarity in concept and facilitate right type of understanding and reflection as intended in terms of learning and training objectives. While using the methods any poor user as in the case of playing the musical instruments it is likely to fail in creating interest and attention on the part of the participants. The trainer before he uses any method in training should thoroughly examine and understand the scope and limitation of each method. The entire thing centres around faculty's communication in the class room.

We can cite examples how the communication should be in respect to each training method. "When to Use and What Kind of Method".

Communication - verbal and non-verbal is a crucial factor in all kinds of human interaction. The individual's very behaviour is his communication, whether it is between two individuals or between an individual and a group or whether it is in the family or in the organisation. Communication plays a very vital role in all human affairs. Communication can be called a most fundamental factor for the growth and development of mankind and civilization. Verbal communication is one factor which differentiates man from other species of life. In communication it is not only the words but the feelings and emotions of respect or disrespect, regard or disregard that is communicated to other people. Team building or a coordinated action in an organisation or giving of instructions to the subordinates, clarifying issues, principles, regulations etc., depend on clarity in communication. Concepts and clarity of concepts matter a great deal in communication. You cannot imagine life especially functioning in an organisation minus communication. It is not just communication but the kind and the content and clarity in communication that matter.

The efficacy of one's communication depends on self-concept or self-image of the communicator. If his self-concept or self-image is weak his communication also is likely to be ineffective. Though clarity of communication is an essential requirement, listening which is an intellectual journey along with the speaker is the major factor in the efficacy of communication. Often we find people as poor listeners. One has to cultivate the habit of patience to listening which not only helps the listener understand what is communicated but it also encourages the communicator. In order to see the efficacy of one's communication he has to seek feedback. In negotiations, in convincing people in order to bring about a desirable change, communication plays a significant role. Whether it is a head of an organisation or the subordinate at the lowest rung in the hierarchy clarity in communication and listening are two principle components for success at any level apart from other factors contributing to the success of any endeavour.

THE COMMUNICATION PROCESS

Communication is a conscious attempt to share information, ideas, attitudes and the like with others. In essence it is the act of getting a sender and a receiver tuned together for a particular message, or a series of messages. "Communication to people in such ways that they act on that knowledge to achieve some useful result. This result may range all the way from a small improvement in doing some production task, to the generation of a sense of national unity and strength in a country. Communication in this sense includes the whole learning process. It encompasses the teacher – the message or material to be taught. The means or media used to carry the message the learning achieved by the audience or participant and actions by which the learning is put into practice.

Communication Problems & Critical Factors

Communication is a process – it has three phases:

1. Expression
2. Interpretation
3. Response

1. Communication is limited by one's concept of the communication process.
   (a). It starts with the recognition of needs which new ideas can help meet and proceeds until people have acted upon them.
   (b). The way one thinks about communication will influence its quality.
2. Communication is a two-way process always involving interaction between those who are aspiring to communicate and the receivers.
3. One must have ideas before one can communicate with others.

4. The system of symbols used to represent ideas, objects or concepts must be accurate and used skillfully.

   (a). Visual and audio-visual aids – All of these are symbols in one form or other employed to express ideas or feelings through **sound, shape, colour or motion**.

   (b). The basic means of communication is words.

5. Cultural values and the social organization are determinants of communication.

6. The environment created by the communicator influences his effectiveness.

   (a) Physical facilities – air of friendliness – rapport - respect for others' – views – permissiveness, etc.,

7. To make sense, the communication effort must be organized according to some specific form or pattern.

   (a) Organization may be informal as a conversation or a discussion or formal as a speech or lecture.

   (b) Other common forms are: a story, a play, a debate, a bulletin, a poster, a panel discussion

   (c) Common ways of organizing a presentation are:

   (i). Chronological or historical

   (ii). Logical

   (iii). Psychological – timing or ordering of ideas according to the anticipated reactions of audience.

8. Cooperation, participation and involvement are essential to Communication

   (a). It takes two to make communication

   (b). Communication is a two way process

9. Standards of Communication influence its success

   (a). Standard of correctness

   (b). Standard of effectiveness

   (c). Standard of good taste

(d). Standard of social responsibility

10. Evaluation is necessary to improve Communication

Plus:

(a). Planning communication

(b). Adapting content and method to the needs, interests and level of ability of the audience

(c). Timing so that given points can and will be communicated for more effectiveness

KEY ELEMENTS OF COMMUNICATION

THE COMMUNICATOR

(a). The credibility of the Communicator as perceived by the audience is a powerful determinant in communication

(b). Good qualities of a Communicator

i). He Knows:

- his objectiveness – has them specifically defined;
- his audience – its needs, interests, abilities, predispositions
- his message – its content, validity, usefulness, importance
- channels that will reach the audience and their usefulness
- how to organize and treat his message
- his professional abilities and limitations

ii). He is interested in:

- his audience and its welfare
- his message and how it can help people
- the results of communication process and their evaluation
- the communication process

- the communication channels – their proper use and limitation
- how to improve his communication skill

iii). He prepares:

- a plan for communication – a teaching plan
- communication materials and equipment
- a plan for evaluation of results

iv). He has skill in

- selecting messages
- treating messages
- expressing messages – verbal & written
- the selection and use of channels
- understanding his audience
- collecting evidence of results

Poor Communicators are guilty of one or more of the following

1. Fail to have ideas to present that are really useful to the audience
2. Fail to give the complete story and show its relationship to people's problems.
3. Forget that time and energy are needed to absorb the material presented.
4. Feel they are always clearly understood.
5. Refuse to adjust to 'closed' minds.
6. Talk while others are not listening
7. Get far too ahead of audience understanding.
8. Fail to recognize others' view–point and develop presentation accordingly.
9. Fail to recognize that communication is a two way process.

10. Let their own biases over influence the presentation
11. Fail to see that everyone understands questions brought up for discussion
12. Fail to provide a permissive atmosphere.
13. Disregard the values, customs, prejudices and habits of people with whom they attempt to communicate.
14. Fail to start where people are, with respect to knowledge, skill, interest and need.

MESSAGE (OR) CONTENT

A message is the information a communicator wishes his audience to receive, understand, accept and act upon.

A successful communication is one in which the major factors influencing the message are controlled as far as possible. This is the responsibility of the communicator.

A good message must be:

- in line with the objective to be attained;
- clear – understandable by the audience
- in line with the mental, social, economic and physical capabilities of the audience
- significant – economically, socially or aesthetically to the needs and values of the audience.
- specific – no irrelevant material
- simply stated – covering only one point at a time
- accurate – scientifically sound, factual and current;
- timely – especially when seasonal factors are important and issues current;
- supported by factual material covering both sides of the argument;
- appropriate to the channel selected
- appealing and attractive to the audience having utility, immediate use

- applicable – audience can apply recommendation
- adequate – combining principle and practice in effective proportion;
- manageable – can be handled by the communicator with high professional skill and within the limits imposed by time.

Applied properly, the foregoing criteria for selecting and sending messages will contribute much to the goodness of the message. Effective communicators use them skillfully. In contrast, poor communicators often do the following:

1. Fail to clearly separate the key message from the supporting content or subject – matter.
2. Fail to prepare and organize their message properly.
3. Use inaccurate symbols – words, visuals or real objects – to represent the message.
4. Fail to select messages that are sharply in line with the felt-needs of the audience.
5. Fail to present the message objectivity-present the material, often biased to support only one side of the proposition.
6. Fail to view the message from the standpoint of the audience.
7. Fail to time the message properly within a presentation or within a total programme.

CHANNELS OF COMMUNICATION

The sender and the receiver of messages must be connected or tuned with each other. For this purpose, channels of communication are necessary. They are the transmission lines used for carrying messages to their destination.

Obstructions or 'noise' that affect – the channels

- Failure of a channel to reach the intended audience

- Failure on the part of a communicator to handle channels skillfully.
- Failure to select channels appropriate to the objective of a communicator.
- Failure to use channels in accordance with the abilities of the audience.
- Failure to avoid physical distraction
- Failure of an audience to listen or look carefully.
- Failure to use enough channels in parallel.
- Use of too many channels in a series.

TREATMENT OF MESSAGES

Treatment has to do with the way a message is handled to get the information across to an audience. It relates to the technique, or details of procedure or manner of performance, essential to expertness in presenting messages. The following are the three categories or bases useful for varying treatment.

(a). Matters of general organization

- Repetition or frequency of mention of ideas and concepts.
- Contrast of ideas
- Chronological compared to logical, compared to psychological
- Presenting one side compared to two sides of an issue.
- Emotional compared to logical appeals.
- Starting up with strong arguments compared to saving them until the end of presentation.
- Inductive compared to deductive
- Proceeding from the general to the specific and vice-versa.
- Explicit drawing conclusions compared to leaving conclusions implicit for the audience to draw.

(b). Matters of Speaking & Acting

- Limit the scope of presentation to a few basic ideas and to the time allotted. Too many ideas at one time are confusing.
- Be yourself. You can't be any one else. Strive to be clear not clever.
- Know the facts.
- Don't read your speech. People have more respect for a communicator who is sure of his subject.
- Know the audience, each audience has its own personality. Be responsive to it.
- Avoid being condescending. Do not talk or act down to people, or over their heads. Never over-estimate the knowledge of an audience or under-estimate its intelligence.
- Decide on the dramatic effect desired. Effective treatment requires sincerity, smoothness, enthusiasm, warmth, flexibility, and appropriateness of voice, gestures, movements and tempo.
- Use alternative communicators when appropriate as in group discussions, panels, interviews, etc.,
- Quit on time.

(C). Matters of symbol variation and devices for representing ideas:

- Word symbols –speech
- Real objects
- Models
- Specimens
- Photographs
- Graphs
- Charts
- Motion Pictures

- Slides
- Drama
- Puppets
- Songs
- Flash Cards

Aspects that help to clarify the exact nature of an audience and how to reach it:

1. Communication channels established by the social organization
2. The system of values held by the audience, what they think is important.
3. Forces influencing group solidarity – custom, tradition, etc.,
4. Individual personality factors – susceptibility to change, etc.,
5. Native and acquired abilities
6. Educational, economic & social levels.
7. Pressure of occupational responsibility–how busy or concerned they are.
8. People's needs as they see them, and as the professional communicator sees them.
9. Why the audience is in need of changed ways of thinking, feeling and doing.
10. How the audience views the situation.

AUDIENCE RESPONSE

Possible Responses

1. Understanding Vs. Knowledge
2. Acceptance Vs. Rejection
3. Remembering Vs. Forgetting
4. Mental Vs. Physical action

5. Right Vs. Wrong.
   - You have to forget your status while communicating.
   - Forget your status and communicate.
   - You are simply wedded to the content and the way it is to be communicated.
   - Personal status may affect the communication process.
   - It is a dictum.
   - Essential attributes of any faculty are humility, modesty and respect for the audience.
   - Participant is a human conduit who is a channel, contributing to the role of a trainer and his conduct, audio-level, norms in communication.
   - Factors that contribute to your communication in the class are: Language, audio-level, intonation, non-verbal communication (body language), examples, analogies, illustrations, spontaneous humour, respect to the participants, sincerity and richness in content.
   - Aalapana, before starting a lecture. Try to know the participants, their interest, and relevance. In the initial stages try to build a rapport with the participants, do not indulge in bragging about you.
   - First impression is the best impression.

COMMUNICATION KILLERS[1]

COMMUNICATION KILLER	EXAMPLE
THREATS (Produces fear, submission, resentment, hostility)	If you're not able to get to work on time we'll have to review your job here: 'Do it or else'.
ORDERS	I'll see you immediately

(Contd...)

(Using power over another)	in my office: 'Don't ask me why, just do it because I said so'.
CRITICISM (Put-downs)	You don't work hard enough: 'You're always complaining.
NAME CALLING ('Branding' the other person)	'Only an idiot would say that; 'You stupid fool'. 'What can you expect from a bureaucrat?'
'SHOULDING' OR 'OUGHTING'	'You should be more responsible': 'You ought to face facts': 'You shouldn't be so angry.'
WITHHOLDING RELEVANT INFORMATION (With a trap at the end)	'You'll love this project'(not saying how much is involved).
INTERROGATION	'How many hours did this take you?'; 'How much did this cost?': Why are you so late?; 'What are you doing?'
PRAISING TO MANIPULATE	'You're so good at report writing, will you do this one for me?
DIAGNOSING MOTIVES	'You're very possessive,'; 'You've always had a problem with motivation'.
UNTIMELY ADVICE (When the person just wants to be heard)	'If you'd just straighten up your desk, you would not be in this panic,'; 'Why didn't you do it this way?'; Just ignore them'.
PERSUADING WITH LOGIC	'There's nothing to be

(Contd...)

	upset about. It's all quite reasonable'.
REFUSING TO ADDRESS THE ISSUE	'There's nothing to discuss. I can't see any Problems'.
CHANGING THE TOPIC	'That's interesting... I saw a funny movie last night'.
TOPPING	'I had a dreadful car accident last week...' 'You should have seen *mine*'.
REASSURANCE BY NEGATION	'Don't be nervous'; 'Don't worry, it will work out.; 'You'll be fine'; 'You look terrific'.

1. Grateful thanks to the author of the above.

6

TRAINING METHODS

Methods in training are the tools which attempt to create a learning climate for the participants. These methods are related to the learning objectives on the part of the participants. Methods again depend on the learning and de-learning which is expected to take place in a training situation. In another sense, methods are the conduits to deliver what is expected to be learnt by the participants. Further, methods are the means enabling the participants to learn what is expected of them in respect to their role or the functions that are to be carried out by them in an organisation. Methods depend upon three principle components of the objectives of training, these components are knowledge, skills and attitude. In some cases, it may be purely information giving that is knowledge based kind of training, in some other it will be social and technical skill development, and in another it would be an attempt to bring about a desirable functional attitudinal change on the part of the participants. In some of the programmes one will find these components in varying degrees. In one, the emphasis will be on imparting of knowledge, in another knowledge plus skill development with a desirable kind of attitudinal change on the part of the participants. Before one goes in for selecting methods in a particular programme, one has to look into the content that is to be delivered, the learning that is to take place and the objectives of the training programme. Once the nature of the contents of the modules are clear, one may go in for choosing the appropriate method.

Learning Objectives

Training methods are to be in tune with the learning objectives facilitating learning on the part of the participants. Since the learning in terms of gaining more information, developing action oriented skills and the right type of attitude in dealing with people require different modes of approaches in helping the participants understand, appreciate, learn and imbibe what is desirable to play his role and carry out the task assigned to him efficiently. Therefore, all the methods funnel down to as mentioned earlier, creating a learning environment wherein the individual reflects as to what he has to learn and the way in which he has to improve in discharging his functions effectively. Each method as discussed below has a different kind of approach focusing on creating a learning situation. These methods try to draw the individual participants closer. As everybody knows, the training is not just something transitory. Some of the programmes that are attempted in helping the participants are of lifelong relevance. In a sense, training deals with neo kind of socialization preparing the individual to fit-in in his role so that he becomes a coordinating functionary in a system or in the organisation. The individual participant is to be enabled to play his role effectively contributing to the goals and the objectives of the organisation of which he is a member.

The entire programme of training provided to the employees/ participants is towards an expected performance in the organisation on the part of the employees. That is the reason that the employees are trained before they enter the organisation and further in the course of their stay in the organisation.

The principal objective of training is to create a learning situation. One of the purposes of a good learning programme is to bridge the differences between the person and the job, so that the individual can perform his job which meets the organisational goals. At the same time, the goals of the individual cannot be overlooked. When an individual's goals are in conflict with organisational goals, the training or education can be a waste of valuable resources. However, it may not always be possible to bring in a positive blending of individual employee's goals and the organisational goals.

It is interesting to note as to what constitutes learning. We are a product of our interaction with the physical environment. The term 'learning' covers every modification of behaviour to meet the environmental requirements from picking up simple habits like nodding to mean 'yes'. Though the acquisition of complex skills like skating up to the most intricate development of personal philosophies of life. It is through learning that one moulds the raw stuff of human nature into a concrete individuality which one possesses.

We cannot see the mind processes which occur when learning takes place.

- Learning is a matter of relation between a goal object, perceived and the satisfaction experienced when the act is completed.
- Learning is basically a change in the way in which we perceive things around us.
- Learning is essentially a change at the level of perception and that changes in behaviour follow from fresh ways of perceiving.
- Learning is basically a way of recognizing our environment in a new fashion so that certain things take on a positive or negative value for us.

The basic and universal law of learning would be law relating to the connection between things, whether things are simple or whether they are complex, and their connections and motivation or the tension state of the individual would be one of the things which facilitate this process of making connections. We may have to regard learning as modifications both of behaviour and of the way of perceiving. Learning is a life long process. Learning is related to expected performance. The following table indicates the relationship.

PERFORMANCE OBJECTIVES Vs. LEARNING OBJECTIVES

Sl.No.	*Performance Objective*	*Sl.No.*	*Learning Objectives*
1.	Cause-Problem Identification	1.	• To identify problems & their causes. • To rank problems according to their nature.
2.	Assessment of Needs	2.	• To understand short and long term needs • To prioritize needs.
3.	Programme planning and Project Formulation	3.	• To gain practical knowledge/ skill in planning. • To understand interdisciplinary nature of planned activities. • To integrate various approaches.
4.	Education and Motivation	4.	• To understand clients' ethos, needs, strengths. • To mobilize groups towards attitudinal change. • To learn skills in organizing and building new communities.
5.	Institutional network analysis.	5.	• To understand structure and functions of various institutions. • To learn the way these institutions influence development and change.
6.	Participatory development promotion	6.	• To understand the indigenous knowledge system and its relation to the change proposed. • To recognize the consistency and usefulness of such knowledge system. • To learn to plan close to people's expectations.

(Contd...)

7. Environment Planning	7. • To gain insight into environmental problems accruing as a result of ill-conceived and hastily implemented programmes.
8. Planning for effective support system	8. • To understand the need, structure & functions of support system for RD • To gain knowledge and skills to coordinate and secure assistance from such system.
9. Monitoring and Evaluation	9. • To understand technical aspects of programme activities. • To understand "WHAT, WHEN and HOW" in project implementation.
10. Planning in Collaboration	10. • To understand the integral and complimentary role of NGOs. To learn the way to encourage and strengthen working with NGOs.
11. Development Administration	11. • To understand ideal administrative organisational setup facilitating development.

(Note:- Source is unknown and grateful thanks are expressed to the author of the above table.)

ISSUES OF METHODOLOGY

Before we move on to describe each method, we may have a brief look at issues of methodology.

It is a mix of methods and techniques the trainer employs and the ways in which they are employed. The techniques importantly are skills that are largely inextricably associated with the trainer, his/her personality and style. The unit of instruction (input) may determine the kind of method of technique. It may be a lecture, a lecture-cum-discussion, a case method, role-play, simulation exercises, games, the sole aim of which is to involve the participants, encourage and provide them learning conditions and opportunity to learn. The trainer needs to make a continuous evaluation of his interaction with the participants and techniques in the classroom situation. He also looks for the feedback. The trainer may have to be a good listener, a keen observer and a good manager of the learning situation.

The psychology which underlies effective adult learning is not different from that which underlies education at any level. Based upon this assumption, one can infer that the difference between child-education and adult learning is not so much in principles as in the curriculum which specifies the selection of method or combinations of methods.

For example, it is the curriculum that pre-determines the content and objectives of learning in relation to instructional procedures such as:

1. Programmed Learning Method
2. Structured Experience
3. Instrumentation
4. Case Method
5. Role Play
6. Syndicate
7. Workshop
8. Seminar
9. Panel Discussion
10. Lecture
11. Field Visits
12. Individual Assignments

In most cases, the curricula and methods, as predetermined and utilized, may frustrate adult learners, because their objectives may not match with those of the course content.

On the other hand, curriculum planning does not imply that a teacher or lecturer in a traditional educational system could utilize inadequate methods and skills, but rather that he/she could get away with less curriculum planning and with less danger of losing participants. In developing a curriculum for adult learners, if attention is not focused on a comprehensive understanding of the content, within which adult education could capture the reflective and concrete experiences of the participants, there would be a high rate of dropouts from the programme.

In addition to the failure to capture the imagination of participants in curriculum planning and the selection of methods, there is also the problem of assessing needs, which are usually based on the universal value systems, instead of the perceived / felt needs of the local people or unique characteristics of specific groups. For instance, the assessment procedures for the selection of instructional methods does not take into consideration aspects like:

a) The experienced participant, who has put in long years of service but is apprehensive of the unknown.

b) The literate 'young star', or new college graduate who is motivated by logical and rational needs.

c) The slow learner, who lacks confidence because his ability to understand is below average.

d) The 'frail linguist' who has difficulty in understanding because of differences in language.

e) The 'alienated bum' who is in an adult learning situation by circumstance and not by choice.

In addition, the training materials and instructional objectives of each input are usually structured so that it is almost impossible for adults with multiple life demands to systematically attend all the sessions of a course. Because each session is not self-contained, the result is that it becomes difficult for adult learners to follow instructions when they miss the classes, but eventually it discourages them to continue in the programme as planned. The dilemma of methodology in adult education also includes the structure of the timetable of activities, and the duration or time within which course objectives are to be achieved. In general, this aspect of adult education does not take into consideration the fact that study habits of adults get rusty, energy levels change and that other things of psychological importance happen within the time-frame of learning. All these determine the participant's reactions to the learning methodologies used in adult education.

The issues of methodology, as discussed, are but eye-openers to adult educators, who must be more sensitive to the psychological aspects and principles of curriculum planning in order to develop more useful course content and instructional methodologies to meet the needs of adult learning.

TRAINING DIAGRAM

Module/ Topic in Training	Nature and Focus of Content					No. of Sessions	Training Methods	A.V Aids	Methods of Evalua-tion in the class
	Knowledge	Skill	Attitude	Activity Oriented	A Blend of All four				
1	2	3.	4.	5.	6	7	8	9	10

There are three types of training depending on the location and the type. These are (i). On the Job, (ii). In the Classroom and (iii). Off the Classroom. We briefly mention the type of training programmes under each head. And a brief description of each type of training programme and the methods that are followed in training are described.

Note:- Please see the Appendix-III for the details of each training method at a glance.

I). On the Job

a. Orientation Training

b. Job instructions

c. Apprenticeship

d. Internship and Assistantship including job rotation and coaching

e. Junior board

II). In the Classroom

a. Lecture

b. Conference and Discussion

c. Seminar
d. Symposium
e. Panel
f. Workshop
g. Syndicate
h. Case
i. Instrumentation in Training
j. Vestibule Training
k. Business Games
l. Structured Experiences
m. Role Play
n. Laboratory Training
o. Simulation
p. Demonstration
q. Exercises
r. Films
s. Buzz Method

III). Off the Classroom

a. Field Visits
b. Correspondence
c. Programmed Instructions

I). ON-THE-JOB TRAINING

Because it requires no special space and equipment, on-the-job training is probably the most common way that employees receive instruction in industry as well as in other organisational settings also. The chief reason for this approach is doubtless its practicality. The employee produces and earns while he learns. In small businesses especially, managers often feel they cannot afford the luxury of off-the-job training. They think on-the-job training is better for their purposes, either because the trainee is performing necessary work that they could not accomplish otherwise or because he is paying his own way, at least in part, by working while he learns. The truth of this latter argument depends on how long training takes and how costly training turns out to be measured by the trainee's effectiveness while learning on the job.

On-the-job training methods are sometimes chosen to help maximize certain principles of learning. For example, the problem of transfer of training is virtually eliminated when the trainee is taught in the physical and social environment in which he eventually will perform his new task. On-the-job training also allows him to practice precisely what he is expected to do after training ends. While becoming adjusted to the daily operating procedures, he is able to associate with the same people he will work with after training. Finally, on-the-job training offers the opportunity for maximum control and use of the relevant reinforcements, because they are usually the same both during learning and subsequent performance.

On-the-job training may be used because a sufficient number of skilled and knowledgeable employees have the time to engage effectively in person-to-person training. The personality characteristics of the coach determine, to a large extent, his ability to create favourable learning environment. If he is highly authoritarian, what the trainee learns probably will be quite different from what he would learn with a highly permissive coach. The trainer on the job then, may compare unfavourably with a professional instructor.

Other likely disadvantages of on-the-job training may be that expensive equipment and workspace are tied up during training. Waste may be high. And the trainee learning under the pressure of job demands, at a pace set for already trained workers, will have to have his progress appraised according to his productive output; as such, the appraisal is likely to reveal little to him about the reasons for his mistakes and failure.

A final word of caution is in order concerning techniques for on-the-job training. Although, in theory it is possible to create maximally favourable conditions for learning on the job, in practice it is extremely difficult to achieve. The chief reason militating against such ideal conditions is that on the job the primary function is production, not training – which under the circumstances, must take second place.

In the Indian context, it should be of Guru-Sishya relationship wherein the Guru is interested in teaching his disciple and the latter too is equally motivated and guided in learning.

ORIENTATION TRAINING

Regardless of where the bulk of an employee's training occurs, some minimum amount of orientation training on the job is essential. Each employee, whether he is newly hired, transferred, or promoted, must be formally introduced to his specific job environment, to the people with whom he will be working, and to organisation policies and objectives that concern him. This introduction must be comprehensive and clear so the new jobholder and he does not start off with vague misconceptions and misinformation. Typically, he is ready and eager to learn about his new environment-perhaps more so than he will ever be again and the initial impression he gets may be a lasting one.

Although, it is impractical to specify all the background information a new employee should receive, the following procedures may serve as guidelines:

1. The new employee should be 'sponsored' or directed by an experienced worker or supervisor in his immediate environment who can respond to questions and keep in close touch with him during the early induction period.
2. Orientation should begin with the most relevant and immediate kinds of information and then proceed to more general organisation policies.
3. The new employee should be gradually introduced to the people with whom he will work, rather than be given a superficial introduction to all of them on the first day. The object should be to help him in every way to get to know them.
4. The new employee should be allowed sufficient time to 'get his feet on the ground' before the demands on him are increased.

In some unskilled jobs, orientation plus some simple instructions on the line may be all the training that is necessary. Next is a procedure for job instruction of skilled workers.

JOB-INSTRUCTION TRAINING

After an introductory statement of the purposes of the job, the trainee receives a step-by-step review and demonstration of the job operations. He then tries to perform the operations himself, explaining as he proceeds. The instructor is encouraged to ask the trainee questions during this demonstration and to correct mistakes as they occur. Practice continues until the participant reaches a satisfactory level of performance; then close supervision is removed. However, the trainer is cautioned to check back later to insure that his performance continues to be satisfactory.

A skilled trainer will help a trainee to focus his attention on the relevant tasks he must learn. The trainer can also estimate the difficulty of each task and make suitable adjustments in the rate of practice, in the number of operations required at specific times in the trainee's development, and the range of error permissible at these different stages. A skilled trainer can detect incorrect patterns and correct them before they become established habits. He can locate areas of weakness and provide the trainee with extra practice and guidance. Most importantly a skilled trainer can provide immediate knowledge of results.

APPRENTICE TRAINING

In formal apprenticeship programme for learning the various skilled trades, the trainee is placed under a supervisor for a specified number of years at the end of which time he automatically becomes a journeyman. If done well, the programme offers the opportunity to move back and forth from classroom instruction to supervised practice on the job. But too often, the programme is not systematically planned. The length of time in training may be unnecessarily long. Although different trainees are likely to learn at considerably different rates of speed, the fixed length of most programmes and the time spent in various phases ignore this difference. In terms of learning the following is a much more efficient programme:

A programme in a machine shop wherein the work is arranged in divisions such as lathe, drill press, bench work, milling machine, and provided a manual for each of these divisions. If an apprentice started on the drill press and worked on the projects assigned, following his manual, when he reached the stage where he thought he had mastered the drill press, he is given a standard proficiency test. If his performance is unsatisfactory, he is given supplementary work on drill press and later took another test. If, however, he demonstrated his competence, then he moved on to the lathe division and subsequently took a test on that division.

Programmes similar to apprenticeships have been recommended for managers. They are generally referred to as coaching but, more specifically, they include internships or assistantships and job rotation.

In essence, internships and job rotation are formalized instances of coaching. That is to say, coaching is made an important part of any plan in which they are used.

INTERNSHIPS AND ASSISTANTSHIPS

In an internship or assistantship, the trainee is assigned a job as a 'temporary' department head or an 'assistant' to a department head. In this position, he is likely to be engaged in a variety of troubleshooting assignments familiarizing him with the many problems of that unit or department. Over a period of time, his supervisor observes his performance and reviews his shortcomings and strong points, thus helping him to improve his performance on future assignments.

JOB ROTATION

Job Rotation provides the trainee with a series of assignments like those described above; the movement from job to job is planned so that he is exposed to successively more advanced learning opportunities. In such a programme, the trainee receives coaching from his immediate supervisor in each different job assignment, as well as from some other executive who is responsible for his overall development.

Systematic job rotation provides the trainee with the

opportunity to acquire valuable perspective and knowledge of interrelationships as he experiences the problems and approaches of the various organisational functions- finance, production, marketing, and engineering among others. A 'Plus' to this system is the constant stimulation that the departments themselves receive from the trainees.

Job rotation may also serve to tie an executive to the organisation as a whole rather than just to the department to which he is finally assigned. An executive who is expected to work in several departments during his training will hesitate to develop strong socio-emotional attachments to any particular group of employees.

To be effective, a job-rotation programme just be tailored to the particular needs and capabilities of the individual trainee and must remain flexible. Simply to set up a standard rotation programme and run all trainees through it can result in considerable waste of time and talent. Some of the men will be marking time on one job when they should be moving on to the next, while others will be forced into new jobs and new learning situations before they are ready.

One solution to this problem is to install a mutual goal-setting process in the system. Such a process is essentially a formalized, continuing plan of coaching. The trainee meets with his immediate supervisor, sets goals with him, and then meets him for periodic review of his progress and modification of his goals. This process increases the trainee's commitment to individual goals and to the total programme because of his personal share in setting the objectives. At the same time, it provides the trainee's supervisors with an excellent means for monitoring his progress so he can be moved ahead in the programme at an appropriate speed.

COACHING

The success of coaching in single internships and job-rotation programmes alike, is almost wholly dependent on the nature of the relationship established between the 'resident' supervisor and the incoming trainee. Coaching will be ineffective if the coach sees the trainee as a rival; if he rejects out of hand the dependent needs of the trainee; if he is intolerant of mistakes; or if he does not allow sufficient time for coaching. Coaching will also be ineffective if the relationship is ambiguous, if the trainee cannot trust the feedback he receives from his coach. Coaching, however, will work well if the coach provides a good model with whom the trainee can identify; if both can be open with each other; if the coach accepts his responsibilities fully; and if he provides the trainee with recognition of his improvement and suitable rewards.

Coaching, itself, can be improved by a systematic programme devoted to raising its quality. If the trainee's shortcomings are emotional or personal, coaching is not likely to correct them. A less direct approach, such as sensitivity training or nondirective counseling, would be more appropriate.

JUNIOR BOARD

Special assignments are often used to supplement coaching. For example, the trainee may be asked to serve on a junior board that investigates a variety of top-management problems on a sustained basis and offers possible solutions. Or he may be sent 'upstairs' to represent the coach and to develop some appreciation of higher-level management attitudes, and aims, as well as to be appraised by higher management. He may be sent out to visit other plants or departments. Or his coach may refer unusual problems to him, such as making a decision on a new sales campaign. He may be asked to work on a special project like making an analysis of transportation costs to various markets. He may even be requested to prepare technical reports and meet with consultants and visitors. The learning value of such special assignments will depend, of course, upon the trainee's readiness for them and the adequacy with which he receives feedback about his performance.

II). IN THE CLASSROOM

LECTURE METHOD

Definition

A lecture is a brief or a lengthy presentation to an audience small or large on a particular theme or subject providing information, facts, describing and analyzing the subject. Basically, it is transmission or sharing of knowledge. It is a traditional mode of communication. Though its efficacy and effectiveness as a medium and method of training and instruction is far less, compared with other methods of training, in practice, lecture as a medium of training is being used extensively.

A lecture could be on any subject on earth – religious, spiritual, scientific and historical, but a lecture as a method of training adults is to be distinguished from the other types of lecture. In the training context it is the adult learners, their background, the mode of their learning and their pattern of behaviour while on training, that are to be taken note of while lecturing to them.

The lecture is, of course, the old standby - the traditional method of transmitting information to others in a classroom setting. It is the most widely used of all the techniques, both on and off the job, despite its serious limitations.

On the positive side, the lecture has its place as an economical means of transmitting factual information to relatively large numbers of people at the same time. This economy, however, may be a false one, since mere exposure to information in no way guarantees learning.

The lecture generally consists of a one-way communication: The instructor presents information to a group of passive listeners. Thus, little or no opportunity exists to clarify meanings, to check on whether trainees really understand the lecture material, or to handle the wide diversity of ability, attitude, and interest that may prevail among the trainees. Also, there is little or no opportunity for practice, reinforcement, knowledge of results, or over learning.

Ideally, the competent lecturer should make the material meaningful and intrinsically motivating to his listeners. However, whether most lecturers achieve this goal is a moot question.

Key Elements of a Lecture

The key elements of a lecture that contribute to its efficacy may be said to be as follows:

- The lecturer himself
- His style of lecturing
- The content

- His grip over the subject
- The media he uses
- His language level and language skills
- His intonation
- The duration of the lecture
- The physical setting
- The size of the audience
- The background and the intellectual level of the audience and their interest in the subject

Delivery

- Start on time.

  Finish on or before time.

  Allow a break between lectures.

- Say what you are going to say.

  Say it.

  Say what you have said.

  (This sequence may occur several times in one lecture).

  Make clear when you are starting a new topic.

- Maintain continuity between lectures. (Say what you said last time). Emphasize headings and display them on blackboard, projector or handout.

  Give signposts of what is to come.

  Use connecting phrases and refer to previous work.

- Vary pace and intonation. Be audible. (Check with back row).

  Voice production is a skill that does not come naturally to all, but it can be improved with practice.

  Do not throw away words.

  Talk at a speed that is comfortable for your audience.

Allow adequate time for note taking.

Use the blackboard and other aids.

Never read from a script.

Use jokes sparingly and do not repeat them year after year.

- Be individual, but avoid annoying mannerisms. Look at your class, but not always at the same participant.

  Do not discourage interruptions.

  Admit mistakes freely.

The Lecturer-Trainer

We may refer to a lecturer as trainer. The lecturer-trainer may take note of the following guidelines in his lecture presentation in order to make his presentation interesting and inspiring and also to sustain the attention of the audience.

- Should have material in stock more than he would use in the class.
- Should not find himself blank, when there is still time slotted for his lecture.
- Modulate his voice not too low of audio-level and not of high pitch, not too slow and not too fast.
- Check the audibility with the audience.
- The media should not drown the speaker.
- To blend the lecture with examples, analogies, illustrations and spontaneous humour.
- Not to indulge in cheap jokes and use references which are in bad taste.
- Establish eye contact with the audience.
- Seek ånd welcome feedback from the audience.
- Be elastic in the subject coverage with respect to time.
- Encourage questioning.
- Let the answers be brief.

- Facilitate discussion.
- Introduce the subject, spell out the objectives of the topic on hand, and conclude the presentation.
- Be what you are and do not try to be what you are not.
- Do not go in for western accent which is not natural to you.

Besides his knowledge of the subject and skill in imparting to the participants, the trainer may remember the participant is a mature individual.

Conclusion

The purpose or objective of lecture is to reach the audience and see that the message is understood and appreciated by the audience. The lecture presenter should remember that his audience is primary and he should try to sustain their interest in the lecture. He should have clarity of expression; he should be a good listener, building trust in the audience and should have respect for his audience. Lecturing is an art with a blend of skills and capabilities. One has to practise it towards perfection.

The profile and limitations listed above in respect to the trainer and participants are not only restricted to the lecture method but they equally apply to other training methods in varying measures.

CONFERENCE OR DISCUSSION

The training technique of the conference or discussion group involves a more or less carefully planned meeting with a specific purpose and goal. Although this method may be used for a variety of objectives, it has proven particularly suitable for acquiring and understanding conceptual data and for the development or modification of attitudes.

Further, conference method is to provide information, to exchange information, to solve problems and to make decisions and to learn about new things.

1. Kinds of Conferences

i. Information giving

ii. Information or opinion collecting – fact finding

iii. Exchange of opinion

iv. Decision-making or problem solving

v. Decision 'selling'

vi. Educational

Numerous comparisons of lectures versus discussions as a means of affecting behavioural change in supervisors and managers indicate that discussion of material in small groups is likely to be more effective, particularly if a change in methods is incumbent first upon a change in attitude.

Discussion method has the following advantages which are quite essential in contributing to exchange of views, opinions and the method brings people together in a productive interacting way:

1. Facilitates different viewpoints – agreement – disagreement – controversies.
2. It is participative
3. The group dynamics – leadership training – action
4. Heterogeneity of the group a welcome sign
5. It should be permissive
6. Equal opportunity
7. Feedback
8. Teambuilding
9. Direct – indirect learning
10. Develops tolerance for ambiguity.

1. Unique characteristics of educational conference.

- Conference leader has a definite body of information or specific procedures to bring out regardless of the amount of discussion.
- Discussion is more limited than other kinds of conferences.
- Ideas and information can be presented dramatically and

can be directed toward getting involvement and commitment.

- Conference members often will accept material better because it is presented in concrete terms and in a logical order.

2. **Trainer Role**

   a. Chairman

   b. Information giver

   c. Discussion leader

   d. Procedural technician

3. **Training Problems**

   a. Difficulties in reducing dependency on conference leader.

   b. Difficulties in encouraging participation

   c. Difficulties in getting leadership shared.

   d. Difficulties in assessing learning.

4. **Some notes on conferences led by consultants.**

   a. Try to establish atmosphere that some controls are in hands of group.

   b. Use questions freely to encourage participation, check communication and stimulate discussion.

   c. Under-participate except when giving information.

   d. Play reality tester role, and encourage respectability of that role.

   e. Try to get group to define problem and talk in their terms.

   f. Devise procedures for getting leadership shared

      i. Group recorder

      ii. Group observer

Discussion has distinct advantages over a lecture if the material being presented is likely to need much clarification and amplification. When the number of persons in a group is so large that general discussion is impractical learning from a lecture can be facilitated if small 'buzz groups' are formed afterwards to share opinions on the lecture, raise questions, and consider alternatives. Each buzz group can then present a summary to the entire lecture room or engage in question-and-answer exchanges with the lecturer. Many individuals who would hesitate to question the lecturer directly will do so via their group spokesman.

The two-way communication achieved in discussion increases the trainees' motivation, enables them to check to see whether they are in error about certain ideas, and allows them to gauge the reaction of the group of their own, as well as the instructor's ideas.

Discussion facilitates the discovery process and thereby increases learning and retention. Rather than present all the answers, the discussion leader can pose questions and create conditions that enable the trainees to discover answers for themselves and then to evaluate them. In this regard, the discussion technique is similar to programmed instruction but with much less system and control over the course of events.

The discussion group itself may be a powerful source of reward and punishment for its individual members. The group can offer acceptance to its individual members or withdraw it, issue verbal punishments, or administer stronger sanctions on or off the job. The discussion leader must be aware of this power of group reinforcement if he is to structure the situation so that the negative effects are minimized and the positive effects maximized.

The conference or discussion technique, then, is not for the novice trainer. It requires skill, ingenuity, and, above all, careful preparation. In fact, it often requires more time to prepare than a good lecture, since the leader must be ready for a variety of unknown eventualities that would not occur, for example, in a lecture.

SEMINAR

It is mostly an academic one wherein at the postgraduate level classes are conducted through a seminar which is mostly participative with the faculty as a facilitator or moderator. The participants will be focusing on different aspects of the same topic.

It facilitates thinking and reflection on the part of the participants and one has the advantage of different viewpoints and opinions on the same topic. On one hand it is educative and it also helps broadening and going in-depth in respect to the multifaceted dimensions of a particular topic or issue. As mentioned above, it is mostly an academic activity conducted on the campus of colleges and universities.

SYMPOSIUM

Symposium also focuses on aspects of a topic. It is only to get more in-depth clarification and elaboration on various aspects of a topic. It is again educative and academic. Normally in training institutes, the seminars and symposia are not very much in vogue.

PANEL

Usually, panel discussion takes place somewhere in the middle of a training programme. Here, some four or five experts in a particular area are invited and each one will be focusing on a particular dimension of a topic or issue and he will share his views and experiences. Initially the panelists discuss among themselves while the audience / participants will be listening to the viewpoints or opinions as expressed by the panelists. So long the panelists continue their discussion among themselves the participants / audience will be just passive listeners and observers. Once the individual panelists finished expressing their viewpoints or ideas, the discussion is thrown open to the audience. Members in the audience may pose questions or seek clarifications from the individual panelists. And it provides an opportunity to know diverse views, suggestions, and solutions to a problem or approaches to any kind of an activity. Advantage in the panel is that people from different walks of life of course, with experience and depth in their own areas of specialization express their views and ideas which really add to the knowledge or information of the participants. One of the panelists will play the role of a moderator. A lecturer or an instructor though he may know what all the panelists have said, sometimes his instructions may not be as effective and as reinforcing as in the case of the panelists. Organising a panel discussion is a process and needs time. We may say that panel discussion is one of the effective methods in training whether it is related to knowledge or bringing about attitudinal change among the participants.

WORKSHOP

Workshop as the name suggests is action and production-oriented. The objective of workshop may be designing a training programme, planning for a particular course of action or any kind of an activity which requires going into details and formulating steps or the course of action and the way in which the action or the task is to be accomplished. Instead of directly teaching or instructing the participants, the participants are involved in working out an aspect related to the subject or an issue. Initially, the group will be familiarized with the subject and they will form into small groups and will workout a concrete plan of action. Depending upon the focus and nature of workshop the small groups again will assemble and share what they have worked-out. In a sense, it is involving the participants to work on some aspects of the topic or problem. In a sense, you may call this learning by doing.

SYNDICATE

Sometimes what you call a syndicate method is used in training programmes. Depending on the size of the participants it would be divided into three or four small groups and each group will choose a leader and these small groups will retire to different rooms and they will discuss various aspects of a particular topic. It may be a problem, it may be resolving a conflict, or it may be a plan of action. Each small group after deliberating over the topic will arrive at some suggestions and conclusions and once all the small groups finish their discussions, they assemble again in a kind of a plenary session and each group leader will present the aspects, conclusions or suggestions the small group has arrived at. The syndicate method provides an opportunity to members in the small group to voice their ideas which may not be that easy and facilitating in a larger group. Further, you have the advantage of diverse views or opinions or suggestions on a particular topic. There is some element of choosing the leader in the small groups and the leader working with the small group and presenting the ideas or conclusions the small group has arrived at in the plenary session. The syndicate method provides some warmth and scope for individuals participating effectively in the discussions. Though, it is also a discussion method in process, the small group has the advantage compared to a larger one. Each small group would discuss one aspect of the topic. The ideas and suggestions are pooled about the topic in the larger group. It is an interesting and quite facilitating in terms of learning and interpersonal relation amongst participants.

CASE STUDY

Case study is based on the belief that managerial understanding and competence can be best attained through the study, contemplation, and discussion of concrete cases – rather than through other common methods of training.

Many variations are possible in the specific application of the case method; but, in general, the trainee is presented with a written case that describes a concrete organisational problem. He is asked to study it in private group with other trainees, and as a group they discuss the adequacy of some or all of the proposed solutions and try to identify the principles involved.

Case study is designed to promote the trainee's discovery of underlying principles. There are no single correct solutions to most cases. Thus, the trainee is encouraged to develop flexibility in his approach to organisational problems. Rather than seeking a single answer, he is faced with the task of ferreting out appropriate and useful questions that may suggest several alternative solutions.

The following questions may be kept in view while writing / presenting a Case Study:-

1. When did it happen?
2. Where did it happen?
3. Were you involved in this case you are presenting?
4. If you were not involved then state the source from where you received information about the case.
5. Was the information received oral or written; published / unpublished?
6. How widespread was the knowledge of the case?

7. What was the number of people involved in the case?
8. How did the case surface? That is who brought it to the notice of whom?
9. Differential perception of the case – how differently was it perceived by different groups involved in the happening? How did the outsiders perceive it? How was it interpreted by different people?
10. What were the responses to the happening?
11. How did this case affect the programme / course of action? How pervasive was its influence on the programme / activity?
12. What was the aftermath of the case?

No two trainees will view a given case in exactly the same way; although they will generally agree on the existence of certain issues, their individual interpretations are likely to be very different, encouraged to project themselves into the situation, they must exercise their own judgment. The extent to which the trainees actually do their own interpreting of the case determines to a large degree the richness of the discussion sessions.

Further, the following are some of the advantages in using a case as a method in training:

The case method helps understand a situation. It stimulates thinking. One could draw inferences, motives, behaviour of people, the way people act, or react. The participant not only understands the issues involved in a situation whether it is a conflict or policy or decision making but also by his participation in the group his views, attitudes, bias and prejudices or in one word his understanding of the situation is revealed. This is one way of understanding the individual through introducing case method in training. Further, the efficacy of using case method depends on the skills on the part of the trainer, skills to develop confusion, insecurity and vagueness into clarity and insight. Case method also helps in drawing diverse conclusions indicating there are several ways of dealing with a situation. And it also reflects the behaviour of the people involved in the case and also of the participants who discuss the case.

At the same time that the trainee is urged to 'be himself', he is also asked to develop skill in objective diagnosis of cases that is, to learn to deal with relationships and elements in a situation with a minimum of personal bias. The process of working through a case with other trainees in : 'free' discussion provides an excellent 'checks-and-balances' system in this regard, since others are often able to detect the influence of personal attitudes on solutions much sooner and more accurately than the individual expressing himself.

The case method is quite flexible in that virtually any kind of problem may be presented in varying degrees of detail, depending upon the specific level of the trainees and the specific objectives of training. Actual cases vary from a paragraph statement of a minor personnel problem to a 50-page detailed history of business firm along with a description of its current status and the problems facing it.

At the one extreme, a case can be presented for discussion without directing the participant's attention to any of its specific aspects. At the other extreme, the trainee may be offered a series of choices that have been pre-tested and scaled to assess his ability to detect and employ the important cues in the situation.

In the presentation of the case, the philosophy underlying decentralization and the accounting problems associated with it come under surveillance, as well as communication patterns and questions of motivation. Role conflict and various types of authority are also of concern. An executive-decision procedure is described so that the participant can examine its value in selecting financial objectives and appraising operating results.

A really adequate demonstration of the value of case discussion should show that it stimulates thinking processes (although stimulation without feedback regarding the adequacy of the activity provides no learning). Learning may occur, however, to the extent that the participant's colleagues sufficiently evaluate and reinforce his conclusions and the ways he arrived at his answers. The method at least sets executives to thinking in terms of multiple answers.

We can see now that although the individual analysis of a problem is initially important, the ultimate success of the case method depends upon adequate group discussion. In general, the earlier remarks concerning the conference leader's skills and the conduct of the conference session are applicable here. Discussion should be generally focused but, at the same time, it should be free, informal, and experimental. It should also promote mutual agreement and mutual understanding among those talking and listening.

VESTIBULE TRAINING

In order to give more attention to trainee needs and to employ instructors who are specialists, a vestibule school may be set up in an area off the production line. Equipment and materials are similar to those used in production, but the emphasis here is on training rather than on production. Programme may last a few days or several months, depending on the complexity of the job to be learned.

Vestibule training has the obvious advantage of minimizing transfer problems; furthermore, it permits the instructor to arrange other ideal kinds of learning conditions, such as immediate reinforcement, accurate feedback of knowledge of results, ample opportunity for practice and repetition, and a learning sequence progressively arranged in order of difficulty. Finally, the learner's active participation helps to ensure successful training.

The most obvious disadvantage of vestibule training is the high cost of providing duplicate equipment that is used solely for this purpose. Such a setup may be more costly than on-the-job training if only a few workers are in the programme at one time.

BUSINESS GAMES

The most recent and most popular development in simulation is the business game. Business games vary from relatively simple non-computer simulations to some complicated ones.

Most business games simulate a total business environment that includes several companies competing in a common market. Game play is usually divided into several operating or decision periods (often called plays) during which the participants must make a wide range of decisions. Such decisions usually concern the classical function areas of real-life companies, such as finance, marketing, production, research, and development. Many games also present major problems in personnel, executive teamwork, and internal organisation. The consequences of each play are revealed as rapidly as possible so that they may be utilized in subsequent decision periods. The nature of this feedback varies from calculating a profit and loss statement by hand in the simpler games to detailed computer print-outs of factory operations, research and development reports, market surveys and extensive financial reports in the more complex ones.

Specialized games have been developed for wide variety of specific executive activities from warehousing to stock-market portfolio management. Players may compete individually or in teams against each other or against computer models of the environment.

ROLE PLAYING

Role Playing involves participants' assuming specified roles and acting out significant events. Instead of just talking about solving the problems at hand, participants spontaneously 'play out' solutions to these problems as they think the persons whose roles they are playing might view them.

Role Playing, however, can be effectively used in conjunction with the case method; here trainees are asked to play out a part of the case they are studying.

Role-playing dramatizes the situation under discussion and helps the participant to become aware of other people's positions and feelings. It describes a procedure called role reversal; whenever a strong difference of opinion appears between two persons, the trainer may ask each person to exchange role with the other and continue the scene. A variant of this technique is called role rotation; then two executives are asked to exchange roles, but not jobs, for the purpose of a mutual education. A critique follows their playing out of the roles. These two techniques are especially useful in circumstances in which real conflict exists between persons who need to cooperate for total organisational effectiveness. Not only are divided opinions ameliorated but, hopefully, each player is expected to acquire more insight into what the opposition feels and wants.

Role-playing has proved to be an effective technique for promoting real attitude change. Some studies revealed that regardless of whether the player is satisfied with his overt performance, his being forced to improvise a defence for a different viewpoint increases the likelihood that he will end up convincing himself of its validity.

In multiple role-playing, a large audience is divided into small teams, each member of which is given instruction to play a particular role. Following the role-plays within each team, the entire audience reassembles and shares experiences. Without their being aware of it, different teams can systematically be given different instructions, so that the effects of those differences on what occurs as the players interact are dramatically revealed during the critique.

For instance, half the audience may be asked to play the role of supervisor while each of the other half may be asked to play the role of subordinates. Supervisors and subordinates then meet in pairs to rank order the importance of a series of management objectives. Unknown to the subordinates, one third of the supervisors are instructed to use their power to be coercive or authoritarian, or to assume complete authority for the decisions made on the appropriate rank order of objectives. Another third of the supervisors are instructed to share their power, to be permissive or democratic and to collaborate with the subordinates in reaching the required decisions. The last third of the supervisors are instructed to give all the power to the subordinates, to avoid attempting any leadership, and to allow the subordinate to decide whatever he likes. The design is completed when each subordinate meets (in systematically varied order) with each of three types of supervisors. As might be expected, afterward subordinates report by far the most satisfaction with the permissive, democratic supervisor and the least, with authoritarian direction. They also feel the greatest sense of responsibility for the decision (as do the supervisors) when they make them in collaboration and the least, under an authoritarian boss.

Most of the several thousand real-life supervisors and executives who have been involved in this 'power-spectrum' role play are not hearing for the first time about the utility of permissive, shared leadership, but it is often the first time that the negative effects of coercive, authoritarian leadership have had such a dramatic impact on them personally. Presumably, it will now be more difficult for them to forget the effects they are likely to have on real-life subordinates if subsequently they are coercive and authoritarian in their relations with them.

Although, role playing may be used in a wide variety of ways for different purposes, the chief emphasis in management development training seems to be upon the development of insights into interpersonal problems, changing attitudes towards other (or the enhancement of empathy), and providing practice in developing human-relations skills.

Role-playing has several major shortcomings. Participants may resent the technique as childish. The instructor must then orient the players beforehand so that they accept role-playing as a legitimate training experience. Also, some players are likely to over-dramatize and overact, putting more emphasis on acting than on problem solving. For example, the trainee playing the role of supervisor may unrealistically 'needle' the participant playing the subordinate, or the 'subordinate' may act ridiculously subservient to his 'boss'. Players often need to be instructed in the nature of their role in order to promote an effective learning circumstance.

Moreover, how much is learned depends on the context in which the role-playing takes place. For instance, in one study the extent that role playing increased supervisory trainee's measured sensitivity to an employee's feelings and point of view depend on whether the play acting was part of the analysis of case material and whether adequate discussions were held after the role play.

Reinforcement is often a problem in role-playing situations. The players receive immediate feedback on the effects of their behaviour from each other and the participant observers. The problem arises when this feedback is in the form of approval, and the approval is for acting rather than for insight into the problem. This kind of a situation is extremely difficult to control since the success of role-playing depends in large part on the spontaneous freedom the players have to express themselves. If the faculty, however, does not provide a few corrective controls at some critical points, players may learn that the way to handle a difficult interpersonal problem is to 'crack' a good joke or simply to overact, since their fellow participants seemed to approve this behaviour in role playing.

Role-playing and case study suggest the following differences between the two:

CASE STUDY	ROLE PLAYING
• Presents a problem for discussion.	• Places the problem in a lifelike setting.
• Derives problems from previous events.	• Involves problems with ongoing processes.
• Typically deals with problems involving others.	• Typically deals with problems involving the participants themselves.
• Deals with emotional and attitudinal aspects in an intellectual frame of reference.	• Deals with emotional and attitudinal aspects in an experiential frame of reference.
• Emphasizes the importance of facts.	• Emphasizes the importance of feelings.
• Typically involves discussion from a psychological position 'outside' the problem situation.	• Deals with participants who are psychologically 'inside' the problem situation.
• Facilitates intellectual involvement.	• Makes for emotional involvement.
• Furnishes practice in analysisl of problems.	• Provides practice in interpersonal skills.
• Provides for development of ideas and hypotheses.	• Provides for testing ideas and hypotheses.
• Trains in the exercise of judgment.	• Trains in emotional control.
• Defines the action or solution.	• Provides for execution of the action or solution.
• Involves action whose consequences are usually undetermined.	• Involves continuous feedback.

Source:- The present author got the material in typed form which did not include the names of the authors of the source. The author expresses his sincere thanks to the authors and source of the above publication.

LABORATORY TRAINING

It is experiential learning and the experience that the participant gains in the small group setting, much of it cannot be explained in words. However, if we were to describe the process, it helps the participants in (a) articulating the un-articulated, (b) making the invisible visible, and (c) owning up the disowned and (d) acting the withheld. It is said that growth of a man into being lies by directing his effort to extend these four boundaries in his own life space. The Lab is geared to answer the specific needs for the mobilization of the self and the system in which the individual functions.

Further, the experience-based learning would help individuals and systems to develop socio-psychological infrastructure for anchoring major programmes of change and development. It also enables individuals and systems acquire a realistic appraisal of internal resources and constraints to action and mobilize themselves for alternative action choices which can break the pattern of stagnation and usher in new ways of maximal utilization of human resources in the organization.

SIMULATION

Simulation is a method that has been extensively used in the past for the training of technical and motor skills. Vestibule training, for example, is a relatively pure form of simulation. For years, the armed forces, as well as commercial airlines, have used 'mock-ups' or the simulation of airplane cockpits and flight conditions for training pilots and flight engineers. No doubt the most sophisticated and most costly form of this kind of simulation is now in current use in the manned space programme. Astronauts must go through hours and hours of tedious training in various circumstances that simulate the conditions of outer space. The technique's adequacy for this kind of training gains support from its remarkable success in this and other similar endeavour.

More recently, simulation has been developed into a highly useful research and training technique for investigating and teaching almost the entire gamut of organisational behaviour. Since it has gone far beyond the relatively limited applications of vestibule training, it deserves to be considered separately.

The typical features of simulation when used as a training device in organisational behaviour or skill training follow:

1. The essential characteristics of a real-life organisation or activity are abstracted and presented as a case-not to be studied and analyzed as in the usual case method, but to be experienced by the trainee as a realistic, life-like circumstance.
2. Trainees are asked to assume various roles in the circumstances and to solve the problems facing them. They are asked to be themselves – not to act.
3. A simulation often involves a telescoping or compressing of time and events; a single hour may be equated with a month or a quarter of a year in real life, and many events are experienced in a relatively brief period of time.
4. Trainees are required to make decisions that have a real effect in the simulation and about which they receive rapid feedback.
5. The simulation is followed by a critique of what went on during the exercise.

THE IN-BASKET SIMULATION

The in-basket is probably the least complex form of simulation used as a technique in industrial training. The typical management in-basket is a paper-and-pencil affair, as follows. The trainee is given a set of written materials, containing background details on a firm and one of its managers whom the trainee is to replace, along with various memos, letters, and notes that present a series of problems which the trainee (as the new replacement) must solve or, at least, attempt to solve. The amount of information available for making decisions is limited, as is the time allowed for the process.

Trainees vary consistently in their ways of handling problems under such circumstances. Some concentrate on the preparation of decisions, while others take final action immediately. A group critique normally takes place after the trainees have individually responded to all of the problems.

The in-basket has the big advantage of being relatively easy to administer to almost any size of group. In a sense it is a compromise between the case method and role-playing in that it is based on a case in which the participant is asked to play an active role. Properly administered, it combines the best aspects of both methods.

DEMONSTRATION

Demonstration as a method is to show how a particular thing is to be carried out. For example, the way in which compost is to be made by the farmers is demonstrated, digging the pit, and filling up of that pit with cow dung and other organic matter including leaf and covering it up with a thin layer of mud. Whether it is a gadget or a particular machine or a way of operating it giving a lecture on such things, it is demonstrated how it is to be assembled and how it is to be operated. Demonstration is visual, practice – skill-oriented kind of thing. It is quite facilitating in teáching a particular task, introducing a new procedure or technique or to illustrate or dramatize some point in a training programme. Demonstrations of any kind are more suitable for small groups. Sometimes it may be extensive and time consuming. Wherever a visual practice skill oriented thing is there in any training programme demonstration as a method is a necessary input. The requirements for demonstration are facilities, visibility, equipment and knowledge on the part of the instructor. It is to help the participants to observe, understand and operate. It mainly deals with what to do, how to do and when to do.

[Note:- For aspect-wise and point-wise details, please refer to appendix – *"Training Methods - At A Glance"*.]

DISCUSSION GROUP

Discussion is an important part in several training methods such as seminar, workshop, conference, panel and in a sense it is facilitating the views and ideas among the participants. It is interactive learning which provides an opportunity to the individual participant to express his views and check with other co-participants and the facilitator, his ideas and the way he would like to do things. It generates usually, zeal and enthusiasm among the participants. Discussion brings participants closer together psychologically and intellectually. It is quite essential and it plays a very vital part in making the participants understand and gain a comparative perspective and in a word it makes them articulate. Discussion as a technique is a very lively and contributing factor, of course, depending on the type of participants and the quality of facilitation. Discussion not only focuses on issues but it stimulates the participation of the group members.

EXERCISES

Exercises are usually, individual and occasionally groups comprising 2-3 members are involved in exercises. With a preliminary or an introductory lecture in the classroom, exercises related to any issue or any learning or any problem solving, are given to the participants so that they could use their knowledge, experience and work on them. Exercises in a sense are self-learning. A participant is assigned a particular task or a problem through an exercise. It is sometimes a useful and encouraging technique in training programmes. It involves the individual to apply his mind to a particular issue and once the participant comes out with his exercise completed and when it is placed before the class, there could be comments on such solutions or answers arrived at by a participant. As in the case of discussion groups, exercises involve the individual to a greater extent. Exercises may be in the classroom or they may be home-based exercises. They may have a range of time depending on the nature of the exercises.

FILMS

Films are very useful and effective media which provide both audio and visual aspects of a theme. Films are so structured providing information as to what is what and what is how and so on. Films are of an enduring type providing information not covered in the modules in the training. They provide an opportunity of exposure to other systems and cultures and often they serve as a break from the regular training and also serve as entertainment. The advantages of films are, they are invariant and once developed they are suitable for a wide range of subjects. Making an educational film is expensive but later on it can be shown repeatedly for long time. To include a film in a training programme, one should just see the relevance of a film to the learning objectives.

A particular theme may be repeated depending on the level of understanding on the part of the participants. The film also provides a basis for discussion. Films are of informative, educational and of entertainment in their nature. As technology advances we have a range of electronic media films. The DVD is becoming very popular gradually. The only limitation with a film is, it may not give the total picture but it may cover partially and it is non-interactive. In the case of a faculty, the participant could interact with the faculty but in the case of a film, they cannot interact but that part is to be played by the faculty or the instructor in the classroom. The film is an aid to the faculty.

BUZZ METHOD

Buzz may be called a method or technique which is used to involve a large audience directly in the discussional process by dividing the members into small groups of 5-7 for limited time ranging from 5-15 minutes to discuss a specific topic each member contributing to the discussion. Time-wise it is economical. It is a technique to cover additional information for a reserve speaker and for setting up questions each group may have a different role to play. In dividing the groups each group is instructed to select a leader and recorder, the leader's job is to see that everyone has a chance to speak. The recorder summarizes the discussion. At the end of the session, the leader or the recorder of each group reports to the full gathering. The organizer or an assistant collect and summaries all the reports and process them. The buzz groups present a situation or a problem for discussion. It facilitates problem-solving technique. It provides an opportunity to get new ideas and views on a particular issue and it also helps people have patience and ability to respect and consider the views expressed by other members. Another advantage or contribution of buzz group is tolerance towards ambiguity. Further, buzz groups provide relevant details and help to identify alternative solutions and develop analytical problem solving skills. But the limitation in respect to buzz groups is, it is time consuming. It may stimulate some and irritate others.

III). OFF-THE-JOB TRAINING

In most of the off-the-job training, what goes on in the

classroom cannot be so closely related to the job as on-the-job training; usually, it is supplemental, rather central, to learning work task. Off-the-job training varies from a short course in rapid reading to intensive instruction in an executive-development programme that lasts for several weeks or months. Courses may be taught by professional personnel on the organisation payroll, university professors, or staff members from private training organisations.

Formal off-the-job training offers several distinct advantages over on-the-job training, the chief one being that for many positions, organized training becomes feasible only when trainees can give their full attention to it. Day-to-day immersion in the normal job activity makes it difficult to encourage the broad changes in behaviour and perspective that are the main objectives of most management-development programmes.

The chief advantages chalked up for such a programme are as follows:

1. It lets executives get away from the pressures of the job and work in a climate in which 'party-line' thinking is discouraged and self-analysis is stimulated.
2. It provides resource people and resource material-faculty members,.fellow executives, and books - that contribute suggestions and ideas for the executives to 'try on for size', as he attempts to change, develop, and grow.
3. It presents a challenge to the executive that, in general, enhances his motivation to develop himself.

Another obvious advantage of off-the-job training is the availability of many courses and programmes that an organisation could never conduct by itself. Even in those instances in which an organisation can conduct similar training on the job, off-the-job programmes are often superior because they are concerned only with training and thus can pay more attention to the circumstances of learning.

The major weakness of most of off-the-job programmes is the failure to incorporate materials that will facilitate transfer of training. Very seldom is real effort made to provide for the application of principles learned. A great deal of potential benefit to the organisation and the participant is also lost because no internal plan exists for capitalizing on the new perspective and new ideas. Unless the organisational climate provides some reinforcement on the job for 'classroom' learning, the goals of off-the-job training are not likely to be realized; and as a result, the trainees may experience frustration. Moreover, a prerequisite for the success of any training programme (especially, off-the-job programmes) is that top management must actively support the training as well as reinforce what the trainee has learned.

FIELD VISITS

Field visits are carefully arranged group visits to an object, place or an institution for on site observation and learning. It should not be used for recreation, though that element may be there as a bonus on field visits. Field visits require careful planning, coordination and analysis of the learning upon return.

Field visits are supplementary and complementary to what was discussed in the classroom. It is observing things, verifying, comparing, confirming in respect to issues, problems, solutions, means, methods discussed in the class pertaining to any topic. For example, in the programme on training methods and skills which runs from three to eight weeks wherein the training methodology is taught, the participants are taken on visits to different types of training institutes, so that the participants could see and interact with the director, principal and faculty of that institute and know how they go about the entire process or cycle of training.

Field visits depend upon the duration of the programme, the learning and training objectives and availability of funds. The course director or the faculty in charge of the field visits has to identify the places of visit, inform the authorities of the institute, department or the villagers, if it were to be a visit to a village about the planned visit of the participants indicating the date, time and number of participants visiting and the purpose of their visit. The faculty has to brief the participants, the purpose or objectives of the visit and what to observe and the kind of data the participants have to collect. These details depend upon the objectives of the visit. The participants may also be provided with an interview guide or a questionnaire indicating the kind of things to be observed, the people to be contacted and the kind of information to be obtained and so on. When the participants get back from the field visit, they are to be provided an opportunity to share their field observation in the class. Despite limitations such as time, cost, logistics of movement, acceptance of the visiting organisation (sometimes) allowing free study of their organisation, field visits in some courses are essential methods in training which facilitate individual learning by seeing and interacting and exchanging ideas and views with the co-participants.

PROGRAMMED INSTRUCTION

In programmed instruction, a subject matter to be learnt is presented in a series of small carefully graduated sequential steps so that the participant achieves mastery over the subject presented and it is self-paced. Programmed instruction is meant for self-study. The individual whenever he finds time, he can at his own pace, go through the material and learn. Programmed instruction may be used sometimes at lower levels in respect of employee training. The material or the mater in programmed instruction is built in such a way that it facilitates the individual to learn by himself. Programmed instruction material sometimes, can be provided to the participants irrespective of their levels as additional sources of learning and information. Sometimes, it also serves as reading material. Speaking of programmed instruction, we may site the examples of learning from the computer. Computer based training is becoming popular where the individual at his own pace can move forward or backward using the computer as medium to learn. Of late, videos and DVDs have come as means of self-learning.

SPECIAL STUDY

Often, suitable reading material for the better-educated trainee serves the same aims as the lecture but with greater success. As a reader, he can stop when necessary, make notes more easily than in a lecture, check back on earlier portions of the material to clarify meanings, consult other books as he progresses, and discuss his reading with other trainees. Consequently, organisation and departmental libraries are becoming important management aids. Distribution of reading lists and journals to executives and professionals are commonplace. Some executives spend time every working day reading journals and books to keep up with their areas of specialization. Technicians are particularly sensitive to this need to keep up with the current literature in their fields. Electrical engineers, for example, who fail to keep pace with the rapid changes in their profession, will find themselves obsolete ten years after graduation. They can avoid obsolescence by continually reading in their field and attending professional meetings.

University programmes for executives are aimed at keeping middle and upper management abreast of recent developments in such areas as the behavioural sciences, applied mathematics, economics, business and the social and political sciences.

TEAM BUILDING IN BUREAUCRATIC SETUP AS A TRAINING METHOD

We may briefly look into two concepts related to the above title; one as to what constitutes team building and the process and functions of a team, the kind of tasks which necessitate constituting and working through a team in accomplishing tasks. The second concept is bureaucratic setup which is a familiar concept. A bureaucratic setup is characterized by rules and regulations, fixed procedures and individual responsibility and accountability. The basic characteristic of bureaucracy is centralization of decision-making, power usually is vested with the higher authority and as we come down along the hierarchy, we find individual employees playing their restricted roles and seldom coming together and working as a kind of team. Teamwork is related to the organisation tasks. It is more prevalent in private and business organisations. In a bureaucratic setup, the functions are mostly carried on adhering to the set rules, procedures and regulations. The individual seldom deviates from these boundaries and decision-making and communication is mostly carried through file notings. Normally the people at the lower level, middle or higher level do not come together and discuss the issue and resolve the issue or any problem. Teamwork is rather alien to bureaucratic setup. Often it is a mechanical way of doing things and collective responsibility is far less in a bureaucratic setup and even to go in for any change in the structure and functions in a government setup is time consuming and you have go in for issuance of government orders which are very time consuming. As mentioned above it is the flow of files and file notings and even if the employees in a department are seated in the same room, in proximity to each other, normally they do not discus a question or problem but the communication is through notings in their files. It is files that move not the people. This tradition of structure and functioning in government departments has been there for several decades. May be here and there, there is a little relaxation wherein people meet, discuss the problems or the issues.

There is a great need now to build teams within the department. In building a team you are not going to recruit people, but the employees are already there occupying different positions with their roles and responsibilities. One has to take into account the function of a particular department and see in what way there could be reorganization of the work bringing people together and making them shoulder collective responsibility. An employee at a particular level may say that he has done his job and be evasive in accomplishing the task of the unit in the department. Task is primary and when a task is to be accomplished it is the responsibility of the entire department. One has to examine the time that is consumed in arriving at a decision or passing some orders and see in what way the time could be shortened bringing people together and resolving the issues. In this respect it may be relevant here to briefly look into the concept and essentiality of team building and working through teams. Usually, in decision-making, we find very limited involvement of subordinates. The employees in the bureaucratic setup are principally guided by the rules and regulations. Not that you do not have rules and regulations in private sector but there they are rather flexible and the human factor is rather larger in private and business sectors where as, the decision making in the government framework is mostly a long drawn affair one passing the buck on to the other. The rules and regulations are man made but they become the rulers of administration and there is a need to look at this traditional way of functioning in government. You have several departments in government, some are administrative, some are regulatory, some are service-oriented and some are developing kind. In some of the departments teamwork becomes an essential factor, a sensible, meaningful way of doing things. In a government setup sometimes you cannot blame the individual employee for any dysfunction or delay for he is bound by the rules and regulations and procedures. He is forbidden in overlooking these procedures.

Team building constitutes a team for a common task, making it harmonious, functional, constructive and productive with individual as well as collective responsibility.

It may be relevant here to look into the merits of teamwork. Organizations are essentially about people working together and yet so often they fail to capitalize upon the full potential of this. A team can accomplish much more than the sum of its individual members. Most organizations have meetings which dampen inspiration and departments which seem to devote more energy to maintaining their own organizational position than to the common good of the organization as a whole. Teamwork is individuals working together to accomplish more than they could alone, but, more than that, it can be exciting, satisfying and enjoyable.

Over the past few years we have seen many approaches aimed at increasing organizational effectiveness and organizations today pay more and more attention to the training and development of their people, particularly those who hold managerial positions. Most of that development activity is centred upon the improvement of individual skills. Knowledge and experience, but organizations are increasingly finding that this is not enough, that a real key to success is the way in which individuals behave towards each other and the way in which groups of people relate to and work with each other. Teamwork improves these things.

In many organizations the symptoms of grumbling and retaliation are easily seen. Because, people cannot express themselves through the system they do it privately in discussions in the corridors, lavatories and car parks. Often bar room chat is a better indicator of organizational health than the most elaborate attitude surveys. The organizations that experience poor teamwork also seem to spend a lot of time on retaliations. They do not use mistakes as opportunities for increased learning and improvement but as excuses for punishing those who made the mistakes, and they do this in the many and varied ways in which organizations are able to hand out punishments.

In many organizations the quality of relationship between managers and those they manage is so low that effective teamwork just cannot get off the ground. Where people cannot confide in or trust their manager, where they are fearful of him or where their conversations are on a superficial or trivial level then real teamwork is unlikely to exist. Essentially teamwork engenders high quality relationships. Another sign of low quality relationships is often that the leader becomes increasingly isolated from his team. He does not represent their view and they do not subscribe to his. The effective team leader needs to be very much a part of his team.

The degree to which people help and use each other is another indicator. Where effective teamwork-does not exist people tend to work in isolation and neither offer nor receive the help of their colleagues. All of us need that help in order to perform at our optimum level.

As teams become increasingly effective so the characteristics they display and the procedures they adopt also change. Even where teams have not tried consciously to improve their methods of operation and effectiveness there can be tremendous differences, but where serious efforts are made to improve these things observers have noted that there are common characteristics which tend to be exhibited according to the stage of development. Before exhibiting the signs of effective teamwork which were listed in ' What is teamwork?' often a team will need to pass through several stages of development during which other signs or characteristics will be exhibited.

Teamwork is increasingly being seen as an important subject and teambuilding is now one of the most popular and effective ways of improving the health of an organization. There is then a very acute danger that teambuilding solutions may be applied inappropriately, that well-meaning but misdirected people may go through the 'ritual dances' of teambuilding when the problems of the organization are really quite different.

In this context, we will briefly look into the need for building teams in government departments which function under bureaucratic setup.

Teambuilding is a process and a necessity depending on the task to be accomplished. A team may be for a particular task, time bound and once the task or the job is accomplished the team may be dissolved and yet the employees will continue performing their roles. Wherever there is an activity which requires concerted, coordinated shared kind of performance, teams are essential. It is the job or the task which necessitates a temporary or a long period team work.

The present day administration in government departments resolving an issue or making a decision is mainly carried on largely impersonally through file notings. Sometimes, it is passing on the buck of decision making upward and downward, a tendency to shirk one's responsibility. Though, as mentioned above building a team in government departments appears to be an uphill task. In this respect, there is extensive literature on the ways to build teams motivating teamwork and sustaining teams for better performance. It may not be out of place here to briefly look into some of the aspects of team and team building. Teams may be constituted depending on the tasks to be accomplished. It is the task that necessitates a team approach. In a sense, teambuilding itself is a kind of training on the job and within the organisation wherein members of a team may or will have different roles and accountability. In a team, we have shared contribution and relative responsibility among the members of a team. The teams may vary in size and the composition also may be different in terms of the demography of the group – degree to which members of a group shared a common demographic attribute such as age, sex, ethnic background, educational level, or length of service in the organisation. This composition will have impact on the performance of the team. As mentioned above, it is the nature of the task that necessitates a team approach and collective endeavour in accomplishing a task. Team building is not that easy. Several divisive forces operate and role and personal conflicts also arise. If the goal in the department is accomplishing a task through which the public interests are served, team approach and teamwork is a necessity. And here, the suggestion is as a process of training and educating the employees in a particular section or department, form them into a team, explaining to them and enlightening them how teamwork is far better and facilitative in carrying out a function effectively.*

In building a team in a government department, the employees are there already at different positions. The idea is to bring them together and counsel them that they have a shared and collective

---

* M Woodcock and D. Francis – "People At Work – A Practical Guide".

endeavour in planning and executing activities entrusted to the department. Even in such a team, though the hierarchical positions are there, based on such a structure, there could be a leader of the team and there may be no difficulty in choosing a leader from middle or the higher level. But the nature of functioning or the quality of functioning in a team will be rather far from authority exercised in a bureaucratic set up. The levels and statuses of the individual employees will remain and there will be no encroaching upon their authority but once the employees are constituted into a team with an assigned responsibility there will be a qualitative change in their interaction or the behaviour as team members, may be for a moment forgetting their respective higher, lower statuses in the department. It should be like a hunting team, fishing team or a sports team where there is the captain or leader wherein the individual status differences do not become dominant. Accomplishing the task that is the goal and who did it and who is master is rather secondary.

Team building in a bureaucratic setup is an idea which may be explored and we may say that this is one kind of training to the employees. The importance of people working together is greater than people working individually. Constituting a team and team functioning is not that easy. Problems will crop up in terms of importance of an individual, his contribution and who is to enjoy the reward. These are all natural and humane. You cannot have a team functioning with absolute understanding and openness. Human frailties, egos, will play but there is a need to turn around these things and build up harmonious, functional teams which will be economical and effective in accomplishing departmental tasks and responsibilities.

While building teams in a bureaucratic setup based on the aptitude and capabilities and innovative nature on the part of the employees who are to be formed as team, the following roles and identification of members do matter in the team who will be designated to play the roles assigned to them. The roles that the members would play are listed below:

1. *Creators and Innovators*: - Those who take initiative and endowed with creative ideas.
2. *Explorers and Promoters*:- Those who have champion ideas after they are initiated.

3. *Assessors and Developers*:- Those who could analyze and make right decisions and options.
4. *Thrusters and Organizers*:- People good in providing structure.
5. *Concluders and Producers*:- People who have the ability in providing direction and follow through in accomplishing things.
6. *Controllers and Inspectors*:- People who are adept in checking for details.
7. *Upholders and Maintainers*:- People who safeguard the organisation from external threats, who fight external battles.
8. *Reporters and Advisors*:- People who are diligent enough in seeking full information.
9. *Linkers*:- People good in coordinating and integrating.

The above-mentioned roles are the ones which normally are expected to be carried out by the members of the team working as a unit. Team building in a bureaucratic setup is not that easy. It would be a slow process fighting against established norms of working in a department but looking at the advantages of working through teams, it is essential to make an attempt to build teams in the departments and carry out the work which would be far better than the individuals working at their desks in a limited restricted way.

TRAINING TECHNIQUES INDICATING LEARNING EFFECTIVENESS

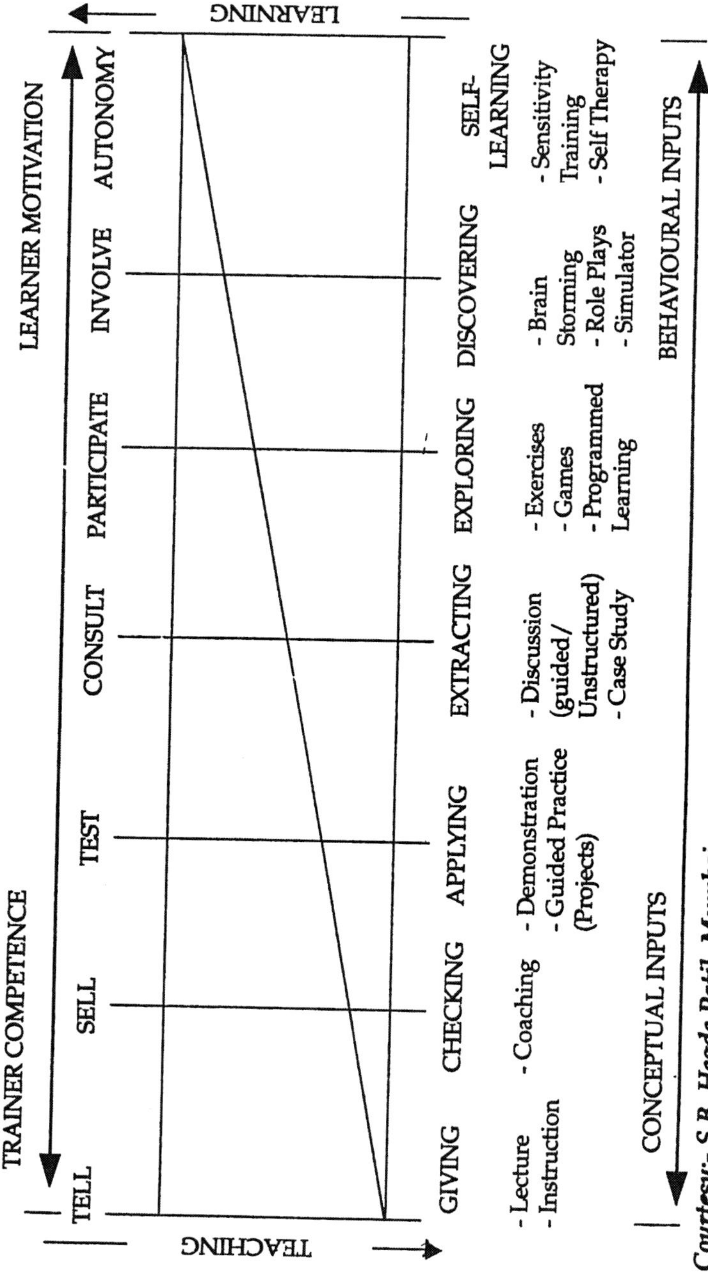

Courtesy:- S.B. Hegde Patil, Mumbai.

7

THE USE OF AUDIO-VISUAL AIDS

The Audio-Visual aids as the name goes are supplementary to the teaching / training methods. One part comprises hearing and the other seeing. The traditional visual aid has been chalk and board. There have been changes in the chalk and board too. The usual black colour of the board has changed to light or dark blue and the chalk now comes in multi-colours. The quality of chalk has changed from dusty and brittle quality to dustless and hard ones. We have advantage with chalk and the traditional board, of course, with a dustless chalk. With chalk and board one can go fast, erase, write, erase and it is cost effective compared with white boards and markers. There is one problem with the markers. After you use it you have to immediately put the cap to the marker. If delayed or forgotten to put the cap, the ink dries up. Using of white-board and markers may be fashionable but it does not facilitate speedy and writing at length. The author is of the opinion that we may go back to the board and chalk, of course, with dustless chalk.

AUDIO VISUAL AIDS

Audio	Visual	Both
Tape-recorder, microphone	Visual Board, flip chart, map, charts, OHP (Over Head Projector) for transparencies, pictures, objects, power point	TV Set

FLIP CHART

It is a large pad erected on a stand and bound so that one page can be turned over at the top to reveal the next. Unlike in the case of black or blue board, the writing on the sheets can be retained and referred back. The pad may consist of several sheets of paper and the matter written on the sheets can be retained for revision and when doubts arise or the faculty were to go back to a point as a matter of revision or emphasis he can go back to the particular page. It also facilitates the participants noting down some points written on the chart during or even after the session is over.

Flip chart is quite handy and we can use either a marker or a ball point pen or a fountain pen. Flip chart fits in well when the number in the class is small, because, for members sitting at a distance, the writing on the flip chart may not be visible. Apart from this limitation the cost of papers is another constraint, in using flip chart.

CHARTS – MAPS

Depending on the subject matter and the context, charts and maps may be displayed on the walls or boards as visual aids in the class. A chart as a sheet of information in the form of a table, graph, or diagram is a useful visual aid in making the details clear and also it aids in remembering things. Similarly, in the context of referring to a place, state, or a country, maps are very useful visual aids. Further, written or printed posters also add to the visual communication.

OVER HEAD PROJECTOR (OHP)

Over Head Projector has become a common and extensively used gadget in the classroom as an aid in using transparencies. Transparencies and the matter reflected on the screen or wall is a visual coordinate to oral communication / discussion in the classroom. We may briefly look into some do's and don'ts in using OHP and transparencies.

Do's	Don'ts
• Placing the OHP in the right angle for proper focusing.	• Not to use transparencies just for the sake of it.

- To switch off the OHP once the display of the transparency is not needed.
- The transparencies should contain around ten lines in bold letters preferably capital letters.
- It could be in type or hand written as discussion proceeds, the lines on the transparency can be moved. It is for focus of attention on a particular point.
- Once the discussion related to the matter on the transparency is over, switch off the OHP.
- Preferably not to project the whole sheet in full.
- While transparency is on projection the faculty should see that he does not block the view.

POWER POINT PRESENTATIONS

It is an advanced version of OHP. It is quite useful, but needs preparation and facility to use it.

TAPE RECORDER

It is another aid to play or record the talks or discussions of participants and to play back as a feedback to the participants. It is useful in respect to training in communication and also can be used to play some recorded voices as feedback so that, the speakers could check the way they have communicated.

TELEVISION

It meets both audio and visual needs. It can be used, of course, depending on the relevance in a number of contexts in the classroom. It should not predominate the classroom lecture-discussion.

While TV permits no interaction between trainee and trainer, like films it can make use of the most skillful instructor and the most efficiently organized subject matter. It can provide close-ups of apparatus and demonstrations regardless of the size of the class. These advantages tend to balance out the disadvantage of lack of contact with the instructor.

When a lecture or demonstration is presented in person or by live TV it does not seem to affect learning or retention one way or the other.

FILMS

Films offer some unique advantages over other off-the-job techniques. Skillful editing can increase the extent that the film conforms to good learning principles. And once it is 'canned', it is available repeatedly thereafter. The subject matter can be organized optimally and the most skillful lecturer available can then present it. Animation can also be employed to make dynamic diagrams, which could be shown in a straight lecture only in static forms. In a film, cause-effect relations can be dramatically illustrated to trainees. The film-trained operators learned more factual information than did trainees who did not see the film.

Instruction by film can be profitably supplemented by holding discussions or lectures before or after the film is shown. Similarly, subjects in another study who spent a half hour discussing a film on prejudice later retained most of the change the film had made in their attitudes.

Films can also be effective if they do not try to cover too much ground too rapidly – that is, if they concentrate on a limited amount of material. Finally, they will be more effective if they are planned from the trainee's viewpoint by considering his current level of readiness to learn, his interest in learning, and the difficulties he is likely to encounter in the process.

MICROPHONE

It becomes essential when the group is larger. A few simple aspects in using the mike: not to keep it too close to the mouth nor at a distance. A collar phone is preferable, which facilitates, the movement of the speaker in the classroom while lecturing/ discussing.

The AV aids, as the name goes are only aids and extension of the speaker. One should not expect that the aids used will compensate the deficiencies on the part of the speaker or his lecture or discussion in the classroom. Some faculty have a tendency and practice of overloading themselves with the AV aids while their actual communication is minimal.

USING OF LIBRARY BY THE PARTICIPANTS

Most of the training institutes have their own libraries, may be large or modest in size, of general type of books and periodicals pertaining to the subjects related to the courses that are offered. Library is a source and a facility for the faculty and participants. Use of library by the participants depends on the following factors.

- Interest on the part of the participants
- Time available for them in the course of the training programme
- Whether it is a residential or non-residential programme
- Duration of the course

In the case of residential programme, the participants will have time in the evenings, early nights and on holidays. Of course, as mentioned above, the use of library depends on the interest of the participants. The training programmes range from one day to several weeks.

Wherever it is possible, one session may be provided as library study, of course, not at the cost of cutting on the coverage of topics included in the programme. Though usually, the participants are provided with handouts-reading material, it is desirable that the concerned course director of a training programme on his own or with the help of the librarian prepare a select list of books pertaining to the programme. It may be on management of change, personality, conflict management, leadership, communication, etc. This select list of books available in the library and germane to the course may be provided to the participants and also placed on a desk in the library with a label indicating books on such and such subjects. If this procedure were to be adhered to, it would make the course director or course coordinator familiarize himself with the kind of literature available at the institute's library pertaining to the course he is directing. It will make him learn and widen his knowledge. The participants may be informed in the introductory session itself, about the display of books in the library and that they may make use of them. If this system which is quite educative is to be followed it would enhance and widen the knowledge of the course director and the concerned faculty.

The training institute's business is to create a learning environment and the very act of providing the participants with a select list of books related to the modules covered in the course and the display of available books on a table / desk in the library contribute to informative and visual aspects of learning.

It has been observed that some of the faculty seldom visit the library and look for literature related to the courses they offer.

Getting back to the participants they may not have aptitude or interest to learn more about an issue or area. Some of them especially from the government, what ever may be their cadre, take training as a routine affair and some tend to think that they know enough and not to bother themselves with further reading.

8

THE COURSE DIRECTOR

The role of the course director in training is crucial and he has to play a multiple role. He may be designing the course or he may make use of a course which has been designed earlier by somebody. Sometimes, in such a case, he may just bring in some alteration in the course. He has to secure reading material in respect to the modules included in the course. He may have to do it by himself or he may have some assistance in selecting, procuring and getting copies of the material to be provided to the participants. He has to look in for faculty, internal and external. In case of inviting faculty from outside, he has to contact them in advance and arrange for their sessions.

A course director is expected to have an outline or a comprehensive idea of the course that is being offered. He may not take all the sessions but he should have an idea as to what should be the sequence of sessions and the quality to be ensured by the internal or the external faculty. When he invites guest faculty it is not to simply inform them of the topic that they are expected to deal with but preferably he should send to such invited guest faculty a copy of the entire programme and also appraise the guest faculty the background of the participants and what has gone on earlier, before the guest faculty comes to take up the module requested of him. The idea here is, the lecture or the discussion by the guest faculty should not be an isolated kind of thing but it should have subject or organic link with what has gone on and what would follow. May be, through letter or over the telephone, he may just brief the guest faculty, so that the congruence and continuity of the theme are established in the topics covered.

Though the internal faculty or external faculty will be taking sessions in the course, the overall responsibility and monitoring depends on the course director. In some instances, the course director will have a larger part of sessions or he may have limited number of sessions. In some cases, especially, in some of the government run training institutes, there may not be expertise and the course director there will be just nominal without having any specialization or expertise in the field of which the training programme is connected with. He may be there as a nominal course director but everything is carried on by other faculty. This is one thing which is found in some of the institutes in a routine, mechanical way. The head of a training institute or the training director / manager will allot a particular course to an internal faculty. The internal faculty may not have any idea of the course that he has to direct. Sometimes, he will not be in a position to tell the authorities that he will not be able to direct the course since, the course theme does not fall within the area of his knowledge or expertise. He mutely accepts that he would direct the course and hang-on on number of people soliciting their help to take up some sessions. It is not a question of insisting that the course director should be knowledgeable of the course that he directs, for in some unforeseen eventuality when the internal faculty is not able to or available and the guest faculty for some personal reasons could not arrive on the campus to take the session that he had agreed to problem arises. On such occasions, one feels that the course director should be in a position to step in and deal with the module. Such a kind of an anchorage will really contribute to the role and the image of the course director and also it prevents discontinuity in the programme. Usually, it is the course director who provides the participants with reading material or what you call handouts.

When it comes to the question of evaluation of the training programme in respect to each session or the overall impact of the programme on the part of the participants, he has to evince a realistic and serious interest in doing this evaluation as mentioned elsewhere. It should not be a kind of a routine mechanical thing. It is not only seeking feedback from the participants but he may also get the feedback from the faculty. This kind of an interaction with the other faculty associated in the training, one can improve the programme subsequently. It is always better to discuss the course or the modules with members of the faculty. In some institutes they even spend months together in finalizing and standardizing a particular training programme. There is a difference in respect to attention paid to the course modules by the faculty and the entire running of the programme between professional training institutes and the ones that are being run by government. There is always an element of bureaucracy in government run training institutes. Sometimes, it is neither of a government type with bureaucratic style of functioning nor it is a professional type of training organisation. It is needless to say that the course director is to be all the time on the look out for means to better his programme and his performance.

In a training institute it is not only the role played by the faculty, but the other functionaries right from the head of the institute whether he is designated director, director general, commissioner, principal, etc., and down to the several other officials who are part of a training institute have some roles to play. In general, the practice in some of the institutes is, the inauguration of a training programme is done by the head of the institute or an official next to the head of the institute. Even in presiding over the conclusion of the programme and awarding of certificates it is the head of the institute who does it or sometimes the institute may invite some well-known personality in the field to award the certificates to the participants. The awarding of certificates to the participants at the conclusion of a training programme may appear something like a ritual but often the participants feel and expect that the head of the institute to award the certificates. Such a practice really contributes to the image of the institute. May be the head of the institute or the other senior administrators or faculty are busy but we will have to take into account the expectation on the part of the participants. For instance, if the participants were of higher levels such as, secretaries, joint secretaries, directors and so on, they expect that senior most functionary: the director general, principal director, the chief secretary or any other senior Indian Administrative Service official to award the certificate. The question here is not the certificate per se but who has signed the certificate from whom the participants received the certificates. This aspect is significant and matters a great deal. The idea here is as far as possible, depending on the schedule of activities and time availability on the part of the head of the institute, it is desirable that he inaugurates the course, signs the certificates and awards the certificates. In signing also he will be a principal signatory and the course director would also affix his signature on the certificates. The question of the head of the institute or a senior member of the administration inaugurating and giving certificates depends again on the largeness of the organisation and multiple training programmes they conduct simultaneously. The principle that is suggested here is, that the non-faculty administrative heads should also establish contact at least minimally with the participants. In the course of a training programme, it is desirable that the head of the institute or next to him in authority just enter the class, spend a few minutes with the participants or he may sometimes take a session also. The above-mentioned practices vary from institute to institute. Sometimes, we have reports from the participants that they have not seen the head of the institute or some other senior administrators in the organisation. Though, they have heard of them or known them by their names, the participants feel bad when they do not get an opportunity of seeing the head of the institute or the other well-known personalities in the institute. There have been instances, wherein the top-level bureaucrats especially people of IAS cadre feel hesitant to interact with the participants of middle or lower order in the organisation. They even decline to inaugurate the programme or at least award the certificates to the participants on the conclusion of a trainir g programme. Training the participants is not simply an interaction between them and the faculty but it is desirable as mentioned above that other officials at the top or at the middle level do interact with the participants in an institutionalized way inaugurating the programme, taking some sessions, being present at the time of farewell function and so on. This kind of a tradition on the part of the officials of the training institute builds the image of the institute and the participants also feel happy that they had an opportunity of listening to the head of the institute or any other eminent faculty or professor at the institute. Training is not to be taken as a stereo type mechanical kind of an activity and the author has come across instances shared by some of the course directors that even though they requested the head of the institute who was an IAS man, he was very reluctant and refused even to meet the participants as a matter of courtesy. Sometimes, the course director with such an IAS head had to plead with him, request him to show his face to the participants. One such IAS head of a training institute was very selective. He only meets participants of higher official level. He cannot come down to the middle level or the to the lower level. Here we are not pinpointing the behaviour of some of the administrative officials but once they come down to a training institute which is a professional body they have to forget that they are from IAS. Once they feel that they are professionals and mingle with the participants at least meet them once in a while their image will go up.

The central focus of any training is the individual and the group and it is the individual and group development which, in turn, contributes to the organisational growth and the qualitative improvement in the larger society. When we have adults with varied backgrounds, experiences, tastes and beliefs that are more or less rigid, we meet with some problems in training them. These problems either could be eliminated or reduced, if each factor in the training process, the participant, his organisation and the trainer and his institute, play its role effectively. In this collective endeavour, the training institute as an agency has a dual responsibility: responsibility to the participant and responsibility to the sponsoring organisation.

9

THE ROLE OF THE TRAINER

Training is a kind of partnership between the trainer and the participant, a cooperative endeavour. Success depends on what one invests in himself and in the other. In the ultimate reckoning, it is the trainer, his personality and his ability in facilitating the learning that matters. The trainer is not to be construed as a bundle of instructional technology.

The trainer is the ultimate "delivery agent" of the learning system. Trainers, therefore, manage the critical dynamic process: acquisition of new behaviour by the learners. This implies skill in bringing to light all the contents and all the methods called for in the training programme. It implies skills in two way communication, flexibility, spontaneity, empathy, compassion – almost everything except feeding multitudes with "but five loaves and two fishes". In sum, the trainer selects methods, media, synthesizes the method and media, into a integrated programme providing outlines and materials put to improve the programme. Further, he evaluates the impact of training programme. As a trainer, he delivers the learning design in the classroom situation, he analyses and responds to individual learner needs, adopts designs to meet the learner needs and he provides ongoing feedback and evaluation to facilitate learning and he also counsels learners. Further, as a trainer he provides feedback to the designers of the training programme about the strengths and weaknesses of the designs which have been put into operation.

ABILITY AND QUALIFICATIONS

A trainer may be fully qualified but may lack the ability to teach, or vice-versa. Absence of any one of these characteristics could be a major setback in training situations and may hinder the effectiveness of the training programme. A good combination of these qualities is desirable in adult training situations since the learners are highly sensitive to these issues.

TRAINER'S LEVEL IN THE ORGANISATION

The position occupied by the trainer in the training organisation is important since acceptance or rejection by adult learners may be highly influenced by it. Since no trainer can either fool the participants all the time, or change his position in the organisation overnight, position cannot be the only factor for the learner's acceptance of the trainer. It is also important to develop person-to-person relationships with the participants. Relationships will pay dividends beyond the trainer's credibility as a result of his position in the training organisation. Further, it may help to establish a good learning environment.

AGE

In may cultures, age and wisdom are considered linearly related though this is not true in all cases. One may find many instances from his own experience that the trainer's age has very little impact on the participants. Time and experience should make the trainer more acceptable and knowledgeable. However, it is not hard to find trainers who just do not learn and improve from their experience. There are also many trainers who make a sincere effort to appear old and win the sympathies of the adult learners. Age of the trainer, in conclusion, is an important but a dubious factor in affecting the training of the adult learner.

In addition to the failure to capture the imagination of participants in curriculum planning and the selection of methods, there is also the problem of assessing needs which are usually based on the universal value systems, instead of the perceived / felt needs of the local people or unique characteristics of specific groups, for instance, the assessment procedures for the selection of instructional methods do not take into consideration aspects like:

a. The experienced participant, who has put in long years of service but is apprehensive of the unknown.

b. The literate 'young star', or new college graduate who is motivated by logical and rational needs.

c. The slow learner, who lacks confidence because his ability to understand is below average.

d. The alienated bum' who is in an adult learning situation by circumstance and not by choice.

In addition, the training materials and instructional objectives of each input are usually structured so that it is almost impossible for adults with multiple life demands to systematically attend all the sessions of a course. Because each session is not self-contained, the result is that it becomes difficult for adult learners to follow instructions when they miss the classes, but eventually it discourages them to continue in the programme as planned. The dilemma of methodology in adult education also includes the structure of the time-table of activities, and the duration or time within which course objectives are to be achieved. In general, this aspect of adult education does not take into consideration the fact that study habits of adults get rusty, energy levels change and that other things of psychological importance happen within the timeframe of learning. All these determine the participant's reactions to the learning methodologies used in adult education.

It is a mix of methods and techniques the trainer employees and the ways in which they are employed. The techniques importantly are skills that are largely inextricably associated with the trainer, his / her personality and style. The unit of instruction (input) may determine the kind of method or technique. It may be a lecture, a lecture-cum-discussion, a case method, role play, simulation exercise, games, the sole aim of which is to involve the participants, encourage and provide them learning conditions and opportunity to learn. The trainer needs to make a continuous evaluation of his interaction with the participants and techniques in the classroom situation. He also looks for the feedback. The trainer may have to be a good listener, a keen observer and a good manager of the learning situation.

The issues of methodology, as discussed, are but eye-openers to adult educators, who must be more sensitive to the psychological aspects and principles of curriculum planning in order to develop more useful course content and instructional methodologies to meet the needs of adult learning.

As we have discussed, the trainer is the lifelong learner. Unless he wants to learn, he cannot be effective in teaching. The kind of rapport the trainer builds between himself and the participants and the atmosphere that he creates are facilitating factors for learning on the part of the participants. In sum, we may say, it is the sincerity, commitment towards establishing a standard of excellence and the personality of the trainer constitute the prime factors making learning a pleasant experience.

10

GUEST FACULTY

If we look at the training institutes of different categories, some are regular professional training institutes which are run on commercial basis and others run by government or a particular department to train their own personnel. The strength of faculty at these institutes varies a great deal. In case of most of the professional commercial training institutes at the state or at the national level are fully equipped with trained faculty belonging to different areas of specialization. They go in for inviting faculty from outside (guest faculty) very rarely but in the case of training institutes run by several of the government departments are of a skeletal strength in respect to faculty. More often, they go in for faculty from outside. The guest faculty comprise individuals who are in the training activity and experienced administrators from the same department. Often we find retired officials of a particular field/department being invited as guest faculty. The practices in respect to inviting and briefing the guest faculty in respect to the overall course and the topic i.e., entrusted to the guest faculty vary very much. It is the course director or sometimes the official heading the training division who will be identifying and inviting the guest faculty. What is to be emphasized here is adequately briefing the guest faculty as to the objectives of the training programme, the background of the participants and the way in which the topic given to the guest faculty is integral part of the course and how it is to be integrated with other modules in the course. You have diverse practices in inviting the guest faculty and introducing him to the participants in the class. Sometimes, the guest faculty may be a very high official in the service or retired. In such cases, the course director sometimes feels hesitant to brief the guest faculty since he is hierarchically of higher order. And even the participants especially from the government departments hesitate to raise questions when a superior officer functions as a guest faculty. Even in the class when the lecture or discussion is on, the participants hold on to a sense of subordination to the guest faculty. They don't feel free to raise questions or seek clarification. We don't question the authority, knowledge or capability on the part of the guest faculty but they are being treated by the host institute as VIPs. There is nothing wrong in treating the guest faculty with all respect and importance, but that kind of treatment should not muffle the quality of his lecture or discussion, he does in the classroom.

We may think of a proper and judicious way of selecting and inviting guest faculty. It should not be a superfluous kind of thing. The emphasis in inviting a guest faculty is to be on the knowledge and capability and communication ability of the individual in respect to the subject and one should not be carried away by his official position. Sometimes, the guest faculty either retired or a person in service may have experience in a particular area which is part of the training programme but he may not have the delivery capacity. The criterion to be emphasized in respect to inviting guest faculty is what he could do effectively, but not in terms of his relationship or acquaintance with the course director or manager of that training programmes. The course director as mentioned above has to brief the guest faculty clearly the focus of the programme and the background of the participants. Sometimes, it may be difficult for the course director to have free discussion or exchange of ideas with the guest faculty depending on his official position.

We have who may be called as professional guest faculty either after retirement or while in service. They will be looking for opportunities to function as guest faculty and on their own they will be contacting individuals or training institutes offering themselves as guest faculty. There is nothing wrong with such type of guest faculty who have taken training activity as a professional economically remunerative activity. Some guest faculty provide in advance or after their session some reading material to the participants. But it is desirable to get such reading material/ handouts from the guest faculty in advance which can be included in the bunch of the material given to the participants. In some cases the guest faculty come and give a lecture and they may not have any reading material to be provided to the participants.

Hospitality provided to the guest faculty varies depending on the resources on the part of the training institute. Some guest faculty are provided transport may be a car or a van. We have come across instances wherein some of the guest faculty of certain degree of status feel rather hesitant to travel by auto rickshaws. Naturally they feel that it is below their dignity to travel by auto to and fro from the institute. Depending on the time, timings of the sessions by the guest faculty, one may think of lunch, or tea etc. In some cases, where the training institute does not have the facility of transport at its disposal, it requests the guest faculty to make his own arrangements to reach the institute. And sometimes, in lieu of providing transport the guest faculty is paid certain amount towards transport. But these small things will make the guest faculty feel rather encouraged, happy and motivated. It facilitates a very healthy relationship between the training institute and the guest faculty. The guest faculty is to be meted out what is due to a guest by the host. It relates to receiving, accommodating and the send off given to the guest faculty. Guest faculty is not only a faculty giving a lecture or contributing his experience to the participants but in a sense he is a resource to the institute and is a spokesperson and representative of the training institute. In some training institutes you find a course director who is only a nominal figure, with his appearance in the first hour in the class and introducing the course. He may not have any sessions at all. The entire course, either it is for three or five days, is totally carried on by the guest faculty. We don't question the erudition or the contribution of the guest faculty, but if a training institute is totally or mostly dependent on guest faculty one can imagine the organic link of the sessions of the training programmes. One can think of the dissipitated nature of the quality of the programme. The ideal thing depending of course on several resource factors is to have institute's faculty, one may go occasionally for inviting guests as speakers.

Sometimes, heavy dependency on guest faculty may affect the

organic link between one session to another session and the quality may be affected. The follow-up also often is difficult. The nominal course director may not have the follow-up from the guest faculty. He is invited, he just comes and gives his lecture, gets the honorarium and goes back, and there ends the interaction. Sometimes, with several guest faculty you may not have the continuity of the theme of a programme.

11

PROVISION OF READING MATERIAL

Usually, in all training programmes, irrespective of the duration of the programmes and the themes covered, handouts or reading material are provided to the participants. These handouts are complementary and supplementary to the lectures and discussions that take place in the classroom. The handouts what may be called the reading material may be typed, photocopied from journals and books or sometimes it may be a printed material. Besides reading material, the course director may also provide to the participants a select bibliography covering the themes and the topics covered in the programme. Of course, this select bibliography depends on the duration of the course and the level of the participants. Some of them may not be interested to look for and read the books but it is desirable and useful such a list of books is provided to the participants. The select bibliography covering the modules in the course would really be complementary to the handouts provided to the participants. These are provided to them in different forms: loose separate units, spiral bound copied and some may give printed books also. Material given to the participants varies in size, quite thin with a few dozen pages to a bulky one running into a couple of hundred pages. Usually or more often, the participants do not read the handouts and they may take home the material and it may lie there as a symbol of the individual having attended such-and-such a training programme. It is not generalization. There may be exceptions in respect to academically and professionally oriented people. This appears to be what actually happens. It is suggested that an abstract of each handout or article provided to the participants may be prepared and given to the participants. That would help the participants and sometimes these abstracts may motivate them to go through the full text of the article or the handout.

Further, while distributing the reading material, the course director may briefly explain to the participants, the contents and the importance and usefulness of the material given to them. Usually, either at the beginning, middle or at the end of the course the reading material is given to the participants. This is done in a matter of fact way as if you are distributing some article or commodity. Seriousness often is not attached to the reading material.

Again a word about the quality of material given to the participants. The photocopies may look very dull. The letters and the figures may not be legible and it will have a poor attraction to read. Providing the reading material involves time for preparation, selection, photocopying and the whole thing costs considerable amount of money. A participant may not remember what all has gone on in the classroom situation, but one thing that he may depend upon is the reading material he was provided with. What is given to the participant should be neat, legible and attractive. Not that it is to be decorated but the very material, the way in which it is bound or put together in a file should be attractive so that the individual may refer to that whenever he needs and he would keep it as a kind of an academic souvenir. Further, the reading material selected from different sources is quite handy. If one were to go in for the original sources, it may take a lot of time. It is useful to mention the sources of books or journals from which the material has been selected. One may not be in a position to buy the original books from which the material has been selected or condensed.

12

ISSUES IN ADULT TRAINING

This chapter focuses on issues one faces in training the adult personnel of different levels drawn from diverse organisations. The 'adults' in the present context is defined as those who have completed their formal education and have entered service. They may be divided into several age groups comprising fresh entrants into service and about-to-retire from service and, in between, several categories of personnel with varying educational qualifications, experience and years of service.

Difficulties sometimes, arise in the training situation since the audience here is different from the audience at a school or university. Further, the duration of the training, the minimal fleeting contact between the participant and the trainer, pressure of time, the heavy schedule of the programme, the sponsoring organisation, the training institute and more important, the trainer, constitute the other factors that matter in the process and effectiveness of training. In the entire training, we can think of four factors, viz., the participant (learner), the trainer (teacher), the organisations of the participants and the trainer and, the training technology employed. Training, essentially, is an interaction between the participant and the trainer. Learning very much depends on the learner and the trainer and, to some extent, on the technology employed. We may briefly look into each of the four factors, the problems that emerge from each and some ways to overcome the problems.

Let us begin with the crucial factor, the participant (learner) and the kind of issues that centre around him.

PROFILE OF ADULT PARTICIPANTS

Age

In most training situations, the age level of the learner has been found to be a vital factor in determining the training effectiveness. If the participants / learners are much younger than the trainer, this may lead to ideological and value differences. On the contrary, if the learners are much older than the trainer (which is the case in most adult training situations), then the learners may either write off the trainer and / or may develop a negative attitude to whatever is taught by him. In summary, there should be only a marginal difference between the age of the learners and the trainers.

Another aspect that has to be considered is the age level of the learners independently. If the participants are too young, perhaps they may exhibit extreme ends on the learning-interest continuum. If the learners are of middle or old age, the interest to learn new information will perhaps be less than that which is normally expected. Aged participants, as evidenced in research studies, may exhibit less involvement in learning activities, rapid memory lapse and low retention.

Sex

Despite the fact that there is no definite answer as to the superiority of one sex over the other in learning abilities, the sex of the participants appears to be a vital factor. In most of the developing countries, one can still see a vast number of male participants and few female participants. Perhaps, due to their minority and the prevailing value orientations, female participants may have to face certain unique problems.

An important aspect for consideration at this juncture would be the matching of the sex of the participants with that of the trainers as and when possible.

Educational Background

The level and diversity of education is another major factor in adult learning. Generally, if the learners are highly educated, rather than facilitating the learning of other participants who are less educated, they may interfere with the trainer. In such circumstances, it is better to take the advanced skills of such learners as a support to the trainer to facilitate training effectiveness. On the contrary, if the learners are of very low academic standards, it is the responsibility of the trainer to upgrade them to the required level and then begin the training programme.

Culture

The culture of the learner is second to none in importance and, hence, has to be well taken care of in the context of learning. Inter-learner and learner-trainer cultural differences may spark off some undesirable issues during the training which may affect the training. A clear understanding of the learner's cultural background and a clear communication of the trainer's culture is a requirement for any adult training programme.

In the entire function of training, sponsoring organisations and training institutes play a pivotal role in making training a success preparing the individual participants for training in terms of requisite knowledge, skills and desirable behavioural change facilitating him to be an effective contributor in meeting the organisation goals. The preparing part, the motivating part and utilizing the services of the individual employee largely depends on the sponsoring organisation and a substantive contribution is also made by the training institute where the employee gets trained. These two organisations are quite vital in the entire development and promotion of department of human requirement.

Besides his knowledge of the subject and skill in imparting to the participants, the trainer may remember that the participant is a mature individual.

- The trainer should appreciate that the participant is a mature person but he needs guidance in a specific area.
- The trainer should consider each participant as a unique person, recognize his needs, appreciate his problems and help him to help himself.
- The trainer should be flexible.
- The trainer should encourage participant's involvement in the learning process.

- The trainer should believe in what he advocates to the participants.
- In the matter of attitudinal and value changes, the trainer should work towards building up the group which facilitates such changes.
- The trainer should know the subject well, have skills to impart it, be interested in doing it and is well prepared for doing it.
- The trainer should not stand on false prestige and remember that he/she is a lifelong learner.
- The trainer should have tolerance for ambiguity on the part of the participant.
- The participant and his learning is the ultimate goal.
- The trainer is one of the group.

The trainer may sometimes have the following problems and tendencies:

- This group seems to be formidable, can I manage it?
- The particular participant is a troublemaker, he is a threat to me.
- I should see what I say prevails, and not what the participants opine.
- I am young in age and experience, my status is low compared to the participants, how am I to manage my sessions?
- I should tell the participants what all I know on the subject.
- The trainer may have personal equations with the participants.
- He may try to experiment on the participants.
- He may fail to get his sessions evaluated (in the class room or outside) by the participants and may not look for or be prepared to receive the feedback.

- Sometimes he is not sure or convinced of what he is talking about.
- He makes the discussion centre around him and not around the participants and their issues and problems.
- He lacks sportive spirit to gracefully withdraw and accept when he goes wrong.
- He is insensitive to the subtle cues given by the participants.

The lecturer-trainer may bear in mind the following likely characteristics of his adult-participants. This knowledge of understanding of the audience is imperative, because the effectiveness of the lecture depends on the profile of the audience and their responses.

PROFILE AND CHARACTERISTICS OF AUDIENCE

- I am an experienced man in the filed, what is there to learn further.
- I am sufficiently old and experienced, should I learn from the young trainer?
- Can I learn anything at this age?
- What use will I have of this training?
- I did not feel the need for the training, my organisation has pushed me over here.
- Should I be trained along with these junior people – junior in age and service?
- This training programme is something alien to me.
- Where am I in the training programme? In the group?
- My importance and that of my organisation has not been recognized by the trainer and his institute.
- It is all theoretical, ideal, bookish and these cannot be put into action.
- Yes, I am convinced of this approach, strategy, but my organisation may not support me when I want to apply it.

- It may be possible here, but we do not have the infrastructure in the back home situation.
- It is just a paid holiday for me; I do not have to bother much about the training.
- I do not agree with the things they tell me here, I will go my own way.
- I do not have any control over my attending this programme, it affects my status.
- I do not like this trainer's style. He is fast/slow, rude, vague, poor in expression, does not recognize me, he talks too much and not impressive.
- I hope that I may find some answers and solutions to the problems I face in my work situation (these may be administrative and technical in nature).

The above list is illustrative of what sometimes may go on in the mind of the participant. These feelings or tendencies funnel down to the following elements:-

- The motivation on the part of the learner.
- His social-cultural values.
- His perception of the training programme.
- His age, length of service and his status in the organisation.
- The importance he attaches to a particular learning, knowledge or skills.
- The learning setting.
- The need for recognition.
- The struggle for leadership in the group.
- The self-concept.
- His coping mechanism in a new situation.

The issues of adult training could become a major challenge to all trainers as these issues put into perspective the essential role that adult education has to play in the development of ability, skills and attitudes in adult learners. Some illustration of problems that are associated with the participants in the training situation may be of order here. The following two cases bring out some of the issues mentioned above.

Case I

It was a two-week training programme for the Managers (extension) of District industries Centres (DICs) of a state in India. The focus of the course was entrepreneurial development. The group consisted of twenty participants. Three participants were senior in the department, having put in about twenty years of service, and the rest of them were newly recruited in the age group of 22 to 27 years, all new entrants to the job. A majority of them were post-graduates with economics and commerce background.

There were two faculty including the author.

Right from the start, we could see some kind of apathy and a feeling of misplacement on the part of the three senior participants. For the first three days they were almost passive, did not involve themselves in any discussion, and sat through with an expression of disgust and seriousness. On sensing their feeling and non-involvement, we just asked them outside the sessions, how they felt about the discussions and the course. What follows is the substance of what they shared with us. "You can see that we are senior people having put in twenty years of service. First of all, why should the government send us for training? We are experienced people. Are we going to do differently after the training? We do not blame you in this. You are doing your job. The second thing is: are we to be trained along with these young, new recruits? Their age is not equal to our service. Further, you all talk theory, what should be, the ideal. It is not possible in the field. No, our experience is different; extension methods would not do. We don't get support from other colleagues and the General Manager. They are target-oriented. They do not know the field problems. What relevance is your training to us?" The burden of their dialogue went on, along these lines. We sensed their problem that they felt bad that they were sent for training despite their long years of service and they had to be co-participants with fresh entrants, whereas, they should have been masters.

They tended to show one-up-manship behaviour. We encouraged them to share their field experience so that it would be beneficial to the younger participants and to us. Their movement began by the end of the first week. But, it made the younger group passive, and as the programme was coming to a close, the seniors started dominating the group discussions with questions, agreements and disagreements.

We had a feeling that the senior participants felt they were recognized and they had their say in the sessions and other activities associated with the programme. Though, we had no answers to all their questions, we managed the training situation by sensing their reserve, their feeling of resentment for being clubbed with young recruits and their need for recognition by encouraging them to share their experiences and views and by empathizing with their problems.

Case II

This refers to a two-week programme on 'Training Methods and Skills'. There were twelve participants. Save one, all were from training institutes of banks, industries and public undertakings. We will briefly mention here the problems relating to two participants. One participant, from a public undertaking (national), was a last minute substitute for another official who was a faculty at the training institute of the organisation. Owing to some personal problems, the person nominated could not attend the training programme. The substitute participant was not in the trainer's role and after his return from the training too, he will have nothing to do with training in the back-home situation. This particular participant made it clear that he was a last minute substitute and he had no use for what was going on in the programme. So, he remained a passive participant showed no interest in the discussions. His attitude towards the programme also, in a way, had some de-motivating effect on other participants. In this case, the fault is that of the sponsoring organisation which failed to communicate to him the reason for his selection except as a substitute.

There was also another participant from a public transport corporation who functioned as a trainer of different levels of mechanics and drivers. He came to the training programme with all earnestness, motivation (as we could observe) to get answers or find solutions to the kind of problems he faces in motivating and training his automobile mechanics. He appeared deeply concerned with those problems, almost verging on personal problems, and as though the problems threw up a kind of challenge to him. He was the man who often posed questions all the time seeking specific methods and techniques to motivate his mechanic-trainees. In many instances, the answers or the remedial measures with respect to his questions, lay in the administrative and managerial aspects of his organisation.

The fellow-participants, sometimes indirectly, expressed their resentment and vexation that there was distraction and waste of time over the repetitive nature of the questions and problems that the particular participant raised in the classroom. Perhaps, the participant was a dissatisfied man when he left after the conclusion of the course. Although it should not appear that the faculty were defending themselves for what they did, they responded generally by appreciating his questions, trying to provide him answers, spending considerable time on his questions and problems at the cost of causing some annoyance to the other participants. However, most of his problems were of a personnel and administrative nature where the training process was not of much help to him.[1]

1. E. Desingu Setty, *The Indian Journal of Social Work*, Vol.XLVII, No.2 (July 1986).

13

THE TRAINING INSTITUTE

Maximal Utilization of Expertise Within the Institute for Training

Training means time, cost and resources. Obviously, the principle should aim at maximal utilization of the professional expertise within the Institute for training of its employees. For instance, guiding or training in the areas such as, preparation of a project proposal, technical and economic appraisal of projects, performance appraisal, motivating subordinates, writing professional reports etc., the expertise is or supposed to be within the Institute and it should be located, encouraged and utilized.

In this context it may be mentioned, as suggested elsewhere in this report, that some of the professional staff may be trained in Training Methods and Skills, which would help them pass on their expertise to other staff.

The training institute has a different kind of responsibility. In most institutes, training is not the affair of one person. It is a team work. Each faculty involved in the programme contributes to the overall effectiveness of the programme. The institute has two distinct functions – training and taking care of the other facilities for the participants. What matters more is the atmosphere it generates and sustains. Small courtesies, a climate of warmth from all concerned, contribute to a conducive atmosphere. It is not enough that the trainer is an understanding type and that he does his job well, but it does matter with the other personnel with whom the participants come in touch, viz., the drivers, the typist, the canteen manager, the bearer in the dining hall or any person in the institute for that matter. Whatever may be the level of motivation on the part of the participant to acquire new knowledge or skills, he is not after a yogi for spiritual guidance or initiation, prepared to undergo any kind of difficulty or deprivation.

Whether the participant has come to the training institute motivated or not, it is up to the institute to provide him such conditions through its programme, faculty and support system, that he is really motivated to learn. Everyone in the institute may contribute to what may be called a learning atmosphere. The training institute may do the evaluation of its programme as a continuous process.

Does the library have enough books and other literature to cover all fields to be learned? Are the faculty competent and capable? Does the supporting staff, (typists, accountants, administrative and the like) contribute to build a healthy learning climate for the participant? Are the other facilities that the institute may provide – canteen, hostel, and transport for instance – adequate to meet the requirements of participants? In hoping to offer training, an institution should first find satisfactory answers to these questions.

MAILING TRAINING PROGRAMMES FOR NOMINATIONS

We have different types of training institutes some run by private organisations, particular department or by the government itself. The very existence and the name of the training institute is not enough and it should publicize the type of programmes it organizes. We may look into the way in which the training institutes publicize or advertise their programmes. It may be through newspapers, brochures and pamphlets. When it comes to detailing a particular training programme, normally, such things may not be clearly announced or advertised, wherein you have the limitation of space and also the cost of advertisement. But when the training institute writes letters to the heads of departments or organisations, normally it does not give all the details and the importance of the training programme while soliciting nominations from the departments. But it is desirable and essential to give, even though briefly, details about the training programme the title, the objectives of the programme, learning that is expected from the programme, the duration, the faculty involved in the training programme, the structure of the programme and the expected or anticipated benefits of the training programme in respect to the individual participants. We mention these things because especially, when nominations are solicited from the government departments the essential details are not provided. The need for giving as far as possible all the details about the programme will help the authorities in nominating the employees for training. Once we give such detailed information about the nature and the expected benefits of the training programme it will help the decision maker in deciding as to who is to be nominated for the training and in what way it would improve the functioning of the department or organisation.

Staff Professional Development Programme

The charity should begin at home as the saying goes. While a training institute's objectives are to train personnel drawn from different organisations it should also focus on training and promotion of the personnel within the organisation in terms of training competence. More often, especially in government sponsored training institutes some of the functionaries who are associated with training activity are seldom encouraged to move forward and they are not inducted into the mainstream of training activity. They are mostly confined to clerical and mechanical functionary kind of activities and not drawn into the professional programmes. In this context, we may briefly look into what the training institute could do in promoting and allowing its own junior staff to the mainstream of training function.

The Programme Associates, Senior Programme Associates and the Training Managers are to be gradually inducted into training, encouraging them and providing them an opportunity to function as co-trainers along with senior faculty and also serve as independent resource persons. This is a simple, straightforward and useful way to provide intellectual and professional incentive to the junior staff and it is a meaningful investment on professional development.

However, possessing competence in the required field is one thing and using that competence effectively, productively is another, for there are other intervening factors affecting the delivery of that competence. The factors are rewards, incentives, career development, promotions, recognition and inter-personal relations and the working conditions (the work environment). This kind of situation equally applies to the Senior Programme Specialists, the PAs and the other supporting staff. Training is supposed to bring in desirable attitudinal change, expand one's sphere of knowledge and improve one's skills.

Quality Control

In order to ensure quality, delivery of the training programmes and sustain the high quality, regular monitoring of the programmes right from the development of the course, its relevance to the participants' jobs and their organisations, the contents, the training methods and techniques employed, the reading material provided to the participants and the suitability and quality of the resource persons invited is to be carried out. Responsibilities are to be fixed among all the staff in maintaining the quality.

Familiarizing With HR Need Analysis In Real Field Situation

It is desirable that a training institute functions as a self-sufficient unit in respect to expertise and core competencies. One such competency relates to the whole gamut of Human Resource Development programmes beginning with client organisation analysis for strategic HR issues, training needs assessment, organising and establishing the HRD training programmes. It is highly desirable that the institute's faculty actually takes up a few past or prospective client organisations of different structure and functions and carries out the whole set of HRD analysis. This first hand, field-based knowledge is essential and would serve as a model and basis for developing HRD training programmes. It also helps in consulting and such organisational studies for arriving at strategic HR issues and competencies required, could be taken up as research projects. Such research projects are a useful investment for strengthening training and consulting.

Besides organisation – based field research, one could also ask the participants in HRD/HRM programmes to work out the HR competencies required in his / her organisation and the kind of training needs. This would also serve as an useful assignment to them.

Efficacy of Face-to-Face Training

The electronic – multimedia have their place and use in training programmes. They are rather supplementary to classroom training. In the Asian context, the nature of the issues, problems and conditions are such that what the participants from Asian/developing countries look for is personalized, face-to-face training interaction. And so, the emphasis is to be laid on classroom training wherein the participants have the advantage of fruitful interaction with the facilitators and thus creating conditions for learning.

Holding a Workshop on Development Strategies

Some of the countries in the Asian Region are in the process of economic restructuring and they are looking for strategies and approaches and aid for development. In order to meet the consulting and training needs of these countries as well as the donor countries' requirements, it is desirable to hold a workshop for a short duration inviting a multidisciplinary expertise. This would serve as a think-tank and during the workshop, major areas for training in the region, in the context of economic restructuring could be identified. There is a need to go beyond the present training programmes and a few cardinal training programmes could keep any training institute on a high pedestal in the Asia-Pacific Region.

HRD Programme for the Personnel of a Training Institute

As we have pointed out earlier, the strength of any training institute and its reputation lie on the competencies of the training staff in their respective fields of specialization and in the performance of their roles as per the norms stipulated by the institute. We may briefly look into the objectives of HRD for the training personnel, the competencies required beginning with institute's Executive Director. In respect of the Programme Specialist and PAs, it is presented in a tabular form. The designations of the head of a training institute and the training staff differ in general and in the present context the above designations are used.

Objectives

- To discover the potential of the training personnel

- To create conditions for translating the potential into productive activity.
- To enhance the competencies and gear up the personnel as a team to develop and deliver client-oriented training programmes.

The Training Personnel

The personnel compromise the Executive Director, the Programme Specialists, the Programme Associates, the Training Managers and the Administrative Staff.

Norms

1. The concept norms refers to set standards of performance of all training activities, in terms of quality and excellence by different functionaries in the training institute. Of each functionary role expectation is the norm and role performance is the output.
2. There are two ways of setting the norms of business, in the context of any training institute, it is conducting the training programmes primarily and doing consulting and research. The norms may be set by the Executive Director or they may be agreed upon and arrived at by all the training personnel. The later is preferable, since it is set by the group, rather self-imposed and the onus of keeping to and performing upto the norms rest with group individually and collectively.

Questions that matter

In HRD programme for the personnel, we may have to address two questions:

1. What kind of competencies,
2. How to develop those competencies and when to or at what stage those competencies are to be developed.

In this respect we may go by organisation hierarchical order beginning with the Executive Director.

Executive Director

What competencies?

As the designation goes, he is the leader of the group. He should have the futuristic at the same time realistic vision for the growth and development of the training institute, embody in himself leadership qualities. Ability to feel the pulse of every activity, wider outside contact, attitude and readiness to encourage and promote junior staff. He is to be an institution builder.

How & When?

a. The Executive Director may have a formal fortnightly or monthly meeting with his training staff, to review the ongoing activities and plan for future programmes. This is besides his informal meetings with the individual and programme special groups.

b. The Executive Director may look into the courses and the contents prior to the offering of the courses and also know in general the likely training methods and techniques that may be employed. A brief perusal of the reading material that is given to the participant.

c. To review each course with the Course Director, Coordinator and other internal resource persons who have handled the sessions after the course is over.

d. Such reviews should not go down as routine activity and ritual.

e. Though it is to be shared by others, it is incumbent on the part of the Executive Director to know the other competitors in the field of training in the region.

f. The Executive Director to compare the training fee charged by his institute with similar programmes offered in the region to know whether the fee offered by his institute is high, reasonable or low. This is in case of a professional institute, charging fee for training.

g. A few observations on the marketing of the training programmes:

- Marketing is not a self-contained discipline that produces results in isolation from other managerial functions.
- Marketing is a shared function.
- Marketing is image building.
- Marketing is everybody's responsibility as corporate unit, but onus may be said to lie on the Executive Director.
- Quality sells itself.
- The overall end product is the training offered to the clients and that is a factor for market response.
- Marketing pervades all training activities, such as:
    - Correspondence
    - Course Director
    - Course Coordinator
    - Resource Persons
    - Living Facilities
    - Reading Materials
    - The impressions the participants carry with them.
- Each satisfied participant is an effective marketing channel. We may have to work towards this end.
- The institute's faculty and the administration may be persuaded to share the marketing responsibility.
- The Executive Director may reflect over the following questions: "Who bothers about market – Whose responsibility is it?" If the staff is paid on the earnings of the centre, then they may have a concern for marketing of the courses. Irrespective of the market, they get their pay. How does it pinch them? The staff, as it is being done now, is to be encouraged with an economic incentive tie-up whenever there is an expected response from the

HRD PROGRAMME FOR THE TRAINING PERSONNEL COMPETENCIES – PERFORMANCE MATRIX

Category of Personnel	What Competencies	The Ways To Attain Them
Programme Specialists	i. Knowledge in the subject matter – a comprehensive understanding of a specialized area in his field.	• To keep abreast of latest things in the field: research findings and other publications. • To keep abreast of latest things in the field: research findings and other publications. • Through interaction with the participants and people in the particular fields. • Through formal and informal discussions. • Through writing and publishing in journals and newspapers. • The Programme Specialists may train themselves in writing case studies and using them as training methods in the course. The participants themselves and their organisations often provide useful and interesting materials for case studies.
	ii. Communication Skills and use of training methods.	• By deliberate practising. • By seeking feedback on one's communication skills: language, accent, speed, and clarity in expression. • By being a good listener

(Contd...)

	• Readiness to accept shortcomings, mannerism's and try to minimize or avoid them. • By a blend of natural humour. • By being audience friendly. • Sometimes by doing voice culture and listening to BBC for English.
iii. Marketing Competency.	• Through designing the courses. • Through effective delivery in the classroom. • Through correspondence with client organisations and funding agencies. • Through discussion with participants. • Through publications. • Through visits to client organisations. • Through popularity gained in consultancy. • The Programme Specialist, while preparing the course brochure may indicate, the way in which it would benefit the participants and their organisation. • The brochure announcing a particular course may indicate the serial number of the course, that is the number of times it has been offered earlier, the total number of participants who attended the course over the years and the countries they came from. It may also indicate participants'

(Contd...)

	appreciation of the course. It could be very brief. Such a structure / getup of the course brochure would make an effective impression and positive response. • In case of Programme Specialists writing to governmental and non-governmental organisations in the throes of restructuring their economies specific mention may be made how relevant the training programmes in question are to their new economies, whether it is HR requirements or economic development planning. • It would be nice that the Programme Specialists write to the former participants personalized letters may be greetings on special occasions. These may appear small things but they add up and make a significant impact positive to the institute's image. Printed material receives less attention.
iv. Competency in Consulting	• By undertaking individual consultancy. • By joint consultancy. • As part of marketing. • To be known to the clients as an expert through training programmes and publications of articles and books.

(Contd...)

	• By preparing technical and financial proposals. • By specializing in particular fields. • By faculty exchange programme, • By acquainting with some consultants' reports in one's own field of interest and expertise.
v. Competency in designing client need – based training programmes.	• Through in-depth study of organisation training needs. • Through expertise in job analysis and employee training needs. • By developing a sense of proportion between subjects to be covered and the time slot for each module. • By developing expertise in matching the training modules / topics with appropriate training methods. • Through knowing clearly what the clients want. • Through discussions with co-facilitators and based on the feedback on the previous training programmes.
vi. Competency in selecting, delivering and preparing training materials.	• It is obligatory on the part of the Programme Specialist / Course Director to read at least once the reading material that is provided to the participants. Sometimes for want of time or lack of interest or both, the PS/CD looks at the titles of the articles in journals and chapters in the books

(Contd...)

	and when they appear close to the modules of the course the material is simply photo-copied and given to the participants as reading material. • Even though, the reading material is given to participants and they are expected to read the material, it is a good practice that either the Course Director or the Coordinator gives a bird's eye view of the reading material, its relevance and importance to the learning objectives in the course. • Besides providing handouts to the participants selected from different sources, the Programme Specialist, who is in-charge of a course may prepare a brief and yet a comprehensive write-up (an essay) on the message the course brings out and the learning elements in the course and their relevance and application to the real life situations. • By scanning through journals in the relevant field by self or asking the Programme Associates to do that job. • Efforts towards minimizing the volume of material given to the participants. • By preparing and providing the participants a select bibliography on the topics covered in the course. • By discussing with the programme coordinator

(Contd...)

		and involving him in the scanning and selection of material.
	vii. Aptitude for and ability to conduct research and publication of papers and books.	• It is a self-motivated and job related activity. • By making use of one's training research experience. • By making use of one's training research experience. • Inspiration comes through personal reflections, thinking, observation, reading and discussions with people. • To keep in touch with research which would enrich training, the Programme Specialist may take up some research study as a continuous activity along with training and consulting function. The Programme Associates may also be associated with such research projects. • The Programme Specialists to keep in touch in writing as an academic activity may attempt to publish at least two articles in an academic year in refereed international journals. This would build up the image of the institute apart from the credit that would accrue to the individual contributor, it would help in marketing the course. • Faculty exchange programme is suggested. • As in the case of teaching faculty of universities,

(Contd...)

		the Programme Specialists and the Executive Director, as an incentive, may have the sabbatical leave facility.
viii.	Positive attitude and willingness to encourage and guide the Programme Associates towards professional growth and development.	• By associating them in academic and training activity. • By discussing with them their individual career development plans. • By discussing with them their individual career development plans. • By encouraging and helping them in their pursuits. • By inducting them into training in desired fields along with the regular participants for the entire duration of the training programme. • By publicly acknowledging their contribution.
ix.	Competency in human relations.	• Should cultivate warm and friendly relationship with colleagues and staff and especially with the participants. • In case of field visits the participants are to be briefed clearly on the eve of the visits, the purpose of the visit, what to observe, what to take note of, whom to meet and discuss and what data and / or information are to be secured, while sightseeing will remain ancillary and incidental.

(Contd...)

Programme Associates, Senior Programme Associates and Training Managers	x. Efficiency and skills in public relations – an effective liaising and coordinating of activities.	• By being authentic and sincere and trying to know briefly the background of the participants. • Meeting the participants individually and establishing contact with them, inquiring and trying to facilitate their requirements. • Paying as far as possible individual attention to the participants and the resource persons. • Provided that time permits and free from other responsibilities, it is desirable that the Programme Associates sit through the sessions of the resource persons to learn and also to assess the relevance and usefulness of the resource persons' lectures, discussions and training techniques employed. • The Programme Associate to prepare a brief report on his learning with his personal observations on completion of a training programme which he has coordinated. • More often, it is the Course Coordinator who scans books and journals to select material to be given to the participants as handouts. In this process, the PA should read the material and then select it. The tendency should be to reduce the bulk as far as possible.
	xi. Effective Communication Skills	• Self-Study and practice.

(Contd...)

and Command Over one's English	• Ability to say 'no' when you feel so and yet maintain cordial relation. • Usually, it is the Course Coordinator or a person temporarily hired who accompanies the participants in their field visits. Such a person should have some minimum knowledge of the areas and organisations visited and should function as a guide to the participants and not remain as a mute spectator. • In a training situation of all the functionaries involved in the training activity, it is the Programme Associate who has the highest frequency of contact with the participants and rather intimate with the participants and his person and role are very important. This fact may be taken note of by the centre, in the context of image building and public relations.
xii. Ardent desire to learn and grow professionally.	• Informal and Formal learning. • Taking initiative and showing interest for professional involvement in training and research. • Building a personal library. • It is desirable that the PAs publish articles for their own academic and career development and also to popularize the institute as a centre of excellence.

(Contd...)

- Cultivate social skills to function as a successful public relations person.
- Avail all opportunities for professional onward movement.
- The PA is an important channel of communication between the participants and the Course Director, resource persons and administration. He is an important facilitator in the day-to-day logistics. He is to be considered by the Course Director and the management as a potential trainer. It depends on the Programme Specialist the way the services of the PA are utilized. The PA is to be considered as a trainer in the offing. Sometimes, the PA's academic potential is not properly utilized in the field of training.
- With the in-service and on the job training, the Programme Associates and other functionaries of this category are to be gradually inducted into training function, encouraging them and providing them an opportunity to function as co-trainers along with senior faculty and also serve as independent resource persons. This encouragement should come from the Programme Specialists.

market. The staff could do their marketing more indirectly through the quality of the courses they deliver to the clients.

- The Executive Director may consider as a promotional measure, as a marketing strategy and also to encourage publication of well-researched and experience-based articles written by the faculty and start a half yearly journal. It would also contain invited articles from experts of certain fields. The journal would serve as a comprehensive information bulletin of the institute's activities and programmes. Over a period of time it would become the mouthpiece of the institute.

TQM in the Field of Training

Of late, though essential, the concept of Total Quality Management is being applied to products and services and there is a greater need to apply TQM in the field of training activity. In order to ensure total quality in the entire process embracing all elements in the training activity, one may have to ensure adequacy and quality in respect to physical facilities such as, accommodation, seminar halls, transport and hostel facilities. In the classroom setting, one has to ensure audio-visual aids, reading material, reference journals and books related to training programmes. There are of course, shortcomings and impediments physical, financial and human resources. As mentioned elsewhere, since training is a very important activity investing on man, the training institute may have to with religious fervour carry on training needs analysis and evaluation of training programmes. Often the training programme evaluations are seldom carried out and even if it is done, it is in a ritualistic manner. The training activity is not a physical instrument or material instrument. It is human activity and it is to be replenished, revamped and kept in readiness as in the case of an aircraft before flying.

14

THE SPONSORING ORGANISATION

In order to make the training serve its purpose, and to make the participant really benefit from the training for his own development and contribute to organisational objectives, the sponsoring organisation may have to do its part. The need for training may arise in the case of a new task, improvement upon the on-going task, it may relate to new organisational changes, expansion or diversification of activity, or to improve the quality of the personnel in their respective spheres. But the question is who is to assess the training needs? This may be done by the organisation or the individual concerned in the organisation. The organisation may do this, keeping in view the organisational goals, the job and the manpower resources. What kind of training? For whom? When? How long? How often? Where? And by whom? Are the questions the organisation may address itself in assessing the training needs.

It is not enough that the organisation nominates an incumbent for a particular training programme, but it should have a clear-cut idea as to how the learning acquired by the person should be used. The organisation should provide opportunities for the trained person to put his new learning into action. What is required is to encourage, support and sustain the enthusiasm and interest of the trained personnel. It should not be a routine affair that an official is nominated for some training, he returns after the training, he begins to do or behave in all earnestness, but his initiative is nipped in the bud, his efforts ignored and his proposals turned down by the management. This would be a futile exercise. It may only contribute to statistics that so many persons were trained and thereby the organisation is fulfilling its paper targets.

It is the responsibility of the organisation to make clear to the person nominated for training the purpose of training, what he is expected to do after his return, the kind of plans or programme the organisation would take up, and the kind of support and facilities that it would provide to the person. Such a clarity of purpose and activity would prepare and motivate the participant before he leaves for the training institute. This kind of an appraisal or briefing to the participant, is necessary because, at every stage of learning or de-learning, he will be reflecting on the back-home situation – the utility of his acquiring new knowledge and skills and how they could be employed usefully in his organisation. And so, the organisation's responsibility does not end with nominating a person for a training programme and welcoming him after his return, but to consider him as a precious human resource and make use of that resource maximally.

The importance the organisation attaches to the training will influence the participant in his learning effort. But often, the problem is: "Has the sponsoring organisation adequately assessed training needs and its usefulness to the organisation?" This can become a serious problem because, in most cases, the sponsoring organisation does not give enough importance to training. For example, often people are sent to training programmes only to get rid of them for a while, or they are being sent on a holiday. This, in itself, does not motivate the participant to learn. He will be saying "I did not want to come here, so why should I bother".

The next point which is also very important is the support the sponsoring organisation will give to the participant after the training. Will he be given the chance to put into practice the knowledge he has just acquired from the course? If the participant knows that his knowledge will not be applied when he goes back to his organisation, he will not find it necessary to learn.

The other question is that the participant will also be worried as to what the sponsoring organization will do with him after he has been to the course. Some of the participants believe that when they come back from a course, they should be placed in a higher grade, or be promoted to a higher post within the organisation. The sponsoring organisation should make clear to the participant, the consequences of attending the course. In most cases, one finds that the course was just too short for a person to be given an incentive, like a promotion, just for attending the course.

Another issue we should consider here is whether the participants are eager from the beginning to attend the course because, in some cases, a person is nominated to attend a course just because the sponsoring organisation wants to get rid of him for a while. In this, they will force him to attend a course which may not even be relevant to his job. The result often is that the participant is not interested to learn, to start with, because he is not wanted to learn.

If sufficient care is taken, and groundwork prepared by the organisation, in nominating the right type of personnel based on their aptitude and interest and organisational requirements, at the right time, for the appropriate programme, backed up by encouragement and support at the back-home situation, some of the problems that we discussed in the case of the participants might not arise, and even if they crop up, they may not be severe.

Organisational needs, employee training needs (man power needs), the way in which the organisations utilize the services of trained personnel, the performance appraisal after the training. Very little feedback communication from the sponsoring organisations and the training institute. No effective dialogue between the sponsoring organisation and the training institute.

15

COMPUTER BASED LEARNING

The advent of software has brought in a revolution in the dissemination of knowledge. It is cost effective and to a larger extent learning through the computer dispenses with the trainer. The individual depending on his interest, aptitude and also based on his role requirements can go in for computer-based learning. In one sense, computer based self-learning is similar to and extension of programmed learning which is one of the training methods. The computers have become libraries of knowledge. There are different ways of learning. Once the guidelines pertaining to what is to be learned, to what extent it is to be learnt are provided it will enable the individual to go in for learning on the computer at his own pace on time.

The Traditional Training Vs. Computer Based Self-Learning

When you look at the traditional type of training beginning with the assessing of organisational needs, manpower requirements, job related needs, the organisation has to provide training to the employees, nominating the individual for particular training and sending him to a training programme, the training being conducted by a training institute followed by the follow-up and evaluation. As of today, it is a long drawn process involving considerable expenditure. The computer based self-learning is cost effective. While dealing with the computer based learning the following aspects do matter:

1. The learning that is expected on the part of the employee
2. To what extent the training programmes cover this expected learning
3. The cost involved in training the employee in an institute.
4. Sometimes the shortage of manpower.
5. Some training programmes may require long absence of an employee in training programmes. It may not be possible to cover the entire knowledge areas required on the part of the employee for his effective performance. Some modules may be covered in the classroom training and the residue or further learning can be on the computer at the employee's own pace. Further, the extent of aspects or details covered either in the classroom lectures and discussions or in the handouts provided to the participants may be limited and inadequate. This limitation of information, knowledge coverage can be made good through the computer.

It is an unthought of revolution that the software has brought in in learning and communication. Today, the computers have become electronic libraries. Books in toto and articles on diverse areas one can think of are fed to the computers. For instance, several volumes of Encyclopedia of Britannica running into thousands of pages are fed into the computer. One need not go to those bulky volumes for any article or reference. In order to guide the employee to go in for computer based self-learning, it is up to the sponsoring organisation or the training institute to provide the employee, periodically the list of books and articles that he may browse through. The employee by himself may scan the computer and locate the areas of interest and things that are relevant to his job in his organisation.

One may think of the methods of learning the mankind has gone through over the centuries. For example in India, during the Vedic period learning was purely based on the teacher orally communicating to the pupil. This oral communication was the only basis for learning for several centuries. In oral communication, physical presence of the teacher is essential and after a few centuries we move on to the palm leaf as a means for recording the matter. The ancient literature in India right from the Vedas, Upanishads, and epics and even during the later period, most of the important historical records, plays, etc. were only written on palm leaf. With the advent of paper, we moved on to using paper and writing on paper to communicate. The paper based communication through books, newspapers etc. contribute and still are continuing. With the advent of the software, it has become unimaginably, quite easy and accessible wherein one can have the entire world literature on the Internet.

Here comes the question of the training needs and guiding the employee providing him the right type of training. One may think of a situation wherein left to himself, the employee as we have mentioned elsewhere may not go in for training, seek training but it is the organisation which identifies the learning and training needs that are essential on the part of the employee. And therefore there arises the need to examine what the individual has to learn on his own through the computer.

Computer Based Learning[1]

Computer based training (CBT) has been around for quite some time now. CBT uses computer hardware along with specially developed software to deliver training and learning programmes through the computer monitor. It can be used on a stand-alone basis or on the mainframe computer, employing multiple terminals.

Going a step further, we might have 'smart computers' which would instruct learners to refer to books or videos or even carry out assignments. Try imagining the machine referring the student to a particular chapter in a book, and then retesting knowledge levels. Not impossible. CBT can also be linked to video players, this would add an appealing visual dimension as an integral part of the programme.

The main advantage of CBT is that programmes can be tailor-made and used at the same time for employees based at dispersed locations. It can prove particularly cost-effective for large organisation. Another point in favour is that standardized material can be provided to all learners and it can be easily updated and improved without much effort.

One drawback is the hardware investment. In order to recover the costs substantially, CBT must be widely used. The programme quality must be carefully screened. A badly designed CBT programme is only as good as a boring presentation. It must be creatively done up, and provide for information and interest value. Another issue to be addressed before implementing CBT is user-readiness and familiarity with technology. There is no point introducing a technique unless users are motivated enough or at least have the basic skills to use it.

In the near future, CBT will travel towards more hi-tech interactive programmes, touch-sensitive screens and interactive disks. In organisations, we might well see individual learning plans coordinated by a central computer facility and local learning centres for individuals to obtain guidance on suitable CBT programmes, feedback on progress and even gain certification. There may be electronic libraries-cum-study centres available both in-company and for public access. As this system develops further usage will increase, costs will decrease and this will accelerate the process more.

Learner-focused development will mean new roles for traditional trainers. Instructors will be replaced by facilitators, who will need to enrich themselves as tutors and mentors. Their primary role will be to enable learners to manage their own learning. As use of technology as a medium for training delivery increases, they will need to first equip themselves with information technology skills. As training designers, they will need to visualize and create new and effective learning environments for technology-based training (TBT) to succeed.

In a digital world where muscle power is being replaced by machine power, hi-tech training will clearly shine through, making an impression stronger than any training technique has made before. But like all other training methodologies, TBT has its own areas of application. While it may be the ideal choice for disseminating information and educating employees on 'How to use the Internet effectively," it may be very inappropriate for bringing about 'attitudinal change' or for an exercise on 'effective stress management.'

Let us not allow the technology factor to become an overriding constraint in developing effective training courses. Rather, a judicious mix of available methods is necessary to cater to specific learning application areas. For example, if you are planning a teambuilding exercise, nothing may succeed better than a wilderness trek. A brainstorming session may be ideal to stimulate creative thinking or problem solving, while case studies may work best for management development. Similarly, sensitivity training for counseling, debates for presentation skills, in-trays for time management, role plays for interpersonal skills, fishbowl techniques for decision making and seminars for conceptual inputs are and will always continue to be evergreen hits.

The Internet has brought a whole new dimension to learning. Instead of a traditional face-to-face situation, the learner has access to an electronic learning environment. Internet technology is still relatively young and many people are only starting to explore its potential.

Several universities offer a variety of courses, including business management via the Internet, so that a student living in Taiwan can study the same course as his peers in Madison or Toronto. The facilities include electronic access to campus library and virtual access to other students across the world and tutors. Technology is helping to achieve what would have been considered impossible some years ago.

In the light of these developments, it is hardly surprising that organisations have started exploring possibilities of using the technology of Internet for more effective training to employees. Similarly, other futuristic technologies like desktop video conferencing are being employed for specific training purposes.

Technology Based Training (TBT)

The boom in information technology is impacting training delivery in a major way. The world of training is no longer dominated by 'training courses'. Instead, the emphasis is shifting to structured on-the-job learning, supported by the right technology. This new approach can result in effective learning of a kind which, by itself, classroom-based activity cannot achieve. Some of the more popular technology based training methodologies include use of the Internet, multimedia, simulation and virtual reality.

Using TBT, training can be delivered to a large number of employees at the same time, so that the unit cost of TBT courses is much lower than the equivalent delivered in the classroom. The initial capital outlay may be high and the investment would require careful thought, costs can be recovered with wide use and reuse of courseware. TBT is a flexible, independent study method where the learner controls his own progress, practice through simulations and most importantly, obtain immediate feedback on his performance.

Electronic Future of Training[2]

In a traditional classroom setting, the instructor and learner meet at the same time and place to exchange information and pursue activities to meet agreed objectives. In India particularly, the guru-shishya tradition makes it necessary for physical proximity between the trainer and learner. However, in the multimedia-based interactive learning, the media is the instructor and the emphasis is on self-learning.

Situation in India

Rapid changes in technology have made the computer an integral part of personal and professional lives. Changes in computer technology have brought major changes in how computers are used to enhance learning and training. As technology has become more prevalent and less expensive, more and more individuals as well as organisations have begun to use it for learning and training.

Benefits of Multimedia

Amongst the benefits of multimedia programmes the key benefits are:

- Learner's flexibility of content (learn only what is relevant by choosing topics from the programme)
- Learning convenience (as per own pace)
- Learning efficiency (since the learning is self-paced and auto feedback is inherent, understanding and involvement in enhanced).
- Uniform input to each learner (particularly important when a large, disparate and dispersed training, audience

has to reach a common standard of performance/ behaviour.

- Unlimited amount of review and relearning for each learner, at no extra cost (retraining/reinforcement/ refresher training becomes free).
- Once initially intended audience (for whom the multi-media programme was acquired) has been trained further incremental training become as good as free with multi-media programmes.

Because of its vastly superior capabilities and as mindsets of trainers and learners undergo a paradigm shift, it is very likely that in the future CD-Rom will supersede other methods of learning in the corporate sector. Multimedia interactive training is best suited for those organisations where:

- Training audience is large and geographically dispersed.
- It is difficult for training audience to be relieved from regular work schedule in a predictable pattern.
- Large number of persons have to be trained in a short span of time.
- Large number of persons have to be trained regularly on the same subject.
- Training audience is heterogeneous in entry profile, grasping ability and learning style.
- It is economical and at a time infinite number of people can learn.
- No restrictions on time, any time that the individual feels like he can sit before the computer and browse through. There is no need for him to take notes and the material is always available on the machine.
- It is a kind of luxury to use the computer for learning. Any published material which has been fed to the computer anywhere in the world is accessible at his door step just in front of him.

There is to be some incentive for the self-learner. One may think of conducting of some tests or examinations periodically to see what the individual has learnt on his own through the computer. This will have an important aspect of reward or punishment. Considerable amount of money is largely spent to meet the traditional training expenditure. Part of it could be provided to the employee based on his performance in the tests measuring his learning. He could be rewarded in terms of money or it could be promotion and so on. The thing that matters here is, you will have to develop a system wherein the individual is motivated on his part to acquire more knowledge by himself using the computer. And this as mentioned above, requires a periodic testing of the learning on the part of the employee. It will become an established tradition a new kind of training through the computer by the employee himself.

The Limitations In The Use Of Computer For Self-Learning

One limitation is the availability of hardware, and the cost involved in providing the hardware to the employees both in urban and rural areas. Though there is increase in the use of computers today, it has not funneled down to all the segments of administration and to all levels in an organisation. We find that in most of the cases only the heads of departments and senior officials are provided with the computers and the employees at the middle and the lower level do not have access to the computers. There is another limitation, while an employee is in the organisation, he may not find sufficient time for his learning on the computer. If one may think of learning through the computer, may be to begin. With, some of their employees are to be provided with computer facilities at their homes, so that they can learn during leisure hours and on holidays making use of the computer for this kind of learning purposes. When he is on the job in the organisation he may have to attend to his job and it may not allow him any time for this kind of learning on the computer. This is a question to be taken note of. Further, to enable the employees to learn on the computer they are to be trained in the operational aspects of computer.

- Supply of hardware to the employees at all levels.
- Training of the employees to make use of the computer.
- The cost of supplying computers to a large group of employees.

The number may run into thousands, may be the government or each department may have to plan a kind of programme especially in providing computers and training the employees in making use of the computers for self-learning. Each department may have a programme or a scheme over a couple of years and over a period of time once this plan is put into action everybody would have become computer literate and also a self-learner in terms of knowledge and skills expected of him in his effective performance in the organisation. One may be provided with the computer but there may not be Internet connection to that.

The System of Testing

The employee in an organisation left to himself may not go for acquiring relevant advanced knowledge related to his job. He should go in for enhancing knowledge in his particular field of work. Making the individual learn on his own may not work with everyone and so in order to make the individual employee take this self-learning seriously, we should have a periodic testing of his knowledge through assessing instruments or it could be through oral testing. Once the individual is found up to the expectations, he may be encouraged with monetary reward, an increment or professional upward movement. In case of those who are found below the expected level are to be meted with some kind of punishment. It may be postponement of his increment and or promotion. This reward and punishment system is only as an incentive. This type of self-motivated learning and the learning on the computer facilitate the learner to be on his own without any inhibition or shyness in the presence of any trainer or a superior officer. In the classroom training sometimes, the participants even though they may have some doubts or areas over which they feel like seeking clarification, they do not raise their doubts or seek clarification. The reasons are several. They do not want to show their ignorance amongst the co-participants. May be the instructor is of a superior position or their own boss in their organisation. Such personal disturbing and inhibiting factors are absent when the employee sits before his computer and he is the master at his own command. The participant in classroom situation may feel diffident of his own communication. He feels shy and therefore he would be a kind of mute passive listener in the class. Sitting before the computer and learning at his own pace he will have the sense of satisfaction and confidence. We should encourage this method which is more of self-reliant, reducing the dependency on external sources for advancement of knowledge.

Conclusion

An increased need to quickly share information and knowledge, develop skills, reach learners in multiple locations, the cost of transporting trainers and participants, and off-the-job downtime are all leading to an increased use of technology for instruction.

Since it is impossible to provide training at multiple locations simultaneously, efficiently and in a cost effective manner, use of multimedia-based instructions is becoming more important. As an alternative means of delivering high-quality instructions, it has several benefits. Research has clearly shown that it is both effective and efficient when implemented properly. In the fast changing business environment and serious efforts towards good governance, constant need to train and retrain gives rise to self-learning by using electronic media.

The learner need not stir-out from his seat to pick up a book or journal to read or refer to, but he needs only click the mouse, the needed information presents itself on the screen of the computer. The world of knowledge is in front of him. It is an unimaginable luxury, the learner enjoys as a contribution from advanced software technology.

REFERENCES

1. *Human Capital*, Vol. 1, No.12, May, 1998, New Delhi.
2. Hemant Kumar, 'Electronic Future of Training', *Human Capital*, September, 1998, New Delhi.

16

EVALUATION OF TRAINING PROGRAMMES

The evaluation of training programmes is a necessary and organic functionally related component of the entire training process. The idea of the training department as a passive provider of a menu of courses appears to be giving way to the concept of training as a management function which contributes to the growth and development of the organisation. As a result, the role of the training manager is changing. There is a growing trend for all institutions – political, educational or even medical to be required to be provided evidence of their effectiveness. With the training departments this evidence has usually been provided by established reputation of the trainers, training manager and the contribution of programmes to effectiveness. The training programmes are designed taking into account the needs of the organisation, employees, and the tasks to be carried out. Even though, normally, every effort is made in designing training programmes and imparting training with the requisite modules employing relevant methods, sometimes you are not quite sure of the learning impact on the part of the participants and their subsequent contribution to organisational growth and development. As such, in order to improve the entire cycle of training evaluating the training programmes has become an important requirement. Evaluation is a kind of check and the source of information to remedy and improve the contents of the programme and the manner in which the contents are delivered.

EVALUATING THE TRAINING PROCESS

The process by which training is delivered and the modules on which it is based can be evaluated against the learning and the performance and change in interpersonal relations on the part of the participants.

Feedback evaluation provides quality control over the design and delivery of training activities. Feedback to the participants during training will be an essential part of the training process. Timely feedback to the trainers about the effectiveness of particular methods and about the achievements of the objectives set for the programme will help in the development of the programme currently being run and those planned for future occasions. The information which needs to be collected for feedback evaluation is

(i). Before and after measures or levels of knowledge, concepts used, skills, attitudes and behaviour.

(ii). Sufficient detail to be able to review each topic covered during the learning event and each learning situation.

(iii). Evidence of transfer of learning to the workplace.

The main purpose of what we are calling feedback evaluation is the development of learning situations and training programmes, improving what is being offered. There is a secondary aspect, as identifying what is good and what is not so good improves the professional ability of members of the training department; reports based on feedback evaluation tend to have conclusions in them which the training department can consider and act on or not.

Evaluation of training programmes depends on the interest of the training institute as well as the faculty involved in the training programme. The head of the training institute and other important administrative functionaries as well as training faculty may have to consider evaluation of training programmes as a contributing factor. They have to take it with serious concern because some of the feedback we get from the participants and even from the faculty will enrich the future programmes in designing, duration of time allotted for the programme, the modules included, reading material provided, methods used in the training and the facilities provided on the campus in respect to food, accommodation and library facilities. The seriousness to be given to evaluation of training programmes needs revamping or emphasis continuously. Sometimes, in the initial stages one may attach a lot of importance to evaluation of training programmes and unfortunately over a period of time, the seriousness tapers off. Of course, once we have standardized a particular programme in respect of all of its facets and are quite sure of the impact of a training programme and its efficacy, may be, you may take the learning and performance behaviour on the part of the participants for granted. The training institute which may be offering different types of programmes orientation, induction, refresher and management courses may over a period of time standardize all the elements of training programme and be assured of its expected results in terms of learning and performance on the part of the participants. In a training institute as mentioned above, there are certain regular and routine type of programmes and sometimes they will be designing new type of programmes which may be experimental and in such cases they have to really go in for evaluation to see in what areas or in what aspects the programme is to be improved. There are two sources for improving any training programme. They are the participants and the faculty. When the faculty are competent in the subject matter and efficient in delivery of the content and the participants are eager and inclined to learn and absorb what is communicated to them may be considered as highly desirable. This kind of a matching between competence and efficient delivery on the part of the faculty and the learning aptitude on the part of the participants may not require sometimes much of the in-depth evaluation of the programme. However, it is desirable that at least some of the results of evaluation / feedback is discussed by the faculty in a meeting. So that, ways could be thought of for improving where some shortcomings have been indicated by the participants. It is something like keeping the instruments sharp all through. This instrument i.e., training is a complex multifaceted kind of activity. There is a greater need to keep it all the time sharp. As we have mentioned elsewhere there are different types of training institutes some run by private organisations and some by government departments. The evaluation of training depends again on the seriousness shown towards the feedback from the participants as well as organisations to which the participants belong. Though as an ideal and as a principle, evaluation of training programmes is taken as an important activity of the training institutes more often and in most of the cases it is not religiously and rigorously followed. Some may do the exit evaluation of the programme in respect to each individual session and evaluating the total programme as such. People use different types of instruments and formats with questions in evaluating the programmes. But what happens usually is, the participants at the fag end of the programme fill in these formats or instruments in a hurry and they are collected by the course director and he may get some feedback of the course and once the filled-in questionnaires go back to the section they may lie there. There is rarely a serious pursuing of the feedback and analyzing the feedback in order to improve in terms of designing, inclusion of modules and the way in which the contents are to be delivered. As mentioned above, in most of the cases it goes as a kind of a routine and formal activity. Since training is an important continuing kind of an activity to improve upon the performance on the part of the employees, serious attention is to be given to evaluation of training programmes.

COMMENTS

It is difficult to understand why the rigorous evaluation of training programmes is the exception rather than the rule in North American business and industry. Grove and Ostroff (1990)* described four barriers that discourage training evaluation:

1. *Top Management does not usually require evaluation:* Frequently, top management seems ready to take on faith that certain training programmes are valuable. Moreover, some top managers reward their training staff for merely staying current with the latest training fads. When sales and profits are good, top management appears to have no problem embracing the value of most training efforts. Further, when a needs analysis implies that training in certain areas is 'good to do', it appears to be especially easy for top management to rest assured that things are being done properly by the training department.
2. *Most senior-level training managers do not know how to go about evaluating training programmes:* Evaluation of

* Wexley K.N. & G.R. Latham, *Developing and Training Human Resources in Organisation*, New York, Harper Collins, 1991.

training is a complex procedure. Most people simply do not know how to evaluate training programmes properly.

3. ***Senior-level training managers do not know what to evaluate:*** Many people are not clear on what questions should be answered by an evaluation. Should they focus on the number of key people who want to attend the programme? The costs per trainee? The degree of enjoyment expressed by trainees? Changes back on the job? Grove and Ostroff (1990) argued that the major contributor to this problem is a lack of clear training objectives. A review of a sample of corporate training catalogues substantiates their point. They described one manager of a corporate learning centre who cut out of his own company's training catalogue all of the different stated course objectives. Then, he tried to match these objectives to the various course descriptions. He was not able to do this because the objectives were so vague! This problem can be corrected by tying the training to the organisational analysis where the corporate objectives and strategies for attaining them are identified.

4. ***Evaluation is perceived as costly and risky:*** There at least two forces acting on training specialists that work against evaluation: cost and risk taking. Many training specialists would rather spend their limited funds on developing new and highly visible training offerings that hopefully will be seen favourably by top management rather than spending scarce dollars on evaluation. The risk with evaluation is that the results may show that a training programme which top management and others like is not attaining the objectives for which it was designed.

To counteract these four barriers the following actions are recommended:

- Top-level management needs to be educated on the importance of rigorous evaluation and the dangers of taking on faith that a certain training development strategy is worthwhile.
- Training managers and their staffs need to be taught the

how to's of training evaluation. They need to be given hands-on training where they are shown how to design questionnaires, use the correct experimental design, statistically analyze data, and calculate utility.

- Training managers and top-level management need to discuss what exactly needs to be evaluated. Training needs to be incorporated into the business strategy. It is important that the organisation's overall strategy and the human resource management's strategy are aligned.
- If top management really wants to reinforce rigorous evaluation, it needs to make it clear to the training director that a certain proportion of the training budget should be targeted to evaluation.
- The risk-taking component of evaluation needs to be minimized by rethinking the purpose of evaluation. Rather than thinking of evaluation as a live or die decision for a training programme, evaluation needs to be thought of as a way of finding out if there's anything wrong with the programme and, if there is, correcting it.

We can have different types of evaluation instruments / questionnaires but here below, we just include a few types of evaluation instruments / questionnaires which relate to the evaluation of an individual faculty's lecture / session and the overall impression of the training programme on the part of the participants.

Note:- The questionnaires that are provided in Appendix-IV are models for different aspects of training evaluation

APPENDIX-I (A)

I. Courses for Personal Growth and Efficacy

Laboratory for Executive Development: Sensitivity Training

Duration:- 6 days

Laboratory for Executive Development is designed to help each individual realize his own potential for growth more fully and to increase his ability to work effectively with others in a variety of situations. By learning how to develop effective teamwork, individuals can join forces to bring about organizational change and improvement.

Objectives

The important objectives of the module comprise the following:

- Self-insight
- Better understanding of other persons and awareness of one's impact on them
- Better understanding of group processes and increased skills in achieving group effectiveness
- Increased recognition of the characteristics of large social systems, and
- Greater awareness of the dynamics of change

The laboratory tries to create a climate encouraging learnings, understanding, insights, skills in the areas of self, group and organization.

Methodology

The lab will be conducted by experienced Sensitivity Trainers with a series of L. Group (Learning Group) labs, interspersed with individual and group exercises. There will be no lectures save brief interventions by the facilitator. It would enable the participant to discover his real self (not in the sense of self-realization) and understand how he is perceived by others wherein the group would function as a mirror reflecting the real individual.

In this process the individual would experience real revelations of himself and others getting at the raw feelings and the inner working of the individuals, and the façade they put on in their worldly interactions.

For whom

Highly desirable and useful to Secretaries, Deputy Secretaries, Heads of Departments, Divisions, Sections and Officials from Administration and Personnel.

2. ***Management of Motivation***

Duration:- 6 days

Motives determine human behaviour-whether it is in the home, factory, office or club. To understand motives, then, is to understand human behaviour.

To deal effectively with the behaviour of individuals and groups in work situations, managers and administrators need to understand human motivation as it operates in and impinges upon each work situation. Motivation easily constitutes the most important task of a manager.

What motives individuals to join organizations? How can motives be recognized? What motivates individuals in organizations to produce more? What motivates them to greater commitment? Do workers and managers have the same motivation? How can motivation be changed? How can motivation be channeled into productive activity? These questions and the like are of great importance to the modern manager in all organizations.

Managers who know the answers to these questions are better

equipped to create an organizational environment which provides for the members of the organization maximum opportunities for high performance and high need satisfaction. They are able to recognize, utilize, direct and if necessary, change their own motives and those of the individuals and groups in organizations for the common good.

Objectives

The objectives of the module are to provide opportunities for the participant to:

- increase his knowledge of the current theories behind motives and motivation:
- improve his skills in recognizing and utilizing the motive structure within himself and those interacting with him and
- learn to develop strategies for his work group organization which will maximize opportunities that will motivate individuals to higher standards of performance and greater commitment to the group/organization.

Contents

- Current theories of motivation
- Motives as determinants of human behaviour
- Motives and emotions and their inter-relationship
- Identification of motives and emotions
- Measurement of motives
- Motives in relation to organizations
- Understanding the motivation of men at work.
- Motivational needs and maintenance needs
- Motivation of managers and motivation of workers
- The achievement motive
- The role and inter-play of the need for achievement, the need for power and the need for affiliation

- Building motivation into work
- Formulation of organizational programmes/strategies that facilitate high performance and high need satisfaction.

Methods

Training methods in the module will include unstructured learning groups, role plays, management games and simulation exercises, instrumentation and lecture-discussions.

For whom

The programme is open to senior and middle level executives in key positions in the Government all the Departments.

APPENDIX-I (A)

II. Courses in Inter-Personal Relations and Managerial Skills.

Organizational and Inter-Personal Relations and Communication

Duration:- 6 days

Whether we speak of functions within a Division carried on by a couple of layers of hierarchy and authority as well as the Divisions, the functions are several and at the same time collective. This collective action among several personnel, superordinate and subordinate depends upon healthy inter-personal relations.

Effective communication is an indispensable prerequisite for the human resources management system to function effectively. Communication has a pivotal role to play in all its sub-systems like HRD and OD too. Effective communication is the basic ingredient in effective human resources management. Inter-personal communication is all the more important for harmonious and productive functioning of an organization.

Objectives

The module would enable the participants to understand and appreciate the dynamics and fruits of working together and what happens when people do not understand their respective roles and their inter-dependency in carrying out the organization's activities. Further, this module will help the participants to enrich their knowledge in terms of the right structure and functions of communication, both verbal and non-verbal and enable them to be effective and productive in inter-personal communication.

Course Contents

- The concept of Inter-personal Relations – its significance and function in the organizational setting.
- Superior-subordinate relationship.
- Inter-divisional relationship
- Inter-personal communication
- Decision making
- Conflict management
- Group dynamics
- Trust building
- Leadership development
- Negotiation skills
- Team building
- Nature of communication
- Scope of communication
- Functions of communication
- Process of communication
- Channels of communication
- Communication in organizations
- Types of communication-informal, formal, vertical, lateral
- Barriers to oral and written communication
- Factors making inter-personal communication effective.

Methodology

This module will comprise lectures, case studies, exercises, assignments, classroom practising of oral communication and role-play.

For whom

Top and middle level staff of all Departments and staff of Administration.

2. *Management of Change and Conflict in Organization*

Duration:- 6 days

The incidence of change and conflict in any organization may be considered a natural phenomenon. Change in values, traditions, practices, lack of understanding, procedures and changes of technological and economic nature and vested interest may lead to conflict and the resolution of conflict itself may lead to change in any organizational setting. People do respond to changes and resolve conflicts in diverse ways, but there are proven means, methods and approaches to face the challenges of change and conflict and that is what the module focuses upon.

Objectives

The module would enable the participants:

- To gain an insight into the phenomenon of change and conflict;
- To understand the sources and the multiple causes behind change and conflict
- To know the ways to initiate and carry out a desirable change
- To work towards understanding barriers and stimulants to change and
- To acquire the skills for resolving conflicts.

Course Contents

- Understanding change as a process
- A brief introduction to theories of change
- Setting change objectives
- Types of change and change models
- Organizational culture, values and change

- Change implementation
- Barriers and stimulants to change
- Technological changes, innovation and human process techniques
- Conflict management; Containing, stimulating and proactive resolution of conflicts.

Methodology

Conceptual sessions, lecture-cum-discussions, case studies and exercises would constitute the chief methods of the course.

For Whom

The course is relevant and useful to all Heads of Departments and second level Supervisors in all Departments.

3. ***Human Resource Management (HRM)***

Duration:- 6 days

Human individuals, their knowledge, skills, leadership, initiative, motivation, capabilities, and aspirations constitute the human side of the resources of an organization. Prudence and wisdom depend on how best these resources of individuals operating at different levels are harnessed, channeled and maximally utilized simultaneously serving the interests of the organization and enhancing the capabilities and job performance of individual staff and also contributing to their career development.

Objectives

The course would focus on:

- Strategies and techniques of optimal resource utilization for enhancing individual organizational compatibility and involving staff in individual and group efforts; and
- Developing people management skills and ways of identifying and managing employee defensive mechanism for positive growth and development.

Course Contents

- Concept and process of human resource management (HRM)
- Psychology of human behaviour
- Organization structure design and HRM
- Manpower planning
- Individual task compatibility
- Personnel selection and training
- Performance appraisal
- Management by objectives (MOB)
- Individual-group compatibility
- Understanding self and others
- Motivation
- Team building and leadership
- Organizational socialization
- Maximum human powers

Methodology

Conceptual sessions, lecture-cum-discussions, case illustrations, individual and group exercises would comprise the methods in the course.

For Whom

Top and middle level professional staff and administrators from the departments of Administration, Personnel and Recruitment.

4. *Training Methods and Skills*

Duration:- 2 weeks

The recent years have witnessed an unprecedented growth in demand for not only new technology but also for new ways of managing organizations and people in the developing countries. This has been widely recognized by most developing economies which are attempting to meet the emerging challenges. A major effort in this direction is optimization of the training function in all organizations. Training today is generally accepted as a developmental, proactive intervention essential for accelerating the existing activities and inducting people into the ever-growing variety of jobs demanding increasingly complex skills. All these are in addition to the important remedial role-played by training in helping to overcome inefficiency, low productivity, poor morale and low profitability.

The number of managers/trainers required today by some of the developing countries in the region runs in hundreds and thousands. The scenario in most developing countries, in recent years, is that of a fairly rapid proliferation in the number of training centres and institutions. However, it is also a fact that most of the nascent training institutions suffer from an acute shortage of competent trainers.

Objectives

The broad objective of this programme is to enable the participants to become more effective in planning, designing and conducting training programmes. The aim is to produce personnel who will teach modern management through the multiplication effect of the teachers. That is, teaching and training the teachers/professionals to pass the knowledge down to a large number of persons. Specifically the course aims at helping the participants to:

- understand and gain insight into the training process
- develop skills in the choice and use of different training methods and material
- develop competence in planning a curriculum and
- develop personal and role effectiveness as trainers.

For Whom

The course is designed to benefit the existing trainers and

prospective training staff both at the State Head-quarters and at the Districts in the State.

5. *Performance Appraisal*

Duration:- 6 days

Performance appraisal is the systematic description of the job relevant strengths and weaknesses of an individual or a group. It serves two major purposes in organizations. (1) improving the job performance of employees and (2) providing information to employees and managers for use in making decisions such as administration, placement, selection-promotion, financial rewards, incentives or compensation etc. The essential purpose in this systematic and periodic appraisal is the accurate measurement of human performance. It attempts to reduce if not to eliminate human bias and prejudice by means of a system that is subject to impartial review and check.

Objectives

The module focuses on the appraisal system, the purpose, the process, the methods and the types and limitations to the system.

Contents

- The performance appraisal as a system
- The purposes
- The process
- Requirements of effective appraisal system
- Legal issues in performance appraisal
- Development of performance standards
- Methods and types of appraisal

Methodology

Concept sessions-lecturers, group discussions and case studies would constitute the main methods.

For Whom

Relevant to the Heads of Departments and First and Second level supervisory staff.

6. *Team Building*

Duration:- 6 days

Most of the activities in organizations are collective in nature carried on by teams ranging from 8-10, each individual playing a specified role and coordinating with others in carrying out a particular activity. Team members synchronize their efforts towards translating a designed objective. Team building can be within groups or at the inter-group level where activities are inter-dependant. The teams may go by different names such as committees, project teams, self-management teams and task groups. The most vital role of an organization is to build teams and foster them towards accomplishing of organizational tasks.

Objectives

This module would enable the participants to understand the functional significance of leadership in an organizational setting and work towards building and sustaining effective leadership and harmonious and productive teams.

Contents

- Types of teams
- Stages of team development
- Conflict resolution in teams

Methodology

The main methods under this module would be lecture-cum-discussions, exercises, team building games and case studies.

For Whom

Relevant to Heads of Departments, Project Leaders and Supervisory staff.

7. ***Supervisory Training***

Duration:- 6 days

The real function of a supervisor is to get work done through other people. It not only involves expertise in respect to the job to be done, but also a great deal of understanding of the employees supervised. The supervisor combines in himself several roles: a guide, a motivator, a trainer, an understanding and sympathetic friend, both a task and people-oriented man. He should gain mastery and skill in working with people and getting things done by the people.

The course addresses these requirements on the part of the supervisor.

Objectives

The course would enable the participant:

- To understand and play effectively his multiple roles;
- To gain an insight into what motivates people;
- To employ ways to motivate people and get work done
- To develop skills to train employees on the job, and
- To foster team work and boost morale of the employees

Course Outline

- The multiple dimensions of supervision
- The supervisor's job
- Problems encountered by the supervisor.
- Supervisor-subordinate relationship
- Managing and motivating employees
- Supervisor as a guide and counsellor
- Ways to improve performance of the employees
- Supervisor as team builder, morale booster and as a leader.

Methodology

Lectures - group discussions – Case studies, individual and group assignments would be the chief methods in the course.

For Whom

For all the Departmental and Sectional Chiefs in the Government Departments.

APPENDIX- I (B)
ILLUSTRATIVE MODELS OF TRAINING PROGRAMMES

- **Training of Field Level Operators on Communication Skills**
- **Duration of the programme:- 3 days**
- **Introduction:**

Communication assumes various forms and the entire business of human society depends on multiple modes of communication. It plays a basic, essential role in all walks of life. Communication is the ongoing process by which people attempt to share meaning via the transmission of messages. Management constantly is interested in the work performance and the way jobs are done with and through other people in order to achieve the mission, vision, values and goals. Communication provides a common silken thread for all management processes of planning, organizing, leading, controlling and proper coordinating. The management of people through small groups and teams demands continuous communication.

- **Learning Objectives**
  - To know the crucial, functional importance of communication in different forms with different types of audience.
  - To understand and appreciate the implications of clarity in communication, person to person, or person to group.
  - To understand the importance of developing

communication aimed at bringing out changes and motivating people.

- To know the modes of communication and to learn skills
- To know the effective communication needs: language, skills, intonation, understanding of the receiver.
- To respect the cultural, social ethos and folkways and mores in communication.
- To know that it is communication which differentiates a person from person.
- To know that body language as a significant factor in contributing or distorting one's communication.

– **Overall Objective**

- To know the function of communication in all walks of human life.

– **Specific Objectives**

- To create awareness and sensitize the participants in respect to the importance of every element of communication.
- To provide an opportunity to the participants to check the efficacy of their interpersonal communication.
- To pay attention to content, language and expression of emotions
- To stress on the importance of body language.

– **Target Group:**

Officials/executives from the field and organisations/departments. One may think of diversity of target group since these programmes are meant for the officials at the district level, they may be drawn from different departments operating at the district level.

Note:- The details of methods, vis-à-vis modules are mentioned in the programme table.

– **TOT Strategy:**

A brief exposure to different training methods related to the module.

– **Designed by:- Dr. E.D. Setty**

Module/ Topic in Training	Nature and Focus of Content					No. of Sessions	Training Methods	A.V. Aids	Methods of Evaluation in the class
	Knowledge	Skill	Attitude	Activity Oriented	A Blend of All four				
1.	2.	3.	4.	5.	6.	7.	8.	9.	10.
1. Function of Communication						ONE	• Lecture-Cum-Discussion • Illustrative examples	• OHP • Flip Charts • Board & Chalk or Marker • Power Point Presentations (depending on the availability)	• Oral Feed-back, • Written Feed-back, During the Class and After the Class/ Course on different aspects of the program
• Role of communication in general	✓								
• Development communication	✓								
• Interpersonal communication	✓	✓							
• Superordinate and subordinate communication	✓	✓							
• Status related communication	✓								
• Communication as a learning process	✓								

(Contd...)

1.	2.	3.	4.	5.	6.	7.	8.	9.	10.
2. The Channels of Communication									
• Direct, indirect	✓								
• Person to person	✓								
• Electronic & print media	✓	✓					Lecture-		
• AV Aids	✓	✓					Cum-		
• Cultural Medium	✓					ONE	Discussion		
• Leaders	✓	✓						-do-	-do-
• Stories	✓	✓					Illustrative		
• Folklore/folk tales	✓						examples		
• Street dramas	✓	✓							
• Puppet shows	✓	✓							
3. Behaviour as Communication									
• Body language	✓								
• Mannerisms	✓						Lecture-		
• Postures	✓					ONE	Cum-	-do-	-do-
• Interaction with the audience	✓	✓					Discussion		
• Ways of addressing the audience/receiver	✓	✓					Illustrative		
4. The Communication Process									
• Understanding objective of communication	✓						Lecture- Cum-	-do-	-do-
• Understanding the audience	✓					ONE	Discussion		

(Contd...)

1.	2.	3.	4.	5.	6.	7.	8.	9.	10.
• Preparation of the message and delivering of the message	✓	✓					Illustrative		
5. **Verbal and Non Verbal Communication**									
• Oral Communication	✓	✓				ONE	Lecture-cum-Discussion Illustrations	-do-	-do-
• Written Communication	✓	✓							
6. **Factors contributing to the efficacy of interpersonal communication**	✓								
• Key Elements of Communication	✓					ONE	Lecture-Cum-Discussion	-do-	-do-
• Barriers to effective communication	✓								

Note:

- The tick mark in the columns shows the element of that component in the module/topic. However, the training method or methods will throw emphasis on those components through examples and illustrations.
  - Duration of each session - 2.30 hrs.
  - Lunch Break – 1.15 PM to 2.15 PM.
  - Tea will be served in the class itself.
  - Session timings are only indicative and subject to change depending on the local conditions.

NB:

Though, the appropriate training methods are mentioned against the sessions depending on the training experience on the part of the prospective trainers and the availability of time, a brief exposure on different training methods may be provided to the prospective trainers.

A 3-DAY PROGRAMME ON COMMUNICATION SKILLS

Objectives:

1. To create awareness and sensitize the participants in respect to the importance of every element of communication.
2. To provide an opportunity to the participants to check the efficacy of their interpersonal communication.
3. To pay attention to content, language and expression of emotions.
4. To stress on the importance of body language.

TENTATIVE PROGRAMME SCHEDULE

DAY & DATE	*SESSION & TIMINGS*	*TOPIC*

1st Day &	1st
	10-45 AM to 1.15PM
		Registration, Introduction on Communication Function of Communication
		• Role of communication in general
		• Development communication
		• Interpersonal communication
		• Superordinate and subordinate communication
		• Status related communication
		• Communication as a learning process
		  • Lecture-Cum-Discussion
		  • Illustrative examples

	2nd 2.15 PM to 5.00 PM	The Channels of Communication • Direct, indirect • Person to person • Electronic & print media • AV Aids • Cultural Medium • Leaders

		• Stories
		• Folklore/folk tales
		• Street dramas
		• Puppet shows
		  • Lecture – cum –Discussion
		  • Illustrative Examples

2nd Day &	1st
	10-45 AM to 1.15PM
		Behaviour as Communication
		
		• Body language
		• Mannerisms
		• Postures
		• Interaction with the audience
		• Ways of addressing the audience / receiver
		  • Lecture-Cum-Discussion
		  • Illustrations

	2nd
	2.15 PM to 5.00 PM
		The Communication Process
		
		• Understanding objective of communication
		• Understanding the audience
		• Preparation of the message and delivering of the message
		  • Lecture-cum-Discussion
		  • Illustrations

3rd Day &	1st
	10-45 AM to 1.15PM
		Verbal and Non Verbal Communication
		• Oral Communication
		• Written Communication
		  • Lecture-cum- Discussion
		  • Illustrations

	2nd 2.15 PM to 5.00 PM	• The efficacy of interpersonal communication • Key Elements of Communication • Barriers to effective communication • Lecture-cum-Discussion

Note:

- Lunch Break – 1.15 PM to 2.15 PM
- Tea will be served in the class itself.
- Session timings are only indicative and subject to change depending on the local conditions.

ILLUSTRATIVE MODELS OF TRAINING PROGRAMMES

- **Training of Field Level Operators on Leadership**
- **Duration of the programme:- 3 days**
- **Introduction:**

Leadership is an important social tool for initiating action, motivating people, mobilizing resources, directing and accomplishing a task. Leadership is task related. It plays the role of guiding and building confidence among people towards better performance. Leadership in different degrees and modes operates in every social system. It is a process of influencing and directing task-related activities of group members. Motivational skills are critical components of leading. It plays a role in organisation and human resources development. One can think of self-inspired leadership and motivated leadership.

- **Learning Objectives:**
  - to understand the import and imperative nature of leadership
  - to motivate oneself, take the lead in organizing and accomplishing a task
  - to learn skills in mobilizing people and resources guiding them and motivating them and leading them towards task accomplishment
  - to learn the skills in interpersonal relations, communication and to encourage others to take lead,
  - to understand and to have the desirable attitude in following the leader in terms of attaining the desirable goals,
  - to understand the entire objective of leadership towards continuous progress making things better,
  - to understand the implications and purport of togetherness developing the 'we sense'
  - to understand the role/task expected of the individual and the mission and the task of the organisation,
  - having understood the objectives of the organisation how

an individual has to play his role effectively and also contribute to the organisational objectives which implies taking a lead and following the lead of the other

- encouraging others to take lead, utilizing the potential on the part of the colleagues, subordinates and encouraging them develop leadership qualities,
- to take lead in accomplishing the task assigned to them.

_ **Overall Objective of the Training Programme:**

- to instill on the part of the participants the purpose and function of leadership in all walks of life and especially in administrative, productive, service and human resource development

_ **Specific objectives:**

- to enable the participants to understand the functional significance of leadership in an organisation-setting and work towards building and sustaining effective, harmonious and productive teams,
- to motivate the individual assume leadership wherever the necessity arises and also to support a leadership in a constructive way

_ **Target Group:**

- Officials/executives from the field and organisations/ departments. One may think of diversity of target group since these programmes are meant for the officials at the district level, they may be drawn from different departments operating at the district level.

Note:- The details of methods, vis-à-vis modules are mentioned in the programme table.

_ **TOT Strategy:**

A brief exposure to different training methods related to the module.

_ **Designed by:-** Dr. E.D. Setty

Module/ Topic in Training	Nature and Focus of Content					No. of Sessions	Training Methods	A.V. Aids	Methods of Evaluation in the class
	Knowledge	Skill	Attitude	Activity Oriented	A Blend of All four				
1.	2.	3.	4.	5.	6.	7.	8.	9.	10
1. **Function of Leadership:** ● Essentiality of leadership in all dimensions of life, in initiating, planning, organizing, coordinating and controlling activities. ● Need for leadership in every field of activity.	✓ ✓					ONE	Lecture-Cum-Discussion with Examples ● Examples of emergence and function of leadership in all dimensions of life ● Political, economic, social cultural, educational, religious, organisational & industrial	● OHP ● Flip Charts Board & ● Chalk or Marker Power Point Presentations (depending on the availability)	● Oral Feedback, ● Written Feedback, During the Class and After the Class/ Course on different aspects of the program

(Contd...)

1.	2.	3.	4.	5.	6.	7.	8.	9.	10
2. Factors Facilitating Promotion Of Leadership									
• Socio, cultural factors;	✓					ONE	Lecture – cum – Discussion	-do-	-do-
• Individual aptitude and initiative;	✓								
• Task, issues, conflicts generating initiative and leadership;	✓						Case Studies		
• Factors facilitating emergence of leadership, inhibiting leadership,	✓								
• The style of management and emergence of leadership	✓								
• Emergence of leadership in centralized and decentralized systems in organisation,	✓						Lecture - cum - Discussion	-do-	-do-
• Cause/activity is the promotor of leadership,	✓								
• Fluctuations in leadership	✓								
3. Cultural and Social Milieu Behind Leadership									
• Cultural and social values	✓					ONE	Lecture - cum - Discussion, With Case Illustrations	-do-	-do-
• Political authority	✓								
• Economic status and ethnic status	✓								
• Leadership of various degrees	✓								

(Contd...)

1.	2.	3.	4.	5.	6.	7.	8.	9.	10.
• Social stratification and leadership	✓								
4. **Types of Leaders**									
• Autocratic	✓					ONE	Lecture-cum-Discussion With Examples	-do-	-do-
• Democratic	✓								
• Laissafaire	✓								
• Mix of these three types	✓								
• Types unchangeable	✓								
• Situational leadership,	✓								
• Hereditary leadership,	✓								
• Traditional leadership	✓								
• Segmental leadership	✓								
• Functional leadership	✓								
• Professional leadership from outside the organisation or community	✓								
• Transitory leadership	✓								
• Enduring type of leadership	✓								
5. **Scope and Space for Leadership**						ONE	Lecture-cum-Discussion & Examples • Examples of situations in organisation,	-do-	-do-

(Contd...)

1.	2	3.	4.	5.	6.	7.	8.	9.	10.
							wherein there is scope & space for emergence of leadership		
6. Leadership and HRD						ONE	● Individual & Group Exercises, ● Lecture-Cum-Discussion ● Case Studies	-do-	-do-
● The role of HRD in promoting leadership	✓	✓	✓						
● The intimate relationship between leadership and HRD.	✓								
● Various aspects of HRD	✓								
● HRD as a contributory factor towards leadership development	✓	✓	✓						
● Provision of incentive for growth and development				✓					

Note:

- The tick mark in the columns shows the element of that component in the module/topic. However, the training method or methods will throw emphasis on those components through examples and illustrations.
  - Duration of each session - 2.30 hrs
  - Lunch Break – 1.15 PM to 2.15 PM.
  - Tea will be served in the class itself.
  - Session timings are only indicative and subject to change depending on the local conditions.

NB:
Though, the appropriate training methods are mentioned against the sessions depending on the training experience on the part of the prospective trainers and the availability of time, a brief exposure on different training methods may be provided to the prospective trainers.

A 3-DAY PROGRAMME ON LEADERSHIP

Objectives:

1. This module would enable the participants to understand the functional significance of leadership in an organizational setting and work towards building and sustaining effective leadership and harmonious and productive teams.
2. To motivate the individual assume leadership wherever the necessity arises and also to support a leader in a constructive way.
3. To understand the function and purpose of leadership towards accomplishing a right and desirable kind of a task.

TENTATIVE PROGRAMME SCHEDULE

DAY & DATE	*SESSION & TIMINGS*	*TOPIC*

1st Day &	1st
	10-45 AM to 1.15PM
		Registration, Introduction on Leadership
		Function of Leadership:
		● Essentiality of leadership in all dimensions of life, in initiating, planning, organizing, coordinating and controlling activities.
		● Need for leadership in every field of activity.
		  ● Lecture-Cum-Discussion with Examples
		  ● Examples of emergence and function of leadership in all dimensions of life

	2nd 2.15 PM to 5.00 PM	**Factors Facilitating Promotion Of Leadership** ● Socio, cultural factors; Individual aptitude and initiative;

		• Task, issues, conflicts generating initiative and leadership
		• Factors facilitating emergence of leadership, inhibiting leadership,
		• The style of management and emergence of leadership
		• Emergence of leadership in centralized and decentralized systems in organisation,
		• Cause/activity is the promotor of leadership,
		• Fluctuations in leadership
		  • Lecture – cum –Discussion
		  • Case Studies

2nd Day &	1st
	10-45 AM to 1.15PM
		Cultural and Social Milieu Behind Leadership
		• Cultural and social values
		• Political authority
		• Economic status and ethnic status
		• Leadership of various degrees
		• Social stratification and leadership
		  • Lecture-cum-Discussion,
		  • With Case Illustrations

	2nd 2.15 PM to 5.00 PM	**Types of Leaders** • Autocratic • Democratic • Laissafaire • Mix of these three types • Types unchangeable • Situational leadership, • Hereditary leadership, • Traditional leadership • Segmental leadership • Functional leadership • Professional leadership from outside the organisation or community • Transitory leadership • Enduring type of leadership

		• Lecture-cum-Discussion • With Examples
3rd Day &	1st 10-45 AM to 1.15PM	Scope and Space for Leadership • Discussion & Examples • Examples of situations in organisation, wherein there is scope & space for emergence of leadership

	2nd
	2.15 PM to 5.00 PM
		Leadership and HRD
		• The role of HRD in promoting leadership
		• The intimate relationship between leadership and HRD.
		• Various aspects of HRD
		• HRD as a contributory factor towards leadership development
		• Provision of incentive for growth and development
		  • Individual & Group Exercises,
		  • Lecture-Cum-Discussion
		  • Case Studies

Note:

- Lunch Break – 1.15 PM to 2.15 PM
- Tea will be served in the class itself.
- Session timings are only indicative and subject to change depending on the local conditions.

ILLUSTRATIVE MODELS OF TRAINING PROGRAMMES

- **Training of Field Level Operators on Team Building**
- **Duration of the programme:- 3 days**
- **Introduction:**

Most of the activities in organizations are collective in nature carried on by teams ranging from 8-10, each individual playing a specified role and coordinating with others in carrying out a particular activity. Team members synchronize their efforts towards translating a designed objective. Team building can be within groups or at the inter-group level where activities are inter-dependant. The teams may go by different names such as committees, project teams, self-management teams and task groups. The most vital role of an organization is to build teams and foster them towards accomplishing of organizational tasks.

Learning Objectives

- To understand the indispensable nature of working in teams
- To understand the diversity of human nature and behaviour
- To learn skills in working with groups and coordinating team activity.
- To learn skills in interpersonal relations.
- To understand and appreciate the necessity of teambuilding and teamwork in meeting organisational goals / activities.
- To develop team spirit.
- Readiness to sacrifice.
- To imbibe the ability to work with people.

Overall Objective

- To make the participants understand and appreciate the need for teamwork. Since most of the activities in organisations are team oriented activities.

Specific Objectives

- To make the participants understand and appreciate the relevance and necessity of team building
- To enable them to understand the process and methods of team building
- To enable the participants to learn how to sustain the spirit of a team
- To make them know the inter-team rivalry and conflict and the way to resolve them

Module/ Topic in Training	Nature and Focus of Content					No. of Sessions	Training Methods	A.V. Aids	Methods of Evaluation in the class
	Knowledge	Skill	Attitude	Activity Oriented	A Blend of All four				
1.	2.	3.	4.	5.	6.	7.	8.	9.	10.
1. The Logical and Functional Necessity of Teamwork in organisation:						ONE	• Lecture-Cum-Discussion • Illustrations	• OHP • Flip Charts • Board & Chalk or Marker • Power Point Presentations (depending on the availability)	• Oral Feed-back, • Written Feed-back, During the Class and After the Class/ Course on different aspects of the program
• The nature of activity which necessitates teamwork	✓								
• The structure and function of teams, diversity of teams	✓								
• Roles of team members	✓								
2. Means and Methods of Team Building	✓					ONE	Lecture – cum – Discussion Case Studies	-do-	-do-
• Identifying the resources within the organisation and talent, knowledge, skills	✓								

(Contd ..)

1.	2	3	4.	5.	6.	7.	8	9.	10
• Defining and determining the nature of activity to be accomplished	✓								
• Longevity of the project – short time or long time	✓								
• Educating the members as to the objectives of the team activity	✓						Lecture – cum – Discussion	-do-	-do-
• Employees' ideas and opinions on Team's functioning	✓								
• Stipulated activity & Means and Methods	✓						Case Studies		
• Motivating them to work together	✓	✓							
3. **Motivation and Leadership in Team Building**							Lecture-cum-Discussion	-do-	-do-
• Function of Leadership in Team Building	✓	✓				ONE			
• Ways to sustain team spirit	✓	✓					Case Illustrations		
4. **Types of Teams and Coordination of Team work**									
• The types of teams-influence of leadership on team members	✓					ONE	Lecture-cum-Discussion	-do-	-do-
• Methods of coordination	✓								
• Role of attitude in team building	✓		✓						

(Contd)

1.	2.	3.	4.	5.	6.	7.	8.	9.	10.
5. Role Conflicts and Conflict Resolution in Teams						ONE	Lecture-Cum-Discussion	-do-	-do-
• Sources and reasons for conflicts in teams	✓	✓							
	✓	✓					Individual & Group Exercises		
6. Individual and Group Counseling									
• Ways to resolve individual differences and creating an atmosphere of understanding	✓	✓				ONE	Lecture-cum-Discussion	-do-	-do-
• Building team spirit	✓								

Note:

- The tick mark in the columns shows the element of that component in the module/topic However, the training method or methods will throw emphasis on those components through examples and illustrations.
  - Duration of each session - 2.30 hrs.
  - Lunch Break – 1.15 PM to 2.15 PM.
  - Tea will be served in the class itself.
  - Session timings are only indicative and subject to change depending on the local conditions.

NB:

Though, the appropriate training methods are mentioned against the sessions depending on the training experience on the part of the prospective trainers and the availability of time, a brief exposure on different training methods may be provided to the prospective trainers.

- To make the participants understand the functional relationship between leadership and teamwork – the role of a leader in team work.

- **Target Group:**

Officials/executives from the field and organisations/ departments. One may think of diversity of target group since these programmes are meant for the officials at the district level, they may be drawn from different departments operating at the district level.

Note:- The details of methods, vis-à-vis modules are mentioned in the programme table.

- **TOT Strategy:**

A brief exposure to different training methods related to the module.

- **Designed by:- Dr. E.D. Setty**

A 3-DAY PROGRAMME ON TEAM BUILDING

Objectives

- To make the participants understand and appreciate the relevance and necessity of team building
- To enable them to understand the process and methods of team building
- To enable the participants to learn how to sustain the spirit of a team
- To make them know the inter-team rivalry and conflict and the way to resolve them
- To make the participants understand the functional relationship between leadership and teamwork – the role of a leader in team work.

TENTATIVE PROGRAMME SCHEDULE

DAY & DATE	*SESSION & TIMINGS*	*TOPIC*

1st Day &	1st
	10-45 AM to 1.15PM
		Registration, Introduction on Team Building
		The Logical and Functional Necessity of Teamwork in organisation:
		● The nature of activity which necessitates teamwork
		● The structure and function of teams, diversity of teams Roles of team members
		  ● Lecture-Cum-Discussion
		  ● Illustrations

	2nd
	2.15 PM to 5.00 PM
		Means and Methods of Team Building
		● Identifying the resources within the organisation and talent, knowledge, skills
		● Defining and determining the nature of activity to be accomplished
		● Longevity of the project – short time or long time.
		● Educating the members as to the objectives of the team activity
		● Employees' ideas and opinions on team's functioning
		● Stipulated activity & Means and Methods
		● Motivating them to work together
		  ● Lecture – cum –Discussion
		  ● Case Studies

2nd Day &	1st 10-45 AM to 1.15PM	**Motivation and Leadership in Team Building** ● Function of Leadership in Team Building

(Contd...)

		• Ways to sustain team spirit
		  • Lecture-Cum-Discussion
		  • Case Studies

	2nd 2.15 PM to 5.00 PM	**Types of Teams and Coordination of Team work** • The types of teams - influence of leadership on team members • Methods of coordination • Role of attitude in team building • Lecture-cum-Discussion

3rd Day &	1st
	10-45 AM to 1.15PM
		Role Conflicts and Conflict Resolution in Teams
		• Sources and reasons for conflicts in teams
		  • Lecture-Cum-Discussion
		  • Individual & Group Exercises

	2nd 2.15 PM to 5.00 PM	**Individual and Group Counseling** • Ways to resolve individual differences and creating an atmosphere of understanding • Building team spirit • Lecture-cum-Discussion

Note:
- Lunch Break – 1.15 PM to 2.15 PM
- Tea will be served in the class itself.
- Session timings are only indicative and subject to change depending on the local conditions.

APPENDIX-II

A MODEL INSTRUMENT TO ASSESS THE TRAINING NEEDS OF EMPLOYEES IN AN ORGANISATION

1. Name of the Respondent:-
2. Academic Qualifications:-
3. Present Official position:-
4. No. of years of service:-
5. What is your role in the organisation/department:-

6. Briefly describe the tasks related to your role:-

7. Are you clear about your job requirements?

8. Do you feel confident in terms of knowledge and skills in performing your job?

   Yes ☐ No ☐

9. If No, what kind of knowledge/skill you feel required?

10. How important is your performance in respect to the objectives of the organisation / department:

11. How do you rate your performance?

    a. Extremely Satisfactory ☐

    b. Satisfactory ☐

    c. Not upto my satisfaction ☐

12. If you are not satisfied of the performance expected of you, please list out the problems and hindrances which cause your poor performance.

    (a). Lack of physical facilities ☐

    (b). Lack of adequate time for the job ☐

    (c). Lack of right or proper guidance from the superiors ☐

    (d). Inadequate support from my subordinates ☐

    (e). Lack of encouragement from the superiors ☐

13. In performing your role as expected of you, what you think you need in terms of the following aspects for effective role performance?

    (a). knowledge relevant to my job ☐

    (b) skills to perform job effectively ☐

    (c). the desirable / right type of attitude in interpersonal relations. ☐

14. What kind of change in behaviour you expect from your superior officers?

    I want them

    (a). to help me ☐
    (b). to increase my knowledge ☐
    (c). to facilitate acquire the required skills to perform my job effectively ☐
    (d). to be friendly with me ☐
    (e). to accept me as an individual ☐
    (f). to respect me as a human being ☐
    (g). to encourage for my career growth and development ☐

15. How does your superior officer treat you?

    (a). quite friendly ☐
    (b). treats me with respect ☐
    (c). gives me what is due to my position ☐
    (d). he is very harsh ☐
    (e). dictates terms ☐
    (f). not of helping, guiding nature ☐

16. What kind of changes are desirable amongst your superiors?

    (a). they should be more knowledgeable ☐
    (b). they should behave like parents guiding children ☐
    (c). they should encourage and motivate the subordinates ☐
    (d). they should learn to be effective in interpersonal relations ☐
    (e). the language they use, and the way they address the subordinates is important ☐
    (f). they cannot treat the subordinates as numerical entities ☐
    (h). they should clearly communicate the changes they expect on our part ☐

(h) provide time and guidance to the subordinates to improve their performance. ☐

17. How do you find the work culture in your organisation/ department?

(a). quite conducive ☐

(b). quite friendly ☐

(c). quite transparent and open ☐

(d). lack of understanding and effective coordination ☐

(e). poor communication ☐

(f). everybody is recognized as important functionary in the organisation ☐

(g). too much of subordination ☐

(h). Very little internal communication ☐

(i). employees are not informed of the significant changes that are being attempted in the organisation / department ☐

(k). the system is more centralized ☐

(l). decision making is mostly vested with the upper echelon ☐

(m). subordinates are indifferent to superordinates ☐

18. If the subordinates are to perform their roles effectively in meeting the stipulated goals of the organisation/ department, how their performance should be?

19. Of all the employees in your department/ organisation who are to be trained?

20. In what areas they are to be trained?

21. If they are to be trained, please indicate the organisation in which they are to be trained?

22. Do you have any pressure in the work situation?

    Yes ☐ No ☐

23. If Yes, what kind of pressure?

24. What are your suggestions to remove such pressure?

25. Is your work individualistic done by yourself only? Or is it teamwork?

    Individualistic ☐ Team Work ☐

26. Do you like your present job?

    Yes ☐ No ☐

27. If Yes, why? What are the contributing factors?

28. If No, what are your suggestions to improve the work situation?

29. If it were to be teamwork, what is your part in it?

30. How do you describe the spirit in the team?

31. Do you have any deadline in finishing a particular unit of your job?

    Yes ☐ No ☐

32. Supposing you have not finished your work within the stipulated deadline what are the reasons?

33. What according to you are the desirable changes to be effected amongst your superiors/colleagues/ subordinates?

    Superiors

    Colleagues

    Subordinates

34. What according to you is the priority:

    a). Superordinates ☐

    b). Middle Level Officials ☐

    c). Subordinates ☐

35. In the course of your discharging role responsibility do you encounter any external interference (i.e., outside the organisation)?

    Yes ☐ No ☐

36. If Yes, specify.

37. What according to you are the measures to bring about positive, productive, attitudinal changes among the superiors and subordinates

    Superiors

    Subordinates

38. What makes an employee perform better?

a). Monetary incentive ☐
b). Adequate knowledge, skills ☐
c). Right attitude ☐
d). Effective Interpersonal Relations ☐
e). Encouragement given by the superiors ☐
f). Cooperation from the colleagues ☐
g). Liking for the job ☐
h). Support from subordinates ☐
i). Congenial work culture ☐
j). Clarity in communication ☐
k). Recognition of merit ☐
l). Rewards for better performance ☐
m). Security of job ☐

39. Have you, during the recent past, accepted any change in your way of working towards better performance?

Yes ☐ No ☐

40. If Yes, please briefly mention the kind of change that you have adopted.

41. If you had accepted the change was it spontaneous?

Yes ☐ No ☐

42. If not spontaneous was there any initial resistance?

Yes ☐ No ☐

43. If there had been initial resistance, how did you overcome that resistance?

44. What are your suggestions in successfully introducing the desirable changes amongst the staff of your department/organisation?

Thank you

APPENDIX-III

TRAINING METHODS – AT A GLANCE

Sl.No. On the Job		*In the Class Room*	*Off the Class Room*
1. Orientation Training		6. Lecture	26. Field Visits
2. Job instructions	Discussion Methods*	7. Conference	27. Correspondence
3. Apprenticeship		8. Seminar	28. Programmed Instructions
4. Internship and Assistantship including job rotation and coaching		9. Symposium 10. Panel 11. Workshop 12. Syndicate 13. Case	
5. Junior board	Experiential Methods or Simulations	14. Instrumentation in Training 15. Vestibule Training 16. Business Games 17. Structured Experiences 18. Role Play 19. Laboratory Training 20. Simulation 21. Demonstration 22. Discussion Group 23. Exercises 24. Films 25. Buzz Method	

* Buzz group or small group discussions can be used in many of the methods.

LECTURE METHOD

What it is?	Process/ Procedure	Trainer Skill	Requirements	Learning Objectives	Other Consideration	Advantages	Limitations
1.	2.	3.	4.	5.	6.	7.	8.
• A usually carefully prepared, rather formal dissertation by one with claims to be an expert on the particular theme. • The effectiveness of a speech can be improved by encouraging the audience to take notes. • Use visual aids as lecturer's 'signposts' or memory joggers – remember, 'a good picture is worth a thousand words'. • Make good use of stories and anecdotes and other figures of speech to illustrate your points.	• Unilateral oral communications between an individual and a group • - the teacher teaches and the learners learn • Could be combined with question – answer session after the lecture • The chairman introduces the speaker, with a brief statement of his/her qualifications and expertise in the selected topic. • The chairman should ensure the speaker is given a fair hearing, in	• Clarity of thought • Organisation of thoughts and points • Clear delivery • Language proficiency • Also • Use of A.V. Aids. • Humour (appropriate) • Use of illustrations (relevant)	• A large enough room with A.V. equipment (if necessary) special care to see no echo effects prevail • Speaker must be visible to and heard by, the chairman and every member of the audience. • Stage or raised platform (speakers' rostrum) with microphone, amplifiers, and loudspeakers when size of audience requires them.	• When straight factual, descriptive explanatory substance is to be delivered • To present factual material in a logical sequence • To present one or more points of view on a controversial subject. • To recount personal experiences. • To entertain or to arouse an audience. • To call for	• When size of the group is large • Not enough space • Not enough time	• Time is largely scheduled by the lecturer • Lecturer in control over the learning • Facilitates well-defined framework for functioning • Suitable for an audience of any size • Easy to organize. • Some people learn more easily listening than reading. • Simple recall exercises make its effectiveness easy to assess	• Bringing about attitude change (though possible) is difficult. • Checking with participants involvement absorption, etc is difficult • Does not cater to differential needs and levels of participants • The audience's role is passive. • There is a one-way flow of

(Contd...)

1	2	3.	4.	5.	6.	7.	8
• Introduce devices such as repetition to heighten drama • Review and summarize regularly, 'Tell them what you are going to tell them, tell it to them, then tell them what you have just told them'. • Be careful not to cram too many points in a single lecture. • Give out copies summarizing your speech at its conclusion. • Prepare your audience for selective listening. 'We will try to find out tomorrow how much you have learnt today'	the best possible conditions • At the end of the speech, the chairman (with the speaker's prior consent) should call for questions or points for discussion. • Finally, the chairman should call upon a member of the audience to make a brief speech of thanks to the speaker		• Visual aids (projector and screen) when called for by speaker.	action • To stimulate thought, thus opening up a subject for discussion and further study.			information • Efficient listening demands concent-ration • The lecture is the traditional, but very ineffective, method of imparting skills. • Audience feedback is limited. • The expert is not always a good speaker. • Good speakers are hard to find.

CASE METHOD

What it is?	Process/ Procedure	Trainer Skill	Requirements	Learning Objectives	Other Consideration	Advantages	Limitation
1	2.	3	4	5	6	7	8
• Comprehensive oral, written, and/or filmed account of an event or series of related events • Allow plenty of time before the start for members to study a written case • Can be very effective if small groups compete in seeking solutions • A debate on possible solutions can be worthwhile when a capable chairman is available to keep the speakers 'on course' • Some 'red herrings' are desirable in any case study, but take care not to build in too many at the expense of getting	• Method calls for confrontation with concrete human situations in the classroom • The trainer presents the situation – the group considers it, discusses and works out alternative modes of confronting the situation • Thinking begins with generalities and moves to specifics • Chairman introduces the topic and explains the case study and what is required.	• Direct and lead discussions towards the learning goal without superimposing his thinking. • Ability to relate theoretical concepts with actual situations • "Managing Time" • Ability to tolerate ambiguity • Ability to develop confusion and vagueness into clarity	• They will vary with the type of case – a stage or some other, fully visible area will be needed if you are going to 'act out' a problem; a film calls for a blackout and for a suitable screen and projector (check on their availability well beforehand)	• When development of skills for observation, diagnosis, analysis and working out alternatives is called for • Presents a situation problem for discussion • Problem-solving technique • Teaching problem-solving processes. • Builds up a complete picture.	• When senior and experienced levels of participation resists an imposed lecture	• Facilitates appreciation of different view-points about a situation • Different approaches to the situation • Makes use of participants' experience and insight as a major resource • Provides relevant detail • Helps to identify alternative solutions. • Helps to develop analytical, problem-solving skills	• Needs quite sometime to make it effective • Cannot be usefully used if the group does not have the kind of experience required • Can be time consuming • Relevance may not always be obvious • Stimulates some people, but irritates others

(Contd.)

1	2.	3	4.	5	6.	7	8
the main message across • Don't waste time in looking for a scapegoat • The best case studies are built upon actual problems (but take care to hide the identity of the people involved) • A common technique in management courses is to ask each member to describe an office problem as a case study for group solution, and later reveal (and sometimes discuss) how it was in fact handled.							

ROLE PLAY

What it is?	Process/ Procedure	Trainer Skill	Requirements	Learning Objectives	Other Consideration	Advantages	Limitation
1	2	3	4.	5	6	7	8
• A 'real-life' situation (but with no script and no set dialogue) is improvised and acted out in front of the group, which then discusses the implications of the performance for the situation under consideration • Role-playing early in a programme will help to break down inhibitions • Select your actors carefully • Where possible, allow them adequate time to improvise their 'props' and costumes • Encourage a light-hearted approach • Arrange for several role-playing sessions–	• The process starts with the players 'behaving in the given set', then the observers analyze this 'play' facilitated by the trainer After sharing of experiences by the players, generalities are drawn from the specifics discovery learning moving from specific to general • The group leader must clearly define the situation (set the scene) before the role-playing begins • Role-playing can be introduced without any warning, but it is better to give the	• Observation skills • Associating observations of the role-play to the phenomenon in question • Facilitating discovery about behavioural tendencies, need for change (if necessary)	• Role briefs carefully prepared to bring out the intended learning point • Making the role briefs clear to the players • Briefing sheets for observers • Each member of the audience must be able to see the action • Actors seem to prefer being against a wall or on a stage, away from their audience.	• When emphasis is on human relations • Inter-personal communication skills • Decision making skills • To examine a problem in human relationships – for example, an extension worker or a social worker who is required to deal with a 'difficult' client • To seek out possible solutions to	• When experiential exposure can compensate for lack of credibility • There is need to motivate participants through active involvement	• Provides for empathy and thus facilitates attitude change, tolerance to other view-points and better perspective • Helps to realize that it is easier said than done • As players tend to identify themselves with the role, revealing discussions may be possible • An effective way of stimulating discussion that is aimed at problem solving • Gives the actor a chance to assume	• If the role players are not perceptive and do not invest themselves the whole exercise could be futile • Some people are too timid or self-conscious to act a role successfully • Role-playing loses some of its effect when the audience is too large

(Contd.)

1.	2.	3	4.	5.	6.	7	8.
try making the groups competitive. ● In multicultural groups, role acting can be a useful means of helping to breakdown inter-racial prejudices and promote understanding. ● Role-playing is generally spontaneous, while the drama spot is usually rehearsed – there is an important area in between the two in which guidelines are established but the dialogue is spontaneous.	actors a little time to get used to the idea – they will then sometimes produce a very polished performance ● The tutor should set a time limit beforehand· 'You have 10 minutes in which to get your message across'. ● After the first performance has been discussed, it is sometimes worthwhile to have the scene replayed by a second set of actors.			an emotion-laden problem. ● To provide a group with insight into attitudes that differ sharply from their own. ● To practise new skills		the personality of (to think and act like) another human being which should lead to a better understanding of the other person's point of view ● Can be an effective means of avoiding the real-life dangers of the 'trial-and-error' approach. ● Can add variety, drama, and fun to a formal training programme. ● The actors are sometimes able to explain cultural differences simply and clearly.	

PROGRAMMED INSTRUCTIONS

What it is?	*Process/ Procedure*	*Trainer Skill*	*Requirements*	*Learning Objectives*	*Other Consideration*	*Advantages*	*Limitation*
1	2.	3	4.	5	6.	7	8
● Material presented in any one or more of a variety of ways (texts, tape-slides, multi-media, or a teaching machine or computer) as a series of small, carefully graduated, sequential steps, the mastering of witch requires the active participation of the learner at his/ her own preferred pace (self-paced learning) ● The most effective learning occurs from challenging, stimulating, encouraging exercises – variety is the key to teaching and to learning. ● Programmed learning	● Sequentially and logically arranged small steps or units of information is to be learnt with the help of reinforcement ● Each unit is presented in a 'frame' followed by a question regarding the learning of the frame. ● A learning 'package' is divided up into units or modules ● The student is required to follow instructions that are based on the media being used ● Reinforcing exercises are set. ● Each set of work is marked before	● Ability to split the whole into meaningful and logically sequenced small units. ● Ability to frame questions that would reflect on the learner's comprehension.	● Facility to present the frames – could be print – tapes or videos or a combination of these. ● Space for each learner to learn independently at his own speed without disturbance. ● The participant must have a private 'quiet-area' – in his/her accommodation or in the training area.	● To teach factual or technical information that can be broken into meaningful and sequential parts. ● For learning at a distance, by correspondence (particularly adults, in their own home). Ideal for in-service training – where students come to a central training unit in their own time to work in a learning unit.	● May be used as a preliminary to give factual data for subsequent classroom discussion.	● Caters to differential speed of learning in the groups. ● Saves class room time by giving the basic factual information. ● Is effective as conventional method, and sometimes faster. ● Students do their own marking. ● Self-testing produces immediate feedback. ● Participants themselves identify areas	● Time and cost consuming. ● Developing and pre-testing of programmes can be costly in both time and money. ● There is a shortage of programmed learning material ● Too many participants will lead to competition for the machines (computer, tape-slide machine, and so on)

(Contd...)

1.	2.	3.	4.	5.	6.	7.	8
can be boring, or it can be 'fun' – make sure it is also challenging ● Programmed learning can be very encouraging for slow learners. ● Don't make the learning units too small – students will grow bored. ● If possible, make the learning machines available outside working hours; to encourage their use.	the student is allowed to proceed.			● As a break from more-formal training.		that require further study ● In step-by-step study, the learner acts as his/her own pace setter.	● Most participants tend to prefer more-sociable learning systems. ● The inflexibility of what is a highly structured method.

FIELD VISITS

What it is?	Process/ Procedure	Trainer Skill	Requirements	Learning Objectives	Other Consideration	Advantages	Limitation
1	2.	3	4.	5	6	7	8
• Moves from observation to clarification to generalization to application • Characterized by a planned itinerary, usually of a predetermined length, during which a particular environment or past or present 'event' is observed and studied • Whenever possible, someone should make a preliminary tour to check on the details and the timing • If a preliminary tour is not possible, check the schedule and	• Identifying suitable places of visit • Briefing the participants of what and how to observe • This needs clarity on the part of the trainer vis-à-vis objective of the visit • Relating visit experiences to generalities of work life • An organizer must plan in detail and contact every person and place that is to be visited • Schedules must be drawn up and maps and handout material prepared • Every member of the party must be well briefed on what they will see,	• Trainer should have knowledge of field visits as related to the objectives of training • Requires organisational ability both on the campus and in the field • Effective in communication and interpersonal relations with the host organisation or community • Ability to relate observations in the field to theoretical developmental aspects	• Suitable places of visits Transport, Boarding and Lodging arrangements in the field • A definite starting time and easily identifiable starting point • Detailed transport, accommodation and catering arrangements • Maps. information handouts and detailed programmes for each stop. • A final 'get together' to review the project.	• When observational data are required as part of the learning. • To increase observational skills • To help see theory used in practice (when used as a supplement to classroom training) • To relate theory to 'real' problems • To study something that cannot be brought into a classroom. • To stimulate interest and concern • To demonstrate	• To help remove monotony of classroom instruction • To help participant group to move about and work as a group	• Helps see and understand practical use of theories and real life problems • Seeing is more meaningful than hearing or reading alone – it becomes easier to 'relate' to the real thing • A particular practice can be related to its environment • A 'team spirit can be fostered through participants becoming acquainted socially. • Usually more enjoyable than classroom learning • Useful for	• Time cost logistics of movement • Acceptance of the visiting organisation & sometimes to allow free study of their organi-sations • Planning and organising can be time consuming • Travel and accommoda-tion are costly • Definite numbers are often difficult to estimate • Tight schedules are hard to maintain

(Contd)

1.	2.	3.	4.	5.	6	7.	8.
preliminary plans and resolve any difficulties well beforehand by telephone, later confirming in writing whatever is agreed upon ● Build in social activities to provide for recreation. ● No schedule should be too 'tight'-always try to allow for the unexpected or the unpredictable. ● Make sure that each of the contact points is known by everybody who needs to know it. ● Don't take anything for granted – telephone ahead each night, to ensure that the arrangements still stand ● All members must be told what will be required of them before they set out.	the purpose of each visit, what will be expected of them, the amount of spare time that will be available and the time of their return ● After each stop, members should meet to review what they have seen and its significance for them.	discussed in the classroom. ● Interest in keeping reports of field visits		a course of action in the field' or in a work environment ● To talk workers in their worker environment ● To find out details of how things are done ● To study foreign cultures or environments		competitive learning 'Each group may prepare a report on the aspects it ahs studied.	● Certain risks are always involved – injuries or sickness, for example.

CONFERENCE

What it is?	Process/ Procedure	Trainer Skill	Requirements	Learning Objectives	Other Consideration	Advantages	Limitation
1.	2.	3	4.	5.	6.	7.	8
• Large or small group of people with common interests, meeting together by common consent • People need to be told 'What's in it for me?' - a clear objective is needed • Decide on those you wish to invite Find out their background and the extent of their information • Early programme planning is desirable (The best way to finalize speakers is to visit them or tell them by telephone what the conference is all about, what is expected from them and who will be attending) Details	• Deciding the subject or issue for conference • Detailing the objectives of the conference and anticipated outcome of the conference. • It's place in the totality of training programme • Preparation of schedule for the conference or fixing the date • Corresponding with the prospective participants • Physical arrangements • Inviting of experts in the field. • Conducting	• Knowledge in the subject area and skill in organising the conference, • Skill in correspondence and interpersonal relations • Keeping the track of the proceedings in the conference, monitoring the entire programme from beginning to the end. • Interested in generating new ideas, encouraging members in the conference to come out with ideas and	• Auditorium, comfortable seating, small meeting rooms, catering, toilets, transport arrangements, accommodation, special equipment for the media and for speakers, audio-visual, display facilities (notice boards and suchlike.	• A group with a common interest discusses a narrow technical area ('Dairy Farmers' Conference' or 'Overseas Aid Conference') • To develop promotion plans ('Save Our Native Forests' Conference).	• The conferences are organized usually related to administ-rative and managerial functions. The participants will be middle level or top level officials, executives, who cannot spend more time in a training situation, it is limited in duration, and conference is to be well	• Members usually discuss topics of high interest to them. • Members are usually voluntary attenders. • Enthusiasts are brought together to share their expertise and to plan. • Degree of success is often hard to measure.	• Often hard to predict number who will attend • Arrange-ments must often be made to provide for guest speakers, a venue, catering, accommo-dation and various other costs for an unknown number. • Degree of success is often hard to measure

(Contd...)

1.	2.	3	4.	5.	6	7	8.
should then be sent to the speakers. ● A wide range of publicity is desirable. ● Look after your guest speakers well- delegate someone to look after and to fuss over each one of them and don't forget a follow-up 'thank you' letter. ● Post-conference publicity is just as important as pre-publicity – try and get messages to the people who were unable to attend. ● 'Balance the books' and pay the bills as soon after the conference as possible.	the entire programme. ● Recording the discussions, issues that arose and resolutions made or conclusions arrived at. ● Highlighting the outcome of the conference	providing a friendly atmosphere and warmth among all the members of the conference.			thought out and well planned, it is not giving instructions but deliberating every issue, seeking new ideas, generating creativity, arriving at consensus for a course of action Finding solutions to the problems, conference is action-oriented.		

DEMONSTRATION

What it is?	Process/ Procedure	Trainer Skill	Requirements	Learning Objectives	Other Consideration	Advantages	Limitation
1	2.	3.	4.	5	6	7	8
• The performance of an action (or the explanation of a procedure) before an audience, to enable the viewers to perform the same action (under guidance, if necessary) • To demonstrate effectively, you must be familiar with your equipment and skilled in using it. • Make sure the audience fully appreciates the purpose of your demonstration – a visual aid can be used to reinforce your words. • The easiest way to a successful	• Collect the necessary materials and equipment and select a suitable site • Practise techniques beforehand • Explain purpose and objectives, then carry out demonstration. • Invite audience to practise the techniques under guidance • Volunteers are tested to see whether they have acquired the demonstrated skill.	• Organisational skill, securing and readily providing the physical and material requirement for demonstration, • Identifying people, • Encouraging them and involving them to be participants in the demonstration, motivating people to be active participants in the demonstration • He is to be a lively encouraging and stimulating person, one interested in the learning on the	• The provision of adequate facilities is most important Everybody must be able to see and to practise with the demonstration equipment. Power points, good lighting, and a raised platform may be other essentials. For a large-scale demonstration, a barrier may be required to keep people from crowding and to allow more people a view	• To teach a particular task. • To introduce a new procedure or technique. • To reinforce a point • To introduce a new product. • To illustrate or dramatize some point in a training programme	• We may call this as audio-visual, knowledge and skill going together • It is learning by doing, • It is experiential learning of practical nature	• What is seen is more likely to be believed and remembered than what is heard or read • Trying for oneself is a powerful aid to learning. • The pace can be flexible and the action can be repeated as often as necessary. • Can utilize the 'real thing' or a model of it.	• More suitable for small groups • Can be expensive and time consuming • Can raise transport and setting-up problems • Special conditions (such as a raised platform) are often required

(Contd...)

1.	2.	3.	4.	5.	6	7.	8.
demonstration is to build on individual experiences ● Students practise best in their own time, without too many observers – some get very nervous while others are watching and criticizing ● Practice, practice and more practice is the rule for mastering a complicated procedure.		part of the participants					

DISCUSSION GROUP

What it is?	Process/ Procedure	Trainer Skill	Requirements	Learning Objectives	Other Consideration	Advantages	Limitation
1	2	3	4	5	6	7	8
• Two or more persons who come together to talk informally and to deliberate on a topic of mutual concern – experiences are shared, opinions expressed, alternatives discussed and action is planned – interaction between individual embers or between similar groups may provide the catalyst for problem solving and for effective planning	• Be sure your instructions to groups are clear, precise and preferably, written (for easy reference) • Appoint a reporter • Discuss the topic and bring down recommendations to solve the problems • It is suggested that you • Break the topic into workable 'bites' • Arrange your recommendations in their order of priority • Appoint a spokesperson to	• Should be an enthusiastic motivator, providing stimulus for discussion, • Should be tolerant towards ambiguity, interested in encouraging a passive spectator concerned with and creating learning environment • Having concern for all involving everybody, • Having commitment to the entire group	• A skilled chairperson (or leader) is needed to prevent the more dominant embers from taking over the group • Participants should sit in a circle or rectangle, in an informal, relaxed atmosphere that is free from noise and other distractions • 'Face-to-Face' discussion is essential • Discussion is usually less restrained when a group is small	• To identify, explore and seek solutions to problems • To develop plans for action • Where necessary, to change attitudes through an amicable examination of the evidence • To develop leadership skills • As a supplementary technique in many types of training	• Providing opportunity to reluctant type of participants to come out and share their views, • It is democratic in the process, • The quality and outcome depend upon the facilitator	• Groups pool experiences, abilities and knowledge to reach recognized goals • Allows every member to participate fully • Can establish a democratic consensus • Can stimulate a desire to learn and to share • Often one individual's enthusiasm can stimulate the whole group	• Can be time consuming, particularly if persons with strong convictions or widely different backgrounds are involved • Preliminary exercises are needed before serious group activity is possible

(Contd..)

1	2.	3.	4	5.	6	7	8.
	report your findings to the full meeting ● Arrange for your eporter to hand the tutor a copy of your findings. ● Staff off the exercises which are interesting, topical and appropriate for the group.		The effectiveness of group discussion may decline when there are more than seven people in a group or when there are more than 30 in the workshop (A workshop of 28, for example, could be appropriately divided into four groups of seven and if these were balanced in terms of age, personality and experience, conditions would be idea for training) Each group should appoint a chairperson (or leader) and a reporter				

EXERCISES

What it is?	Process/ Procedure	Trainer Skill	Requirements	Learning Objectives	Other Consideration	Advantages	Limitation
1	2	3	4.	5.	6.	7	8
● A work assignment, designed to provide practice in a skill or technique – useful to review skills already learnt and as a basis for self-instructional learning ● During a lengthy workshop, field exercises can provide a worthwhile break for both tutors and participants. ● Every exercise needs to be both challenging and relevant.	● Exercises may be field action-oriented or are related to class or home, book reviews, selection of exercises which are germane to the objectives of training, selecting material exercises in advance, briefing the participants the relevance of such exercises and what they are expected to do and in what way they are to present and what would be the benefit of such exercises, these exercises could be individual or group oriented	● Selecting relevant areas for exercises complementary to the training programme, briefing the participants as to what is expected on their part in working on the exercises knowledge and skill in evaluating the exercises and providing feedback to the participants. Also knowledge at what point the exercises are to be introduced in the training programme	● They depend on the type of exercise. An adequate workspace and tools, a carefully planned appointment schedule, adequate travel and accommodation arrangements; and ● up-to-date maps may all be necessary	● To demonstrate a skill or technique ● To provide practice ● To reinforce or to test learning ● To test initiative ● To review already acquired skills	● It is more academic and participants should also have language and skill in doing the exercises	● Can promote familiarity with the real thing ● Helps to build confidence or independence ● Represents self-instructional learning ● Can be used to provide a welcome break ● Can help to develop initiative	● Worthwhile only when well planned and tested ● Often requires a good deal of organising ● The degree of skill that is acquired must depend upon the individual capabilities

(Contd.)

1	2.	3.	4	5.	6	7.	8
For example, 'Go and investigate and situation and prepare a report to the director Produce your recommendations by (mention date) ● The students must always be given clear instructions on what is expected of them and by them ● A critical but helpful feedback is an essential part of any worthwhile exercise – and don't forget to praise	and it provides the stimulus for individuals' understanding, the exercises have a beginning and they should have an end and it should not be a kind of a mechanical thing that is asked of the participants, it should have an organic link with the modules that are discussed in the training programme, it should be organized in such a way that the participants really appreciate the import of the exercises and derive the benefit by their own doing and as commented upon by the faculty.						

FILMS

What it is?	Process/ Procedure	Trainer Skill	Requirements	Learning Objectives	Other Consideration	Advantages	Limitation
1	2	3	4.	5.	6	7	8.
• Audio-visual, often detailed presentation of a subject, directed by one or more experts. • Wind the power cord around the leg of the table so that any late arrivers who trip on the cord in the dark don't pull the projector on to the floor • Arouse audience interest in the film by individual and group assignments. • Test the audience after the showing to see how much has been learnt – a re-run may be	• Set up and check the equipment in a room that can be darkened at the appropriate time (sun shining on a curtain can interfere with a blackout). • Thread the projector and run the film through beforehand to make sure there are no breaks and that you can work the machine, also, to get the	• Knowledge of the relevance of the film, briefing the participants seeking and summarizing the feedback from the participants after their having viewed the film	• Apart from the film(s), a projector that works and a screen are essential. • A darkened room for showing. • A qualified operator. • A power source. • Everybody must be able to see and to hear.	• To present factual material in a direct, logical manner. • To provide a break in a training programme. • To show things not readily accessible to the individual viewer or the naked eye • To give a time sequence (seasons, for example) • To arouse	• Provides information not covered in the modules exposure to other systems and cultures and also serves as a break from the regular training and also serves as an entertainment	• Tells exactly the same story each time it is shown • Suitable for a wide range of subjects • Can easily be repeated • Its running time is known (or is easily discoverable)	• Is costly to make or to buy. • It can be difficult to find a film on a suitable topic at the right level for your particular audience • There is a wide range of overseas films but few relevant local ones • The film producer takes over control of

(Contd...)

1.	2	3.	4.	5	6	7	8.
worthwhile. ● Select carefully the time you show a film – not right after a heavy meal, for example	sound levels right (but remember that the acoustics of full room necessitate more volume than an empty room). ● Be sure to rewind and rethread the film so that it is ready for showing. ● Rewind the film after the final showing, before you return it to its canister.			or increase interest ● To illustrate various points of view.			your audience ● No one can talk back to a film – it's one-way communication ● Some trainers rely too heavily on the film ● Requires expensive equipment and a degree of expertise

PANEL

What it is?	Process/ Procedure	Trainer Skill	Requirements	Learning Objectives	Other Consideration	Advantages	Limitation
1	2	3	4	5	6	7	8
• A group of (usually) three to five specially knowledgeable persons, in full view of an audience, holding an orderly conversation on a set topic (Differs from a symposium in that, after sometimes making a short, formal statement, the panel members talk only to one another) • Take care in selecting your chairman and the panel members – the extrovert and the good communicator are needed • It is a good idea to explain the 'ground rules' to	• Organizer sets a clear objective • Panel members are selected and briefed. • Meeting is held to discuss the objective and the 'ground rules'. • Programme and publicity are printed and distributed • The stage is set, the sound system is tested, and sufficient seats are set out • Audience assembles and chairman briefly introduces the	• Choosing right type of panelists systematically organising the panel, briefing the participants and integrating panel discussion with the objectives of the training programme	• Each speaker must be audible and visible to every member of the audience • A good stage setting, together with adequate microphones (if need be) and a satisfactory sound system	• To identify and explore a topic, issue, or problem • To weigh up the pros and cons of a course of action. • To assist the audience to understand a complex issue.	• Provides an opportunity to the participants to know the views of experts on a particular topic or issue	• Frequent changes of speaker and viewpoint should maintain a high interest level. • Can be very relaxed and informal and thus establish a favourable audience reaction • If you select the panel members carefully, all sides of an argument can be presented	• A skilled chairman is essential • Panel members need to be selected for balance and for their ability to communicate – any extreme differences of opinion may block progress toward a solution • The subject is not necessarily considered in the logical order

(Contd)

1	2	3	4.	5.	6	7.	8.
the audience beforehand ● The good chairman presents a balanced picture and makes sure that each member of the panel becomes involved – that the questions are shared about ● The group chairman will try to relax the pane members and to maintain a sense of humour ● On many such occasions a summary by the chairman or the tutor is a good way to conclude the discussion ● Don't forget to arrange for a vote of thanks from the floor to the chairman and the panel – and for formal 'thank you' letters to everybody after the event	topic and the panel (stating their qualifications) ● Each panel member may make a brief formal statement (usually five to ten minutes) setting out his/her point of view before the exchange of ideas and comments ● May be followed by a forum to broaden the discussion and to involve the audience (Agreement to this needs to be obtained beforehand from the panel members)						

SEMINAR

What it is?	Process/ Procedure	Trainer Skill	Requirements	Learning Objectives	Other Consideration	Advantages	Limitation
1.	2	3.	4.	5	6	7.	8
● A group whose members may each be called upon to play a formal role during its one or more study sessions, held under the guidance of a recognized authority in the subject ● Right from the start the leader should aim at establishing a stimulating working climate and a relaxed atmosphere. ● Each member must be encouraged to participate to the fullest extent	● Define the seminar's objectives ● Circulate the publicity material (with programme details, and background notes on the leading authority) ● The no of enrolments may have to be limited, depending on the popularity of the topic, the facilities that are available and the wishes of the leader(s) ● A preliminary	● Organisational ability, skill in time management, sometimes summing up the de-liberations of the seminar	● A semicircular seating arrangement is needed to promote group discussion ● A comfortable, relaxed atmosphere is important. ● There should be facilities for note taking and for preparing reports ● Audio-visual equipment should also be available.	● To study 'in-depth', under an expert	● Provides an opportunity on diverse views and personal interaction among experts	● Provides learning through sharing An authority guides the discussion and thus promotes learning ● A well-run seminar will cover detailed and systematic discussion, thorough investigation, and careful inquiry	● Often the right leader is difficult to find ● Often, too, the members are not prepared to devote the necessary amounts of time and hard work to preparing and presenting the reports ● The expert's presence may inhibit some of the members ● Sometimes, it is difficult to research the topics

(Contd)

1	2.	3.	4.	5.	6.	7.	8.
possible – involve anyone who is shy or reserved by asking them questions ● The leader(s) should ensure that everyone who speaks keeps strictly to the topic under discussion – it is very easy to digress ● Many topics are controversial – a balanced approach to them is desirable ● The seminar's success will depend on thorough research, the quality of presentation, the skill of the questioners, and the extent to which each member becomes involved	meeting should define the topic, lay down the ground rules, assign the various jobs to individuals or to working parties, and draw up reference lists. ● All the members should be encouraged to discuss the reports and to question the reporters. ● The seminar should be followed up by an adequate no of summarizing and evaluating sessions						and locate the sources of some of the material ● Members will not make equal contribu-tions – some will play only a passive role

SYMPOSIUM

What it is?	*Process/ Procedure*	*Trainer Skill*	*Requirements*	*Learning Objectives*	*Other Consideration*	*Advantages*	*Limitation*
1.	2	3	4	5	6	7	8
• A series of short (usually five to 25 minutes) prepared speeches by up to five authorities, covering various aspects of a subject – usually followed by an audience-involvement session in which the subject is opened up • Balance the speakers well – try to arrange an informal meeting with them beforehand, so that they get to know one another • The chairman needs to keep a firm control on the meeting and to see that the questions are spread evenly between the speakers – otherwise the last speaker tends to be questioned most often • A spread of 'arranged' questions from the audience can help to present a balanced point of view • Asking a guest authority to sum up finally, at the end of the discussion, is a good technique to follow	• The chairman sets the scene and introduces each speaker with a few brief remarks. • A short question period may follow each talk, or the questions may be reserved for a formal discussion period at the end • A period for the exchange of questions and comments between the speakers may be worthwhile, in addition to the audience's question time	• Organisational ability, skill in time management sometimes summing up the de-liberations of the seminar	• Every member of the audience must be audience able to see and hear in comfort. • A stage and (possibly) loudspeakers may be needed for a large audience	• To present new material concisely and logically • To present several differing views on the one subject • To provide a just analysis of a controversial issue • To clarify conflicting aspects of a complex problem and to depict the relationships of the parts to the whole	• Provides an opportunity on diverse views and personal interaction among experts	• Provides for differing points of view • Time-limited speeches minimize digressions • Brief speeches help to maintain audience interest • A comprehensive coverage becomes possible • Greater resources are available to answer questions	• Must be run as a formal event • The audience does not normally participate until the final stages

WORKSHOP

What it is?	Process/ Procedure	Trainer Skill	Requirements	Learning Objectives	Other Consideration	Advantages	Limitation
1	2	3	4	5	6	7.	8.
● Usually, a group that is 'in retreat' from a common workplace or similar workplaces in order to share work-related common interest, to improve individual work performances, to extend knowledge through intensive study, research and discussion; or to solve their work-related problems by	● Set clear objects and goals ● Planning – How big? When? Where? How long (half day, five weeks)? ● Should 'proceedings' be recorded and published – Who would do the work? How and when would it be done? ● Try to ensure the members are selected for their potential contribution and their experience rather than for reasons of prestige or seniority ● Check on the physical facilities and material requirements well in advance	● Providing guidelines to the participants in terms of what is expected of them in the workshop ● Knowledge in respect to the themes, items for workshop ● Guiding the small groups in their work, ● Meeting the objectives of workshop ● Bringing out the product of the workshop	● A common meeting place, with additional rooms for workshops ● Seats should be arranged in a semicircle (avoid theatre-type seating) ● An adequate library and other resource materials are required for research ● AV materials for recording ideas and reporting back to full groups (large paper pads or	● To identify, explore and seek solutions to work-related problems ● For in-depth study of a situation (background and social and philosophical implications) ● To plan for future activities ● To build up a text or construct proceedings (trainer's manual, for example)	● Sharing of views, experiences, collective endeavour, ● Group work, intellectual interaction, ● Producing something to be acted upon	● Can assemble and take advantage of a great deal of experience ● Designed for a high degree of participation ● Allows for group-determined goals, plans and recommendations ● Competition between 'rival' groups is possible ● A well-run workshop maintains the interest and enthusiasm of its members ● It will generate more ideas than	● Its organization and running are time consuming ● Requires a high staff-to-student ratio ● Requires more space and equipment than normally needed for a lecture series ● It members must be wiling and able to work independently and yet to cooperate closely.

(Contd.)

1	2	3	4	5	6	7.	8
sharing common experiences and knowledge	● Arrange for an adequate no. of carefully chosen resource persons to be on hand ● Draft the detailed timetable. ● Prepare the 'need-know-know' information handout. ● Make sure someone is on hand to welcome each new arrival, to help anyone with and to problems, answer any queries that may arise. ● Follow up the workshop with a final evaluating and strengths and weaknesses session	for further action.	overlays are ideal for this – with the help of 'blue-tack' or masking tape, you can paper a wall with the sheets and thus build up a complete story or compare a series of reports).	● To develop a working philosophy. ● As part of a convention or conference to study brief, related topics or problems.		any individual would produce alone, and will promote confidence in agreed-upon solutions	

'BUZZ' METHOD

What it is?	*Process/ Procedure*	*Trainer Skill*	*Requirements*	*Learning Objectives*	*Other Consideration*	*Advantages*	*Limitation*
1	2.	3.	4.	5.	6	7	8.
● A technique to involve a large audience directly in the discussion process by dividing up the members into small groups of five, six or seven for a limited time (five to 15 minutes) to discuss a specific topic, with each member contributing to the discussion. ● Time is saved by the organizer nominating the leaders and the recorders ● A good technique to gather additional information for	● Calculate approximate number in audience. ● Work out the no of groups you will have (for example an audience of 28 could provide four groups of seven) ● Having decided on four groups you would quickly 'number off' the audience, from one to four. ● Gather all the number 'ones' in one part of the room, the 'twos' in another part, and so on. ● Each group is instructed to	● Skill in dividing the groups. ● Coordinating the sub-groups ● Summarizing the discussions ● Spelling out the major ideas and suggestions that emerged from the buzz group discussion.	● Easily movable chairs to facilitate quick organisation. ● If numbers permit, use . open-formation seating (a circle or a 'U' arrangement is ideal because no one is hidden) – avoid theatre-type seating. ● Cards or papers for note taking (most people carry a pen).	● Presents a situation problem for discussion. ● Problem-solving technique. ● Teaching problem-solving processes. ● Builds up a complete picture.	● Interest in getting new ideas and views on a particular issue ● Patience and ability to respect and consider the views expressed by the members in the groups ● Tolerance towards ambiguity.	● Provides relevant detail. ● Helps to identify alternative solutions. ● Helps to develop analytical, problem-solving skills.	● Can be time consuming ● Relevance may not always be obvious. ● Stimulates some people, but irritates others

(Contd...)

1	2	3	4.	5.	6	7	8
a resource speaker and for setting up questions ● Set up the groups before the lecture and ask each one to carry out selecting listening', for example - ● Group-1 – note points that require further amplification ● Group-2- look for omissions on which you would like the speaker's view a Group-3-list points with which you disagree ● Can be used to get more out of a technical film by providing it with greater purpose.	select a leader and a recorder ● The leader's job is to see that everyone has a chance to speak ● The recorder summarizes the discussion ● At the end of the session, the leader or the recorder of each group reports orally to the full meeting. ● The organizer and an assistant collect and summarize all the reports and process them.						

LABORATORY TRAINING

What it is?	*Process*	*Trainer Skill*	*Physical Requirements*	*Learning Objectives*	*Other Consideration*	*Advantages*	*Limitation*
1.	2.	3.	4.	5.	6.	7.	8
• It is an experiential learning.	• A group comprisinơ 10-15, seating togetheı without any agenda and an individual member raising any issue, of course, mostly related to the present. • Based on the questions on the matter that the members raised discussion will be focused • Primarily it focuses on articulating, un-articulated • Making the invisible visible. • Owning up the disown and acting the withheld. • Interaction in unstructured situations giving scope to open, exploratory sharing of experiences and ideas. • Trainer may introduce structured experiences, use instrumentation or even a case to facilitate useful discussion.	• Tolerance to ambiguity and ability to move the ambiguous situations to insightful learning events. • Empathy with the group appreciates. • Giving of opinions and directions.	• Quiet undisturbed setting allowing for relaxed introspection – needs quite sometime	• Understanding of self and others. • Personal growth – as persons or role incumbents	• Willingnesc to open up • Not indulging in equations. • Not playing one-up behaviour. • Reflections on the self. • Showing empathy to the others. • Patience to receive and understanding	• Helps total growth of a person. • Helps give perspective to both life and roles. • Helps focus on strengths and weaknesses of individuals and experi-mentations	• Time consuming Unless participant is motivated and perspective, not much learning may come about

APPENDIX-IV

EVALUATION QUESTIONNAIRE ON A TRAINING PROGRAMME

1. Considering everything, how would you rate this programme? (Check one)

   Unsatisfactory ☐ Satisfactory ☐

   Good ☐ Outstanding ☐

   Please explain briefly the reasons for the rating you have given:

2. Were your expectations

   Exceeded ☐ Matched ☐ Fallen below? ☐

   (Check one)

3. Are you going to recommend this training programme to other members of your department? Yes________No_______. If you checked 'Yes', please describe the job titles held by the people to whom you would recommend this programme.

4. Please rate the relative value (1 = very valuable; 2 = worthwhile; 3 = negligible) of the following components of the training programme to you:

Videocassettes	______	Role-playing exercises	______
Workbooks	______	Small group discussions	______
Small group discussions	______	Lectures	______
Cases	______	Readings: Articles	______

5. Please rate the main lecturer's presentation (1 = not effective; 2 = somewhat effective; 3 = effective) in terms of :

Ability to communicate ________

Emphasis on key points ________

Visual aids ________

Handout materials ________

6. Please rate the following cases, readings, and videocassettes by placing a check mark in the appropriate column:

	Excellent	Good	Fair	Poor
Overcoming Resistance to Change				
Reviewing Performance Goals				
Setting Performance Goals				
Handling Employee Complaints				
Improving Employee Performance				
Slade Co.				
Superior Slate Quarry				
McGregor's Theory X and Y				
Henry Manufacturing				
First Federal Savings				
Claremont Industries				

7. Was the ratio of lectures to cases (check one): High_____OK____Low____

8. Were the videocassettes pertinent to your work? (check one)

   To most of my work? ______

   To some of my work? ______

   To none of my work? ______

9. To help the training director and the staff provide further improvements in future programmes. Please give us your frank opinion of each case discussion leader's contribution to your learning. (Place your check marks in the appropriate boxes.)

Faculty	Excellent	Above Average	Average	Below Average	Poor

10. How would you evaluate your participation in the programme? (check)

    Overall workload: Too heavy ____ Just right ____
    Too light ____

    Case Preparation: Too much ____ Just right ____
    Too little ____

    Homework assignments: Too heavy ____ Just right ____
    Too little ____

11. What suggestions do you have for improving the programme?

12. Please add any additional comments, criticisms, or suggestions that you think might be helpful for the training group to know before scheduling future programmes.

LECTURE EVALUATION SHEET

Name of the Faculty:

1. Content	:	Rich (4)	Moderate (3)	Faire (2)	Poor (1)
2. Language	:	Excellent (4)	Very Good (3)	Good (2)	Fair (1)
3. Style of Delivery	:	Excellent (4)	Very Good (3)	Good (2)	Fair (1)
4. Examples, Analogies, Illustrations	:	Rich (4)	Moderate (3)	Fair (2)	Poor (1)
5. Humour	:	Rich (4)	Moderate (3)	Fair (2)	Poor (1)
6. Pace of delivery	:	Right (4)	Fast (3)	Slow (2)	Very Slow (1)
7. Posture & Body Language	:	Free (4)	Confident (3)	Nervous (2)	Too Nervous (1)
8. Summing Up	:	Appropriate (4)	Appropriate to some extent (3)	So-So (2)	Incomplete (1)
9. Overall Rating	:	Excellent (4)	Very Good (3)	Good (2)	Fair (1)
10. Any Comment	:				

PROGRAMME EVALUATION QUESTIONNAIRE
(TO BE FILLED IN BY THE PARTICIPANTS)

1. Name of the Institute :

2. Title of the Course & Date :

3. Course Objectives :

4. Did you receive advance information about the programme from the Institute? If so, did you respond to it

5. Have you gone through the objectives and other details of the programme?

   Yes ☐ No ☐

6. Have you discussed with your immediate officer about the programme and its objectives before attending it.

   Yes ☐ No ☐

7. If Yes, what is his response?

8. Give the details about your immediate superior officer like his name, nature of work, designation and address.

9. Give your opinion about the structure and organization of the course in relation to its objectives.

   Yes ☐ No ☐

10. Whether this training programme will be useful to handle your job immediately?

11. Can you describe in a few lines about the practical use of this programme?

12. Do you satisfy with the duration of the programme?

    Yes ☐ No ☐

13. If No, specify with reasons that how many days you want?

14. During the programme did you have a close interaction with your co-participants?

    Yes ☐ No ☐

15. If Yes, how this interaction helps you to handle your job more effectively?

16. Do you find the reading material supplied to you during the programme satisfactory and relevant?

Yes ☐ No ☐

17. If No, please give the reasons.

18. To what extent are you satisfied with the following?

Satisfied fully	Satisfied to a Large extent	Satisfied to a limited extent	Not at all satisfied
(1)	(2)	(3)	(4)

	(1)	(2)	(3)	(4)
(a) Reception & Transport	☐	☐	☐	☐
(b) Food quality & Service	☐	☐	☐	☐
(c) Classroom facilities	☐	☐	☐	☐
(d) Library facilities	☐	☐	☐	☐
(e) Interaction with faculty	☐	☐	☐	☐

19. Assessment of Training Faculty Table – 1 (Session wise evaluation)

20. What were the topics dealt with in the programme are more useful to you?

21. Please mention a few topics that are more useful to you but not included in the programme schedule?

22. Give your impression about the programme in a few lines.

23. Specify whether this training programme has given you a thought to improve your work when you resume your duties.

    Yes ☐ No ☐

24. If Yes, please write a few lines about it.

25. Any comments/suggestions/observations about the programme in brief?

QUESTIONNAIRE TO SOLICIT RESPONSE FROM THE IMMEDIATE SUPERIOR OFFICER OF THE PARTICIPANT WHO HAS ATTENDED THE TRAINING PROGRAMME ON ____________

AT______________DURING__________

(TO BE ADMINISTERED THREE MONTHS AFTER THE COURSE)

1. Have you received any communication from the training institute or your head office about the nomination of your subordinate officer to the said programme?

   Yes ☐ No ☐

2. Have you had any discussion with your subordinate officer who has been nominated to the programme, about its objectives?

   Yes ☐ No ☐

3. Were you consulted before nominating your subordinate officer to this programme?

   Yes ☐ No ☐

4. If Yes, specify how many days in advance.

5. Did you express your views with your higher officers with regard to the benefit of attending this programme by your subordinate officer?

   Yes ☐ No ☐

6. Have you noticed any progress in the performance of your subordinate officer after attending this programme?

Yes ☐ No ☐

7. If Yes, can you briefly describe about the progress in the performance of your subordinate officer in his/her activities after receiving the training.

8. Do you agree with the views expressed by your subordinate officer in the evaluation of the programme in general / and the important topics in particular?

Yes ☐ No ☐

9. If No, can you give a few suggestions about the topics covered in the programme in view of the good performance expected on the part of your subordinate officer?

10. Are you satisfied with the topics covered in the programme for higher performance of your subordinate officer?

Yes ☐ No ☐

11. Were you subjected to any inconvenience when your subordinate officer was sent for attending the programme?

Yes ☐ No ☐

12. Whether your subordinate officer who has been trained in the

programme has been assigned the right type of job to utilize his newly acquired knowledge and skills?

Yes ☐ No ☐

13. If No, please give reasons.

14. Whether your trained subordinate officer is provided with required facilities and equipment to perform his functions effectively, for example, providing computers, audio-visual aids, etc.

Yes ☐ No ☐

15. Would you like to recommend the same programme to your other subordinate officers in view of their improvement in performing their functions?

Yes ☐ No ☐

QUESTIONNAIRE ON COURSE DIRECTOR'S REPORT

1. Name of the Institute :

2. Title of the programme :

3. Duration of the programme :

4. Name of the Programme Director :

5. No. of participants :
   (Please enclose a copy of the final list of the participants)

6. Have you received feedback from all the participants?

   Yes ☐ No ☐

7. If No, please give reasons.

8. Whether the participants or their superior officers were contacted in advance before the commencement of the programme?

   Yes ☐ No ☐

9. If they were in touch with you, how many days in advance?

10. What was their response when they were contacted in advance?

11. Whether the institution has collected any information with regard to the expectations of the participants about the programme in advance. If so, how and when?

12. What are the observations of the Course Director with regard to the organization of the programme?

13. What was the venue for this programme?

14. Whether the programme was residential or non-residential?

15. What is your preference in conducting the programme, residential or non-residential?

16. How many working days were earmarked for the programme?

17. Number of working hours planned for the programme?

18. Number of sessions planned during the programme?

19. Did you face any inconvenience in conducting the sessions as planned?

    Yes ☐ No ☐

20. If Yes, please mention the kind of inconvenience you faced.

21. Please provide the programme schedule and the material supplied to the participants?

22. Have you conducted similar programmes earlier, if so when?

23. If you had conducted similar programme earlier, what is your experience with regard to the cooperation of those participants?

24. Whether any measures been taken to include the suggestions given by the participants of the earlier programme? If so, what are those measures?

25. What are the general comments the Course Director would like to make in relation to this programme and its participants?

EVALUATION QUESTIONNAIRE ON LECTURE

Lecturer:......................................

Date:......................

	RATING:- CIRCLE APPROPRIATE NO.			COMMENTS
VOICE	Clearly audible, well modulated	5 4 3 2 1	Largely inaudible; Monotone	
PACE	Appropriate number of words and ideas per minute	5 4 3 2 1	Too fast or too slow, Too many or too few ideas	
NON-VERBAL COMMUNICATION	Good use of gesture and eye contact, no distracting mannerisms	5 4 3 2 1	Poor or distracting use of gesture and eyes, annoying mannerisms	
ORGANISATION AND PREPARATION	Well organized *eg* Introduction to topic planned repetition, summaries, links between ideas well explained	5 4 3 2 1	Badly organized; confusing presentation	
USE OF OHP, BLACKBOARD, ETC.	Clear; well presented appropriate use; supportive to presentation	5 4 3 2 1	Cramped; illegible; inappropriate use; distracts from presentation	
ATTITUDE	Friendly, responsive, enthusiastic, creates positive impression	5 4 3 2 1	Creates negative impression; dull unfriendly, unresponsive	

Source:- Institute of Educational Development, University of Surrey

GLOSSARY OF TERMS

Sl.No. A

1. **Accountability:-** The extent to which the results of a project, programme or activities can be justified to an organisation in terms of operational goals and financial returns.

2. **Action Plan:-** List of activities, in order of time, (often fully 'costed') designed to achieve an objective – specifies target dates and the person responsible for completion of each activity.

3. **Action Learning:-** A management development activity in which a manager is required to solve an actual problem of an existing organisation. The managers following a programme of action learning meet periodically in 'sets' of four to six managers with a 'set adviser' to discuss their progress.

4. **Action Research:-** Research, especially in the *behavioural sciences*, into a situation in order to bring about some practical improvement in that situation, as well as contributing to the store of academic knowledge.

5. **Action Training:-** *Training* in which *activity learning is emphasized.*

6. **Activity Learning:-** Learning by means of active participation, e.g., in *projects* or discussions, as opposed to passive means such as lectures.

7. **Administration:-** 1. Synonym for *management;* especially in government or public service (public administration). 2. Activities connected with keeping records and information

processing; paperwork. 3. Activities concerned with applying rules, procedures and policies determined by others. 4. The government of the day in a country – i.e., the politicians appointed by the country's political leader to take charge of particular departments. 5. The duties of an *administrator.*

8. **Administrative Theory:-** An approach to developing general principles of management in which attention is concentrated on formal *organisation structures.* The administrative-management approach dominated thinking about management in the 1930s. It replaced the *scientific management* approach and was itself replaced by the *human relations school.* Administrative management theory was particularly influenced by the views of Henri Fayol (1841-1925) who was chief executive of the French mining and metal working firm, Commentry-Fourchambault-Decazeville, which he rescued from the verge of bankruptcy. His article 'Administration, industrielle et generale', ***Bulletin de la Societe de Iindustrie minerale*** (1916, No.3), was translated by J.A. Coubrough as ***Industrial and General Administration*** (Geneva: International Management Institute, 1929). Other important contributors to the theory were two executives of General Motors Corporation, James D. Mooney and Alan C. Reiley, whose *Onward Industry* was published in 1930, the American political and business philosopher, Mary Parker Follett (1868-1933), the American expert on public administration, Luther Halsey Gulick (born 1892) and the British management consultant, Lyndall Fownes Urwick (born (1891). The principal writings of these theorists are: M.P. Follett, *Dynamic Administration: The Collected Papers of Mary Parker Follett,* edited by E.M. Fox and L. Urwick, 2nd edition (London: Pitman, 1973); *Papers on the Science of Administration,* edited by L. Gulick and L. Urwick (New York: Institute of Public Administration, Columbia University, 1937/ reissued 1969 by Augustus M. Kelly, New York); L. Urwick, *The Eleemtns of Administration, 2nd edition* (London: Pitman, 1947) and the second translation, by Constance Storrs, of Fayol's book, *General and Industrial Management* (London: Pitman, 1949). The term, 'administrative management theory' was coined by James G. March and Herbert A. Simon, in *Organisations* (New York: Wiley, 1958)

9. **Adoption:-** The mental process through which an individual passes from first knowledge of an innovation to the actual use of it.
10. **Agenda:-** A list of things to be discussed at a meeting.
11. **Alter Ego (Latin for 'other self'):-** The observer watches the learner in a particular situation and provides an immediate or a delayed feedback on the adequacy of the action.
12. **Annotated Reading List:-** References on a particular subject, usually interpreted by the tutor or student(s), with a short description, explanation, or evaluation of each item.
13. **Appraisal:-** 1. Considered judgment of the value or worth of something or someone. 2. Synonym for *performance appraisal.*
14. **Apprentice(Noun):-** An *employee* who has entered into a special contract with his employer whereby the employer will provide the apprentice with training in a craft or trade for a specified number of years and the apprentice will work for that employer for that number of years.
15. **Apprenticeship:-** A training method (usually formal) under which a novice (apprentice) learns a trade or a craft under an experienced worker, on the job.
16. **Aptitude:-** The capacity of a person to acquire knowledge or skills.
17. **Assessment:-** Evaluation made at short intervals examining measurable outputs of a programme.
18. **Assimilation:-** The merging of groups or individuals into one group with a common culture and identity.
19. **Audience - Reaction Team:-** A representative sample of three to five audience members who, in order to clarify points which might not otherwise be understood, will ask questions of the speaker (or some resource person), either during or at the end of an address. (A useful technique when an audience is very large or whenever it would be difficult to accept questions from the floor.)
20. **Authoritarian Management:-** A *managerial style* characterized by the practice of *authoritarianism* and, usually, belief that human relations are irrelevant to getting work done, that

people are necessarily indolent, self-centred and uncooperative, and that people require strong direction and control if discipline is to be maintained. People practising authoritarian management would accept McGregor's *Theory X*, would have a '9, 1 managerial style' according to Blake and Mouton's *managerial grid*, and would be practising *System 1* management according to Likert's analysis. Authoritarian management is also very similar to *scientific management*.

Under authoritarian management, workers are *motivated* basically by fear of losing their jobs if they disobey orders or having their wages cut if their performance is inadequate. (Also known as 'autocratic management'.)

21. **Authority:-** 1. A person who makes decisions, gives opinions, judgment or information or takes action that affects other people is said to have authority if the people affected believe that, if asked, he could justify his actions in terms that they are willing to accept. Authority may be acquired, for example: (a) by study and experience that make one an expert who will be able to give a rational, intellectual justification for one's opinions or a practical demonstration that what one has said is correct; (b) by *delegation* – from one's superior in an organisation so that his authority is one's justification; (c) by being appointed in a legitimate way to take specified action, so that the method of appointment is one's justification. Also. A person who has expertise derived from study and experience is called an 'authority'; a document appointing someone to take specified action is called an 'authority'. 2. A book that is relied on for information or opinions that are usually believed. 3. A *local authority* or a *public utility*. 4. Competence to speak on behalf of others.

22. **Autonomy:-** Self-determination; especially: (1) the right of a state to organize its affairs without external interference; (2) the discretion of an individual in an organisation to make decisions without consulting other people in the organisation; (3). the capability of an individual to select personal values and withstand social pressures for conformity.

B

23. **Body Language:-** Communicating through physical means.

Our body gestures, expressions, posture, clothes, social behaviour, and so on.

24. **Brainstorming:-** A technique for encouraging creative thinking. A problem is presented to a small group of people who spend a few minutes formulating alternative statements of it and then sometime stating their ideas as rapidly as possible (the ideas may be tape-recorded but are commonly written, often on flipcharts so that the group can see them). During the production of ideas, four principles are observed: (1) quantity is important – the more ideas that are produced the more likely it is that they will include a good one; (2) cross-fertilization should take place – people should try to build on the ideas produced by others; (3) there must be no criticism of others' ideas – this would dampen their enthusiasm; (4) individuals must also suspend judgment and not evaluate their own ideas – an idea may seem extraordinary to one person but may, through the principle of cross-fertilization, get the group to generate useful ideas.

C

25. **Case Study:-** Comprehensive oral, written, and/or filmed account of an event or series of related events.

26. **Coach:-** To tutor, to train – to bridge the gap between learning and doing. "One-to-one" intensive learning through demonstration and practice, in which the coach 'models' the desired behaviour, (characterized by immediate feedback and correction.)

27. **Coaching:-** Systematically increasing the ability and experience of the employee by giving him or her planned tasks, coupled with continuous appraisal and advice.

28. **Colloquium:-** An academic conference or a seminar.

29. **Communication:-** Imparting information and understanding from one person to another.

30. **Computer-Assisted Instruction (CAI):-** A series of highly structured, self-paced learning segments, presented by a computer, which electronically processes the learner's responses and provides immediate feedback.

31. **Concept:-** An abstract idea of the connections between (two or more) objects or events (for example, the 'concept' of evolution).

32. **Conditioning:-** As used in advertising or training – a subconscious response to a stimulus, such as a product, which a person reacts to without even thinking about it. "Brainwashing" is an extreme form of condition.

33. **Conference:-** Meeting for consultation or deliberation. Can be large or small group of people with common interests.

34. **Confrontation, Search and Cope (CSC):-** Three-part experience in which the learner faces a problem or an uncovered need (confrontation), is responsible for seeking out a solution (search), and then applies it to the problem (cope).

35. **Consensus:-** Delineation of areas of agreement by individuals or groups previously in conflict with each other.

36. **Criterion-Referenced Instruction (CRI):-** Learner-controlled process in which skills to be acquired are broken down into specific behavioural objectives, each with its measurement criteria. Emphasis is on reaching required competency standards (not on the time taken to do so). Learner is aware of the definition of 'competency' and of how his/her performance will be tested.

37. **Critical Incident:-** Of, or relating to, concentration of attention or effort on a few important occurrences. As in 'critical-incident approach' (to *group training*) in which the trainer pays particular attention to handling events that could contribute to the development of his group.

D

38. **Delphi Method:-** A method of obtaining forecasts of future developments (e.g., for *market research*) in which a number of experts are asked to give their individual forecasts; these are collected, and summarized; a summary of all forecasts is sent to each expert and each is asked whether he would reconsider his views in the light of what others have said; the process is repeated until the predictions are satisfactorily uniform. (Named after the ancient Greek religious site at which the gods

were believed to communicate answers to humans' questions about the future.)

39. **Demonstration:-** A practical showing how something works (result-demonstration) or is done (method-demonstration).

40. **Diagnosis, Prescription, Treatment:-** Learner's needs and/ or weaknesses are uncovered (diagnosis) and a course of action or a plan of study is developed (prescription), which the learner follows in order to overcome the deficiency (treatment).

41. **Dialogue:-** A conversation on a prearranged subject between two persons in front of an audience. Open and frank discussion to seek a mutual understanding.

42. **Diary Method:-** Technique used in social research in which people are asked to keep records of what they do. Used, for example, to assess the size of audience for television programmes where viewers are asked to write down the names of the programmes they watch.

43. **Discovery Learning:-** Learning through doing. Also called 'Action Learning" or "Experiential Learning".

44. **Discussion:-** Relatively unstructured exchange of ideas between two or more members of a group on a topic of mutual interest.

45. **Discussion Group:-** Two or more persons who come together to talk informally and to deliberate on a topic of mutual concern. Experiences are shared, opinions expressed, alternatives discussed, and action is planned. Interaction between individual members or between similar groups may provide the catalyst for problem solving and for effective planning.

46. **Dynamics:-** Energies and forces derived both from individuals and their interaction, with one another and from the effects of these influences on 'active' (as opposed to 'static') behaviour.

E

47. **Education:-** All-embracing generalization which covers all facets of learning process – art of acquiring and applying knowledge.

48. **Evaluation:-** Objective assessment of strengths and weaknesses of particular training activities – usually aimed at providing feedback and suggesting improvements. May be ongoing, terminal (at completion) or expost (some years after completion).

49. **Exercise:-** A work assignment, designed to provide practice in a skill or technique. (Useful to review skills already learnt and as a basis for self-instructional learning.)

50. **Experiential Learning:-** Learning through doing. Also called "Action Learning" or "Discovery Learning".

51. **Extension:-** The process of extending or reaching out technical services to clients. (Usually, associated with agriculture, health or forestry services).

52. **Extroversion:-** Tendency to be 'outgoing' and sociable, preferring to deal with people rather than with ideas.

F

53. **Facilitator:-** Tutor or trainer who, by acting as a catalyst in the training-learning process, 'facilitates' the achievement of results.

54. **Flip Chart (Paper Pad):-** Large, inexpensive sheets of paper (usually newsprint) mounted on an easel, to be written on with felt-tip marker pens or crayons.

55. **Flow Diagram:-** Diagrammatic representation of the steps involved in completing a particular task.

56. **Forum:-** A public assembly in which everyone is given a chance to voice his/her views.

G

57. **Game Theory:-**(or Theory of Games). A mathematical theory that applies to certain situations in which there are conflicts of interest between two or more individuals or groups.

    Game Theory deals with situations, called 'games' that can be represented by the following mode: (1) there are n 'players' (individuals, corporations, groups) each of whom is required to make one choice from a specified set of possible choices; (2) each player knows what outcome results from each possible combination of choices; (4) each player has an order of preference for the possible outcomes (often each player assigns to each outcome a numerical value called a "payoff' which can be thought of as representing the number of points, dollars, etc., that he gains or loses from the outcome; (5) each player knows the preferences of the other players (i.e., he knows what their payoffs are) and all players are assumed to act so as to gain the most they can from the game; but (6) each player makes his choice without knowing what choice the other players are making.

The theory attempts to answer the question: In a situation of this kind, what choice should a player make? A simple version of the problem is when there are only two players (a 'two-person game'). The payoffs for each player can then be arranged as a *matrix*. The simplest form of the two-person game is a 'two-person zero-sum game' in which, for each outcome, the payoff for one player is exactly opposite to the payoff for the other player (e.g., if one player gains 5 points the other loses 5 points). For further details, see e.g., R.D. Luce and H. Raiffa, *Games and Decisions: Introduction and Critical Survey* (New York: Wiley, 1957).

58. **Group Dynamics (Sensitivity Training or T-Groups):-** Study of forces interacting within a group; now usually refers to various participative learning methods which aim to improve trainees' skills in understanding the needs of others.

59. **Group Training:-** Form of *group dynamics training* in which the trainees meet in small groups and each trainee studies the behaviour and *group processes* that take place in his own group.

    The groups may be given special tasks to perform (as in *Coverdale training)* or there may be very few rules about what it should do (as with a *T-Group*). (See also, *cousins group, family group* and *stranger group.)*

H

60. **Hidden Agenda:-** The matters that are important to an individual at a meeting (eg. Of a committee) but which he cannot discuss or deal with, either because the matters are not on a formal *agenda* for the meeting or because they are personal

emotional matters relating to the meeting (eg. Intense dislike of another member of a committee).

61. **Hierarchy:-** An arrangement of the *positions* in an *organisation* into *ranks* such that the holder of a position in one rank is *responsible* to the holder of a position in the next higher rank for the performance of his job.

62. **Hierarchy of Needs:-** It has been proposed by an American psychologist, Abraham H. Maslow, that *needs* which dominate human behaviour may be grouped into five main classes and that these classes fall into a 'hierarchy' in the sense that needs belonging to one class became apparent (and set up drives) only when needs of 'lower' classes have largely been satisfied. The classes that Maslow distinguishes are: (1) physiological needs (eg. for food; (2) safety needs (eg. for security, stability, protection); (3) belongingness and love needs (eg. for friendship and a position in a group or family); (4) esteem needs (eg. for a constant high evaluation of oneself and for the esteem of others); (5) need for self-actualization. More information is given in **A.H. Maslow, *Motivation and Personality*,** 2nd edition (New York: Harper & Row, 1970).

63. **Human Relations School:-** An approach to the theory of management and of organisations that emphasizes the individual worker's need for satisfactory relationships with other members of his work group and his need to participate in decisions that affect his work (i.e., a requirement for *participative management)*. This approach developed from the *Hawthorne Experiments.*

64. **Hygiene Factor:-** An aspect of a job that can contribute to the dissatisfaction but not the satisfaction of the job holder according to the *motivation-hygiene theory.* (Also known as a 'maintenance factor'.)

65. **Hygienic Management:-** A *management style* characterized by provision of high wages, employee benefits, good working conditions and good supervision in the belief that workers will therefore have high morale and will work harder. In terms of Herzberg's *motivation-hygiene theory,* managers with this style concentrate on ensuring that *hygiene factors* are right, so that there is no dissatisfaction. Herzberg suggests that this

approach does not *motivate* employees to work harder. Hygienic management is sometimes seen as a sophisticated version of *paternalistic management*.

I

66. **In-Basket:-** Reinforcing exercise to stimulate learner's response to a collection of memoranda, letters and directives that pose problems which force learner to set priorities, make decisions, and handle potential difficulties.

67. **Induction Training:-** Training designed to introduce a new trainee into an organisation.

68. **Instructional Objective:-** Statement laying down a set of instructions and a series of tests designed to reveal the extent to which the learner has been able to follow (and to profit from) them.

69. **Internalization:-** An individual's complete acceptance of a social norm to the extent that it becomes the natural, unquestioned thing to do.

70. **Internship:-** Supervised system of acquiring practical experience – used mainly with advanced learners who enter a profession.

71. **Introversion:-** Tendency to be shy and to withdraw into oneself.

J

72. **Job Enlargement:-** 1. Training and encouraging employees to perform a range of jobs related to the ones they hold so that manpower can be used more flexibly. 2. Assigning additional tasks to an employee in order to make his job more varied and interesting.

73. **Job Enrichment:-** Changing features of a job other than *compensation*, physical working conditions and the essential tasks of the job in order to increase the *job satisfaction* of the person performing it.

74. **Job Evaluation:-** Establishment of the relative worth of a number of *jobs* (not employees) in an organisation by considering, for example, their complexity, the amount of

training or experience required, how much the organisation would suffer if they were done badly and so on.

75. **Job Instruction Training (JIT):-** A training programme, originally developed as part of *training within industry*(TWI), in which trainees are taught how to instruct other people to perform simple industrial tasks. In the current UK version of TWI, this programme is known as 'job instruction and communication'.

76. **Job Method Training (JMT):-** A training programme, originally developed as part of *training within industry* (TWI), which provides trainees with an introduction to *method study.* In the current UK version of TWI, this programme is known as 'job methods'.

77. **Job Relations (JR):-** One of the programmes in *training within industry.* It is designed to provide an understanding of human relationships with particular emphasis on the prevention of problems and effective handling of problems that do arise.

78. **Job Rotation:-** Members of a group exchange jobs among themselves for set periods of time in order to gain "job enlargement".

79. **Job Satisfaction:-** The gratification (in the sense of mental pleasure following from the satisfaction of needs, desires or hopes) that a person derives from the job that he is employed to perform.

80. **Job Specification:-** A description of the personal characteristics required for performing a *job.* A job specification normally states the type of employee required for a job, in terms of skill, experience and special aptitudes, and summarizes the working conditions found in the job.

L

81. **Laboratory:-** Environment specially equipped for carrying out experiments and tests.

82. **Lateral Thinking:-** Ability to think in a non-consecutive way and to link otherwise unrelated topics. Various techniques include 'reversing the normal situation' and 'random-word provocations'.

83. **Learning Curve:-** A graph that shows improvement in the performance of a task, by an individual or a group, as it is repeated and more is learned about it.

84. **Lecture:-** A formal dissertation by one with claims to be an expert on the particular theme.

85. **Linear Programmed Instruction:-** *Programmed Instruction* in which the frames are presented in the same sequence for all learners. In each frame there is question for the learner to answer in order to test his learning but the questions are usually phrased so that they suggest the right answer – hence the alternative name of 'constructed-response programmed instruction'.

86. **Line Manager:-** A member of an organisation who is responsible for the success or failure of a section of the organisation in performing part of the principal work of the organisation.

87. **Line of Command:-** The sequence of people in an organisation through whom instructions from the *Chief Executive* pass before reaching a particular employee. (Also known as a 'chain of command'.)

88. **Listening Group:-** Audience is divided into several groups, each of which listens to and observes a specific part or facet of a speech, demonstration, panel, or such line.

89. **Listening Team:-** Its members listen to the speakers, take notes, and question or summarize at the end, thus providing interaction between the speaker(s) and a large audience. Unlike the reaction team, they do not interrupt.

M

90. **Manage:-** To carry out the task of ensuring that a number of diverse activities are performed in such a way that a defined objective is achieved – *especially* the task of creating and maintaining conditions in which desired objectives are achieved by the combined efforts of a group of people (which includes the person doing the managing).

91. **Management By Exception:-** Technique of carrying out the *control* functions of management by paying attention only to

deviations from a *plan*. The process of *monitoring* the system (and, by implication, judging what constitutes a deviation from the plan) is *delegated*. The phrase was first used by F. W. Taylor (see *scientific management*). See also Lester R. Bittel, *Management by Exception: Systematizing and Simplifying the Managerial Job* (New York, McGraw-Hill, 1964).

92. **Management By Objectives (MBO):-** A systematic procedure for planning the work of managers in an organisation which is characterized by collaboration between each manager and his superior in analyzing the manager's tasks and establishing quantified objectives to be achieved by the manager within specified time-limits. Emphasis is usually placed on integrating the objectives set for individual managers with those of the whole organisation and on having a well established procedure for ascertaining whether a manager achieves his objectives and for regularly reviewing objectives. The phrase, 'management by objectives' is usually attributed to the American management consultant, Peter Ferdinand Drucker (born in Austria, 1909) – see P.F. Drucker, *The Practice of management* (London: Heinemann, 1955). For detailed descriptions of MBO systems, see G.S. Idiorne, *Management by Objectives: A System of Managerial Leadership* (New York: Pitman Publishing Corporation, 1965/London: Pitman Publishing, 1970), W.J. Reddin, *Effective MBO* (London: Management Publications, 1971) and J. Humble, *Management by Objectives* (London: Management Publications, 1972).

93. **Management Development:-** An activity, taking place in an organisation, with the objective of making managers into better managers. It includes training, in the sense of acquisition of *skills*, and improvements in attitudes and personality.

94. **Management Game:-** A training or educational activity in which a trainee must take a sequence of decisions relating to a simulation of a real-life management problem and is presented with the results of each decision after he has taken it. A game may be played by trainees working individually or as teams or by a number of trainees competing against each other. In the competitive type of game, the result of an individual decision is the response, or the next move, of the other competitors. In the individual type of game, the response is

provided by a trainer, or by a computer, according to predetermined rules. (Also called a 'business game', or 'game'.)

95. **Management Guide:-** A document used in some systems of *management by objectives.* There is one for each manager in the organisation, showing : (1) outline of the manager's job; (2) the results of the last *key results analysis* of his job; (3) his *job improvement plan.* (Also known as a 'management job description' or 'manager's guide' or 'results guide'.)

96. **Manipulation:-** When the "power-holder" influences the behaviour of others.

97. **Man Power:-** The persons available to do work.

98. **Manpower Planning:-**The practice of planning to ensure that the right numbers of the right people will be available for the right jobs at the right time.

99. **Mass Communication:-** Transferring a message from one person (or several) to a large audience using such means as radio, television, films, newspapers or other publications.

100. **Merit Rating:-** Assessing an employee's performance and personal qualities – usually so that his pay can be determined (see *merit increase*). *Also* such an assessment of an employee.

101. **Method Study:-** Systematic recording and critical examination of existing and proposed ways of performing tasks involving human activity in order to develop and apply easier and more effective methods and reduce costs. (Also known as 'motion study'.)

102. **Module:-** An independent learning unit which should provide appropriate descriptions, explanations, examples, and exercises – designed to bring the learner to a specified level of skill.

103. **Monitoring:-** Continuous or periodic review and surveillance by management of planned activities.

104. **Mores:-** The social norms that provide the moral standards of behaviour of a group or society.

105. **Motivation:-** 1. The causes of particular behaviour by an individual – especially causes (e.g emotions) related to the

internal state of the individual. 2. Process or study of *motivating* people to behave in a particular way.

106. **Motivation-Hygiene Theory:-** The view, advanced by an American psychologist, Frederick Herzberg (born 1923), that an employee derives *job satisfaction* from two separate sources: 'hygiene factors' and 'motivators'.

The 'hygiene factors' are matters not directly connected with the task to be performed in the job; they are, for example, working conditions, remuneration, interpersonal relationships and the managerial styles of superiors. Herzberg suggestss that if these factors do not reach a certain standard then they will cause dissatisfaction but that when they are at an acceptable standard they will not contribute to satisfaction.

The 'motivators' are concerned with the tasks to be performed; they are, for example, the nature of the tasks, the possibility that the job offers for career advancement, and the opportunities for assuring oneself that one has done a good job. If these factors are good then they will cause satisfaction, but if they are poor it is unlikely they will cause dissatisfaction.

Evidence for the theory is given in F. Herzberg, B. Mausner and Barbara Snyderman, *The Motivation to Work* (New York: Wiley, 1959). See also, F. Herzberg, *Work and the Nature of Man* (New York: World Publishing Co., 1966/London: Staples Press, 1968).

107. **Motivator:-** An aspect of a job that can contribute to the satisfaction but not the dissatisfaction of the job holder according to the *motivation-hygiene theory.*

108. **Multiple Management:-** A system of *employee participation* devised by Charles P. McCormick of McCormick & Co. Inc. (producers of spices and foods in Baltimore, Maryland) during the 1930s. Committees are formed to represent the employees in particular areas of a firm and there is also *junior board.* Committees are able to discuss freely any subject and may present unanimous motions to the board of directors for consideration. See, e.g. C.P.McCormick, *The Power of People: Multiple Management up to Date* (New York: Harper and Brothers, 1949).

N

109. **Nominal-Group Technique:-** Individuals work in each other's presence, but do not interact. Their comments, written on cards, are shared among the group. (Device to overcome shyness and prevent domination.)

110. **Non-Verbal Learning:-** New perceptions and feedback from emotions and behaviour, gained through non-verbal communication.

111. **Norm:-** the commonly accepted form of social behaviour.

112. **Normal Curve:-** Bell-shaped curve representing the frequency distribution of many naturally occurring biological and psychological traits.

O

113. **Objective:-** Conditions to be met or a target to be achieved, drawn up in response to a need-should define desired results and answer such questions as: 'What is to be achieved?", By what margin will it be achieved?", and "When will it be achieved?"

114. **Observation:-** The recognition and noting of a fact or occurrence.

115. **Occupational Psychology:-** The study of psychological problems associated with work and which arise in connection with, for example, vocational guidance, design of *aptitude tests*, personnel selection, training, *work study or ergonomics.* (Also known as 'industrial psychology'.)

116. **Off-the-Job Training:-** Any *training* that takes place while the *trainee* is not performing his normal job.

117. **Open-Ended Question:-** A question that does not force the respondent to answer in terms of fixed alternatives, such as 'yes' or 'no'. Respondents answer in their own words from their particular point of view.

118. **Oral Tradition:-** Culture that is transmitted from one generation to the next by word of mouth.

119. **Organisational Behaviour** (US spelling: Organizational

Behavior). The behaviour of people when they are acting as members of *organizations.*

120. **Organization Development:-** The activity of improving an organisation's ability to achieve its goals by using people more effectively.

121. **Organization Planning:-** Deciding on the form of organization appropriate to an enterprise. The process includes grouping activities, delineating authority and responsibility, and establishing working relationships.

122. **Organization Theory:-** The body of knowledge about *organizational behaviour and organizational structure.*

P

123. **Panel:-** A group (usually) three to five specially knowledgeable persons holding an orderly discussion on a set topic in front of an audience. (Differs from a symposium in that, after sometimes making short, formal statements, the panel members talk only to one another).

124. **Parkinson's Law:-** The aphorism, 'Work expands so as to fill the time available for its completion,' written by an English author, historian and journalist, Cyril Northcote Parkinson (born 1909). See C.N. Parkinson, *Parkinson's Law or the Pursuit of Progress* (London: John Murray, 1958). Parkinson also produced a second law, 'Expenditure rises to meet income', in *The Law and the Profits* (London: John Murray, 1960).

125. **Participative Management:-** A *Managerial style* characterized by extensive use of the *group-decision method* and in which each person is given wide opportunity to exercise *discretion* in his work. The style represents a complete contrast to *authoritarian management.* People practising participative management usually believe that people can be emotionally committed to doing jobs well. They would accept *McGregor's Theory Y*, would have '9,9 managerial style' according to Blake and Mouton's *managerial grid*, and would be practising *System 4* management according to Likert's analysis. Norman Raymond Frederick Maier (1900-77), an American psychologist, was a leading proponent of participative management. See, e.g., Norman R.F. Maier & John J. Hayes, *Creative Management* (New York:

Wiley, 1962). (Sometimes known as ' democratic management'.)

126. **Paternalism:-** *Managerial style* characterized by a belief that subordinates are necessarily less mature and less capable of looking after themselves than their bosses – i.e., treating one's subordinates as children. The attitude often leads to an emphasis on behaving in a kindly and fair-minded way and preoccupation with providing welfare facilities. Paternalistic mangers normally listen to the views of their subordinates but insist on retaining decision-making power for themselves.

127. **Paternalistic Management:-** A *managerial style* (especially when practised throughout an organization) characterized by provision of a wide range of valuable rewards for employees and a belief that employees will work well out of gratitude, and out of fear that they could lose the important benefits if they did not work well. Wages are high, promotion prospects are good and there are numerous fringe benefits under paternalistic management. It is usual for people practising paternalistic management to use *consultative management*.

    In extreme forms of paternalistic management, managers believe they are responsible for all aspects of their employees' welfare and living conditions.

128. **Peer Teaching ("Peer-Assisted Learning' or "Peer-Mediated Instruction':-** Small groups of peers act as both teacher and learner by switching roles. (Differs from peer tutoring, in which a student who is gifted in a subject helps another who is having difficulty in it.)

129. **Perception:-** What someone feels and thinks, on the basis of their experience and knowledge.

130. **Performance Appraisal:-** Assessment of how well an employee does his job; especially an assessment carried out as part of an organization's formal procedure in which regular assessments are made, records kept of the results, and action taken to improve performance. (Also known as 'appraisal'.)

131. **Personnel Management:-** Activity, function or study of helping managers in an organization to make the best use of the human resources of the organization.

132. **Peter Principle:-** The aphorism that 'in a hierarchy every employee tends to rise to his level of incompetence'. Named after a Canadian educationalist, Laurence Johnston Peter (born 1919) and explained in L. J. Peter and R. Hull, *The Peter Principle* (New York: William Morrow/London: Souvenir Press, 1969).

133. **Pilot Training:-** A training course that serves as a trial on a small scale before being adapted for large scale use.

134. **Potential Assessment (or Potential Review):-** 1. Assessment of an employee's future career in an organization. 2. Procedure for regularly assessing the future careers of all employees in an organization.

135. **Programmed Instruction (PI):-** Method of self-instruction in which the material to be taught is split up into small items (called 'frames') and recorded in permanent form (e.g. printed or tape-recorded). The material is presented in such a way that the learner can see or hear only one frame at a time. The learner works through a sequence of frames. Usually the learner has to make some response to each frame (such as answering a question) and his response determines which frame he should look at or listen to next. The complete set of material presented to a learner is called a 'programme'. (Also known as 'programmed learning'.)

136. **Programming Language:-** A set of standard symbols (and, often, groups of symbols) and rules for combining the symbols so that they represent instructions for a *computer* to carry out specific operations. (Also known as a 'code'.) A computer is designed to interpret instructions that are written in its *computer instruction code,* which is a very elementary language using a very restricted range of symbols. Computer instruction codes are virtually impossible for programmers to use and much effort has been devoted to devising languages that are more convenient. The first stage is the use of *low-level languages* in which many instructions are represented by mnemonics. The next stage is the sue of *high-level languages* (such as *ALGOL, COBOL, FORTRAN* and *PL/1*) which use *micro-instructions,* often represented by approximations to English words.

137. **Progressive-Part Method:-** A method of training in which the operation to be learned is divided into small parts and the

trainee practises the first two parts separately, then the first two combined, then the third part on its own, then all three combined, and so on.

138. **Project:-** Specially assigned task, such as a book review or report on a field trip, on which each person works independently.

139. **Psychodrama:-** A real-life situation is acted in front of a group which then discusses the implications of the performance.

Q

140. **Questionnaire:-** A document (especially, one reproduced in large numbers) containing a set of questions intended to elicit useful information.

R

141. **Random Sample:-** A *sample* of a given size from a *population* which has been chosen in such a way that any possible sample of that size could have been chosen with a known *probability*. The term usually refers to a 'simple random sample' – i.e., one in which any possible sample has an equal probability of being chosen.

142. **Ranking Method:-** Method of *job evaluation* in which all the jobs to be evaluated are *ranked* according to some consistent system (e.g., by asking someone to put the jobs in order of importance after considering *job descriptions)*.

143. **Rating Scale:-** A method of assigning numerical values to *ratings*. The ratings may be: (1) classified (eg. ratings of 0,1 and 2 meaning bad, average and good respectively); (2) by interval measurement (eg. if A is rated at 45, B at 50 and C at 60 then the difference between B and C is twice the difference between A and B); or (3) on a ratio scale in which there is interval measurement and one rating (usually 0) corresponds to complete absence of the quality being rated.

144. **Refresher Training:-** Training that is intended to improve trainee's performance of their current job. (Also known as 'booster training'.)

145. **Retraining:-** Training that is intended to enable a person to

take up an occupation that is different from the one for which he was previously trained.

146. **Role Reversal:-** Version of *role playing*, during training, in which two trainees role-play a situation and then exchange their roles.

147. **Role Rotation:-** Variation of the *role-playing* technique of training, in which each member of a group of trainees successively plays a particular role.

S

148. **Self-Actualization:-** One's need to become all one is capable of becoming.

149. **Self-Concept:-** A person's own view of himself/herself, particularly of their 'weakness' or 'strength' (in an emotional, psychological sense).

150. **Semantics:-** Study of the relationship between words and their meanings.

151. **Seminar:-** A training method used to present ideas of an expert or a group. Members may be called upon to play a role during its one or more study sessions, held under the guidance of the recognized authority in the subject.

152. **Sensitivity Training:-** Improving trainee's skills in understanding the needs of others. (A sensitive 'do-as-you-would-be-done-by' approach.)

153. **Simulation:-** Representation of a system (a physical device such as an aero plane or an abstraction such as the economy of a country) by a device that imitates the behaviour of a system. For example, the behaviour of a real aero plane can be simulated by a scale model, the behaviour of the economy of a country can be simulated by a computer programme.

154. **Simulation Model:-** Computer information-processing programme, designed to duplicate thought and other processes.

155. **Situational Test:-** A person's behaviour in a standard situation is observed and recorded.

156. **Skill:-** Action or series of actions which has required practice in order to perform it adequately.

157. **Skit:-** A short, rehearsed, humorous (often satirical) stage presentation involving two or more persons. Can be used to gain audience response to a particular problem or situation or to promote group discussion. (Differs from role playing in that it has a prepared and rehearsed script, while role playing is impromptu).

158. **Slide:-** Photographic transparency, the enlarged image of which projected on to a screen, usually to illustrate a speech. (Can be synchronized with an audio tape.)

159. **Social Learning:-** Observational learning, in which reinforcement plays no obvious role.

160. **Sociology:-** The science that deals with human beings in their relationship with each other.

161. **Socio-Technical System:-** A *system* that includes people performing work and which has been identified for purposes of discussion and analysis concentrating attention on the interaction between the people and their methods of working (including the physical production facilities, materials, machinery, tools, quality standards, pace of work, etc.).

162. **Standard Deviation:-** Statistical value used to measure extent to which individual's score differs from the group's mean. (Often interchanged with 'standard error'.)

163. **Stereotype:-** Gross generalization based on certain narrow traits in common, but applied to all the members of a group, regardless of their individual differences.

164. **Stranger Group:-** In *group training* a group that consists of people who do not know each other.

165. **Strategic Plan:-** A *plan* which sets out general methods or policies for achieving specified objectives; especially a plan of future *corporate strategy*.

166. **Strategic Planning:-** The activity, process or study of preparing *strategic plans*. (Also known as 'corporate planning'.)

167. **Strategy:-** 1. A general method or policy for achieving specified objectives. 2. In *game theory* a rule by which one player selects

his choice. The rule may be a 'pure strategy' – i.e., a rule that he will definitely select a specified choice – or a 'mixed strategy' – i.e., a rule that gives the *probabilities* of his making each of a number of choices.

168. **Stress:-** Any unpleasant and disturbing emotional experiences due to frustration or fear.

169. **Subliminal Perception:-** Visual stimuli presented at speeds above or below the threshold of awareness and recorded in the memory without going through the thinking, problem-solving, reasoning or perceiving processes.

170. **Symposium:-** A series of short (usually five-25 minutes), "pithy" prepared speeches by upto five authorities, covering various aspects of a subject – usually followed by further discussion and audience involvement.

171. **Supervisor:-**1. A *manager* whose main role is to ensure that tasks specified by others are performed correctly and efficiently by a defined group of people – especially when none of those people are themselves managers (see *first-line supervisor).* 2. Synonym for *supervisory programme.*

172. **Syndicate:-** 1. A small group of students, from a larger class, formed to discuss and report on a set problem or jointly carry out a training exercise. (Also known as a 'buzz group'.) 2. An association of independent firms formed to carry out business of common interest- e.g., to buy materials used by all the firms.

173. **Task:-** A requirement for the exertion of human effort leading to a recognizable achievement.

174. **Task Analysis:-**Systematic analysis of the behaviour required to carry out a repetitive job in order to identify areas of difficulty and to devise appropriate methods of training people to perform the job.

175. **Teaching Machine:-** A device for displaying a programme in *programmed instruction.* In its simplest form, the programme is on a roll of paper. The trainee winds the roll so that he can read a frame through a window in the machine, reads it, writes his response on a second roll of paper through another window, then winds on so that the correct response is displayed and he can compare it with his own. If he is correct, he winds on

again to the next frame; if he is not correct, he can wind back to re-read the frame and try to resolve his difficulty.

176. **Team Work:**-Work done by a number of associated people who are all agreed on and committed to doing it. Each person does a part of the work and his part is coordinated with the efforts of the others.

177. **T-Group:**-A training method used to surface personal feeling between a pair with the hope of resolving deep-seated interpersonal problems.

178. **Thematic Apperception Test:**- A method of assessing personality in which a testee is shown a set of black-and-white pictures depicting various scenes and is asked to say what is happening in the picture, what led up to the events in the picture and what the outcome will be. An experienced examiner can obtain insights into a testee's personality by analyzing his responses to the pictures.

179. **Theory X:**- A set of assumptions about human behaviour that D. McGregor considered to be implicit in much managerial policy and practice: The assumptions are:

    1. The average human being has an inherent dislike of work and will avoid it if he can.
    2. Because of this human characteristic of dislike of work, most people must be coerced, controlled, directed, threatened with punishment to get them to put forth adequate effort towards the achievement of organisational objectives.
    3. The average human being prefers to be directed, wishes to avoid responsibility, has relatively little ambition, wants security above all. (Quoted from D. McGregor, *The Human Side of Enterprise,* McGraw Hill, 1960) Cf. Theory Y.

180. **Theory Y:**- A set of assumptions about human nature and human behaviour that D. McGregor considered to be more consistent with current research knowledge of those subjects than *Theory X.* McGregor also considered that if a manager assumed Theory Y then his subordinates would be more highly motivated than if he assumed Theory X. The assumptions are:

1. The expenditure of physical and mental effort in work is as natural as play or test.
2. External control and the threat of punishment are not the only means for bringing about effort toward organisational objectives. Man will exercise self-direction and self-control in the service of objectives to which he is committed.
3. Commitment to objectives is a function of the rewards associated with their achievement.
4. The average human being learns, under proper conditions, not only to accept but to seek responsibility.

181. **Training:-** Systematic development and improvement of an individual's ability to perform a specific task or job.

182. **Training and Visit (T&V):-** A management procedure involving regular intensive training sessions for extension workers, followed by a planned schedule of visits to contact farmers.

183. **Training Manual:-** A document setting out prescribed or recommended methods of instruction and other details of a *training scheme* or of a particular training activity.

184. **Training Specification:-** A detailed statement of what a trainee needs to learn based on a comparison between his *job specification* and his present level of ability, training or experience.

185. **Transactional Analysis (TA):-** Method of analyzing the interaction ('transaction') between two persons in relation to three mental ('ego') stages (adulthood, parenthood, and childhood of the respondent.

186. **Transfer of Training:-** Influence (positive or negative) of past learning or training on a new situation.

V

187. **Vestibule Learning ("Induction" or "Introductory Training"):-** Off-line, instructor-led training, designed to bring trainee upto production standards before he/she assumes on-line responsibilities.

W

188. **Work Study:-** (1). Members work partly at their individual studies and partly on jobs more or less closely related to those studies. (Designed to introduce work experience as early as possible in a study programme); or (2). Time-and-motion study.

189. **Workshop:-** Usually, a group that is 'in retreat' from a common workplace or similar workplaces in order to share work-related common interests, to improve individual work performance, to extend knowledge through intensive study, research, and discussion, or to solve their work-related problems by sharing common experiences and knowledge.

Source:

(1). Derek French and Heather Saward, *Dictionary of Management*, 2nd Edition, 1975, Gower Press Limited, England.

(2). Goeffrey Moss, *The Trainers' Handbook for Managers and Trainers*, 1988, Singapore Institute of Management, Singapore.

SELECT BIBLIOGRAPHY
ON TRAINING AND HUMAN RESOURCE DEVELOPMENT

1. Adair John: *Training for Leadership*, Hampshire, Gower Press, 1968, pp. 158.
2. Anthony William P: *Management of Human Resources : A Systems Approach to Personnel Management*, Columbus Grid, 1977, pp. 276.
3. Berger M L: *Group Training Techniques*, edited by Berger M.L. and Berger P.J., London, Gower Press, 1972, pp. 191.
4. Carney Clarke G: *Exploring Contemporary male/Female Roles as Facilitators Guide*, Edited by Clarke G Carney and Sarah Lynne McMohan. California University-Associates, 1997, pp.276.
5. Cohen Arthur M: *Critical Incident in Growth Groups: Theory and Technique*, Edited by Arthur M. Cohen and R. Douglas Smith, California University Associates, 1976, pp. 292.
6. Cooper C : *T-Groups – A Survey of Research*. Edited by CL Cooper and IL Mangham. London, Wiley-Interscience, 1971, pp. 283.
7. Craig Robert L: *Training and Development Handbook: A Guide to Human Resource Development*, (Second Edition), New York, McGraw Hill, 1976.
8. Derek French and Heather Saward: *Dictionary of Management*, 2nd Edition, England, Gower Press Limited, 1975.

9. Desatnick Robert L: *Innovative Human Resource Management*, New York, AMA, 1972, pp.208.

10. Donaldson Les: *Human Resource Development: The New Trainer's Guide* by Les Donaldson and Edward E Scannell. Reading Massachusetts, Addison-Wesley, 1978, pp.151.

11. Dubrin Andrew J: *Personnel and Human Resource Management*, New York, Van Nostrand, 1981, pp. 566.

12. Dyer William G: *Modern Theory and Method in Group Training*, Van Nostrand, 1972, pp. 251.

13. Egan Gerard: *Interpersonal Living: A Skills Contract Approach to Human Relations Training in Groups*, Monterey Brooks/Cole Publishing, 1976, pp. 317.

14. Francis Dave: *Improving Work Groups a Practical Manual for Team Building*, Dave Francis and Don Young, California University Associates, 1976, pp. 261.

15. Frank H Eric: *Human Resource Development: The European Approach*, Texas, Gulf Publishing, 1974, pp. 248.

16. Gane Christopher: *Managing the Training Function Using Instructional Technology and Systems Concepts*, London, George Allen and Unwin, 1972, pp. 183.

17. Gibbs G I : *Handbook of Games and Simulation Exercises*, London, E and F N Spon, 1974, pp. 226.

18. Goeffrey Moss: *The Trainers' Handbook for Managers and Trainers*, Singapore Institute of Management, Singapore, 1988.

19. Golembiewski Robert T: *Sensitivity Training and the Laboratory Approach: Readings about Concepts and Applications*, edited by Robert T Golembiewski, F E Peacock Publishers, 1977, pp. 445.

20. Hamblin A C: *Evaluation and Control of Training*, London, McGraw-Hill, 1974, pp. 208.

21. Harwell Edward M: *Personnel Management and Training*, New York, Chair Store Age Books, 1975, pp. 387.

22. Havelock Ronald G: *Training for Change Agents – A Guide to the Design of Training Programmes in Education and Other Fields* by

Ronald G Havelock and Mary C Havelock, Ann Arbor Institute for Social Research, University of Michigan, 1973, pp. 249.

23. Hemant Kumar, Electronic Future of Training, *Human Capital*, September, 1998, New Delhi.

24. Henderson Richard: *Performance Appraisal: Theory to Practice*, Reston & Reston Publishing, 1980, pp. 310.

25. Heyel Richard: *Performance Appraisal: Theory to Practice*, Reston Publishing, 1980, pp. 310.

26. *Human Resource Development in Rural Areas and Role of Rural Institutions: Educational Training and Institutions for Rural Human Resources Development in Asian Countries*, Geneva, ILO, 1975, pp.237.

27. ILO, Geneva: *Introductory Course in Teaching and Training Methods for Management Development*, 1972.

28. ILO, Geneva: *Human Resources for Industrial Development: Some Aspects of Policy Planning*, Geneva, ILO, 1971, pp. 155.

29. Johnson David W : *Human Relations and Your Career: A Guide to Interpersonal Skills*, Englewood Cliffs, Prentice-Hall, 1978, pp. 385.

30. Jones John E : *Annual Handbook for Group Facilitators: The Tenth Annual*, edited by John E Jones and J William Pfeiffer, California University Associates, 1981, pp. 296.

31. Kelly Colleen: *Assertion Training: A Facilitator's Guide*, California University Associates, 1979, pp. 382.

32. Kennedy John: *Manpower Training and Development: An Introduction* by John Kennedy, Institute for Personnel Management, 1979, pp. 288.

33. Kirschenbaum Howard : *Developing Support Groups: A Manual for Facilitators and Participants* by Howard Kirschenbaum and Barbara Glaser.

34. Krug Robert E: *Impact of Participant Training on the Attainment of Development Goals : Analysis of Two Sectors*, Washington American Institute for Research, 1976, pp.50.

35. *Laboratory Method of Charging and Learning: Theory and*

Application, edited by Kenneth D Benne and others, California Science and Behaviour Books, 1975, pp. 589.

36. Lynton Rolf P : *Training for Development*, by Rolf P Lynton and Udai Pareek, Bombay, Taraporevala, 1973, pp. 408.
37. Malennan A: *Educating and Training Technicians*, London, Commonwealth Secretariat, 1975, pp. 136.
38. Malgavkar P D: *Training for Entrepreneurial Development : Review and an Approach*, Delhi, Cabinet Secretariat, 1974, pp. 86.
39. *Managing Human Resources*, London, Heinemann, 1976, pp. 179.
40. Martin Desmond D: *What Every Engineer should know about Human Resources Management* by Desmond D Martin and Richard L Shell, New York, Marcel Dekker, 1980, pp. 176.
41. McGrath E.H. : *Training for Life and Leadership in Industry*, Delhi, Prentice-Hall, 1973, pp. 356.
42. Mehta M M: *Human Resources Development Planning with Special Reference to Asia and the Far East*, Delhi, Macmillan, 1976, pp. 192.
43. Michalak Donald F : *Making the Training Process Work* by Donald F Michalak and Edwin G Yagner, New York, Harper and Row Publishers, 1979, pp. 512.
44. Mill Cyril R : *Activities for Trainers : 50 Useful Designs*, San Diego University Associates, 1980, pp. 226.
45. Miller Lawrence M: *Behaviour Management: The New Science of Managing People at Work*, Chichester, John Wiley, 1978, pp. 404.
46. Mondy R Wayne: *Personnel: The Management of Human Resources* by R Wayne Mondy Robert M Noe and Harry N Mills, Boston, Allyn and Bacon, 1981, pp. 599.
47. Mumford Alan: *Manager and Training*, New York, Pitman Publishing, 1971, pp. 152.
48. Nadler Leonard: *Corporate Human Resources Development: A Management Tool*, New York, Van Nostand Reinhold, 1980, pp. 199.
49. Nadler Leonard: *Developing Human Resources*, Houston Gulf Publishing, 1970, pp. 262.

50. NTL Institute for Applied Behavioural Science: *Laboratories in Human Relations Training*, Virginia, 1971, pp. 81.

51. NTL Institute for Applied Behavioural Science, Washington: *Problem-solving Programme for Defining a Problem and Planning Action*, Washington, 1969.

52. NTL, Washington, *Group Development*, Washington, 1961, pp. 106.

53. NTL, Washington, *Issues in Human Relations Training*, Washnngton, 1962, pp. 121.

54. Nylen Donald: *Handbook of Staff Development and Human Relations Training: Materials Developed for Use in Africa*, Edited by Donald Nylen, J Robert Mitchel and Anthony Stout, Washington, NTL Institute for Applied Behavioural Science, 1967, pp. 309.

55. Odiorne George S: *Training by Objectives : An Economic Approach to Management Training*, London Macmillan, 1970, pp. 354.

56. *Organisation of Training* by Ivor K Davies and others, London, McGraw-Hill, 1973, pp. 113.

57. Otto Calvin P: *Management of Training – A Handbook for Training and Development of Personnel*, Edited by Calvin P Otto and Rollin O Glaser, Reasing Addison-Wesley, 1970, pp. 410.

58. Pettman B O: *Training and Retraining : A Basis for Future*, London, Transcripta Books, 1973, pp. 133.

59. Pfeiffer J William: *Handbook of Structured Experiences for Human Relations Training* by J William Pfeiffer and John E Jones, Iowa City University Associates Press, 1969.

60. Pfeiffer J William: *Instrumentation in Human Relations: A Guide to the Behavioural Sciences* by J William Pfeiffer, Richard Heslin and John E Jones, 2nd Edition, California, University Associates, 1976, pp.324.

61. Rapoport Robert N: *Mid-Career Development: Research Perspectives on a Developmental Community for Senior Administrators*, London Tavistock, 1970, pp. 290.

62. *Research Management and Technical Entrepreneurship: A US Role*

in Improving Skills in Developing Countries, Washington, National Academy of Sciences, 1973, pp. 40.

63. Robert R Carkhuff et al., *Art of Helping: Trainers Guide*. Human Resources Development Press, Amherst, 1977.
64. Sayles Leonard R : *Managing Human Resources*, by Leonard R Sayles and George Strauss, 2nd Edition, Englewood Cliffs Prentice-Hall, 1981, pp. 510.
65. Sikula Andrew F : *Personnel Administration and Human Resources Management*, Santa Barbara, John Wiley, 1976, pp. 456.
66. Singer Edwin J : *Human Resources : Obtaining Results from People at Work*, by Edwin J Singer and John Ramsden, London, McGraw-Hill, 1972, pp. 197.
67. Smith B Babington : *Training in Small Groups : A Study of Five Methods*, Edited by B Babington Smith and B A Farrell, Oxford, Pergamon Press, 1979, pp. 144.
68. Stammers Robert : *Psychology of Training*, by Robert Stammers and John Patrick, London, Methuen, 1975, pp. 144.
69. Suessmuth Patrick: *Ideas for Training Managers and Supervisors: Useful Suggestions, Activities and Instruments*, California University Associates, 1978, pp. 328.
70. Taylor Bernard: *Management Development and Training Handbook*, edited by Bernard Taylor and Gordon L Lippitt, London, McGraw-Hill, 1975, pp. 650.
71. Thayer Louis: *50 Strategies for Experimental Learning* (book One), La Jolla University Associatse, 1976, pp. 230.
72. Tracey William R : *Managing Training and Development System*, New York, AMACOM, 1974, pp. 480.
73. *Twenty Exercises for Trainers*, edited by Cyrcil R Mill, Washington, NTL Learning Resources Corporation, 1972, pp. 48.
74. Udai Pareek: *Designing and Managing Human Resources Systems with Special Emphasis on Human Resources Development*, edited by Udai Pareek and T. Venkateswara Rao, Oxford and IBH, New Delhi, 1981, pp. 347.

75. Walker Alfred J: *HRIS Development: A Project Team Guide to Building an Effective Personnel Information System*, New York, van Nostrand Reinhold, 1982, pp. 243.

76. Wellens John: *Training in Physical Skills*, London, Business Books, 1974, pp. 194.

77. Whatley Arthur A: *Personnel Management in Action : Skills Building Experiences* by Arthur A Whatley and Nelson Lne Kelley, St. Paul West Publishing, 1977, pp. 305.

78. Whitaker Galvin: *T-Group Training: Group Dynamics in Management Education*, edited by Galvin Whitaker, Oxford Basil Blackwell, 1965, pp. 82.

79. Woodcock Mike: *Team Development Manual*, Westmead Gower Press, 1979, pp. 221.

INDEX

❑❑❑